27 ESSENTIAL PRINCIPLES OF STORY

Master the Secrets of Great Storytelling, from Shakespeare to *South Park*

By

Daniel Joshua Rubin

WORKMAN PUBLISHING
NEW YORK

Library of Congress Control Number: 2020938343

ISBN 978-1-5235-0716-0

Workman books are available at special discounts when purchased in bulk for premiums and sales promotions as well as for fund-raising or educational use. Special editions or book excerpts can also be created to specification. For details, contact the Special Sales Director at the address below or send an email to specialmarkets@workman.com.

Cover and interior design by Becky Terhune

Workman Publishing Co., Inc.
225 Varick Street
New York, NY 10014-4381
workman.com

Printed in the United States of America
First printing July 2020

10 9 8 7 6 5 4 3 2 1

For Karen and Sally,
my two favorite stories.

And Tim Erjavac.
We had some laughs.
See you on the other side.

Contents

PART THREE: ESSENTIAL PRINCIPLES OF SETTING, DIALOGUE, AND THEME

INTRODUCTION

Old School, New Adrenaline

This book was inspired by the way martial arts are taught. The best schools focus relentlessly on drilling fundamentals. Here, the fundamentals are old-school principles of plot, character, setting, dialogue, and theme—the same ones Aristotle wrote about more than 2,100 years ago, but updated and given a shot of adrenaline. No matter what form your story takes, whether you're writing a novel, screenplay, TV series, podcast, web series, graphic novel, comic book, song, or just telling a story, these universal principles apply.

This is classic dramatic structure made simple. By "classic dramatic structure," I mean stories with a beginning, middle, and end that build tension, keep your audience guessing what will happen, are fueled by intense emotion, and resolve in a meaningful way. If you want a path to follow to help you tell a coherent, authentic story, you will find what you need here. If you are more of a free spirit, you can study each principle in isolation and use only the ones that feel essential to you. The key word here is *you*. Storytelling is a personal and revealing art. You write stories to express the truth as you see it. My hope is that each chapter will help you figure out how to execute each principle in your own unique way.

You won't find any literary theory, academic puffery, or slick jargon. All twenty-seven principles are stated simply, in plain

English. This is important for two reasons. One is that it makes it simpler to understand and master each principle. Terms you may have heard, or learned in class, such as *inciting incident* and *climax*, can be problematic because, in the context of story, they don't mean what they usually mean. A "climax" is a high point of tension. But in story, the climax refers to when the Central Dramatic Question is answered, which is often *not* the high point of tension. It's simply the moment we learn how things turn out. But more important, cutting out the convoluted terminology creates space for you to fill with your own unique intellect, personality, and heart.

For example, Chapter 12 is called simply, "Provoke dilemma." When you force your characters to struggle through impossible choices, you reveal who they are. Because this concept is so simply stated, your mind immediately goes to work, thinking up dilemmas for your characters to face. And no two writers construct the same types of dilemmas. So, you get the benefit of executing a timeless and fundamental principle, but in your own way. You get to have your cake and eat it too.

The twenty-seven principles will give you enough direction to avoid getting lost, but not so much that it strangles your creativity. And you can use this book any way you want. You don't have to read it cover to cover or start with Chapter 1. Some writers find inspiration in a line of dialogue or an idea or a personality—that's fine. You can start by reading one of the chapters on dialogue—or one on theme or character. The emphasis here is on practical value. This book exists to serve your needs. If you're already in the middle of a story, but feel stuck—the dialogue's not sharp, the characters don't feel distinct, you're not sure what it all adds up to—you will find an answer to your problem.

If you invest a small amount of time—a few weeks tops—actually doing the work of carefully working through these chapters, you'll be astounded by how much insight you gain. You don't need to invest north of $200,000 in a fancy degree. You need fundamental principles and the confidence that comes from knowing you've truly mastered them.

Each chapter is structured the same way. Up first is a Quick Take that explains the basic idea. Then we'll break down the mechanics of How It Works, just like car nuts break down auto parts to see how they work. Next, in How a Master Did It, we'll detail how one of the greatest storytellers throughout time, in all media, executed the principle. This is not theory. I will show you how they did it. Then, in How You Do It (it's always about *you*), we'll bullet point, step by step, how you execute the principle in your own work. This will teach you how professional writers think through story. Then you'll take a Mini Final Exam. These are fun little stories that relate to the principle at hand and are followed by a single multiple-choice question. The goal for these is to reinforce the principle, and to give you that extra shot of confidence that comes from knowing you have command of it. And it doesn't end there. In Continuing Ed, you'll be told about another story that beautifully executes the principle, along with some questions to think about so you can further explore the principle on your own. When you finish a chapter, it will feel as if you've installed the principle in your brain, just like putting software onto a hard drive.

Again, this methodology is inspired by martial arts. You will never hear a black belt complain about working on fundamentals. They spend countless hours on the basics: breathing, striking, kicking, blocking, stances, mentality, and movement. But here's the key thing about martial arts: No two people will execute the moves in the same way. Inevitably, we bring our own personality and style to everything we do. This is not about assembling bookcases from Ikea that all look exactly alike. We're talking about you telling *your* story. The goal is to help you engage in more constructive, insightful conversation with yourself, to discover what you truly think and feel.

One of the pleasures of writing this book was diving deep into the stories in How a Master Did It—they are all extraordinary and no two are alike. To my knowledge, this is the most diverse collection of stories ever assembled in a book on writing—it's not the Western Canon. You'll find a wide variety of media and genres, and storytellers from different time periods and all walks of life. You'll explore a new generation of masters including Junot Diaz, Jhumpa Lahiri, Alison Bechdel, Samanta Schweblin, and Eminem. This diverse lineup is not about being politically correct. Fuck that. I'm the least politically correct guy on earth. It's about developing a more complete picture of what it means to be human.

Now you might be wondering who the hell I am and what gives me the right to lecture the world on story. It's a fair and important question. I'm not Stephen King and I don't fancy myself to be some know-it-all guru. But I've paid my dues and then some. I've written on staff for shows on the WB and NBC. I've been Playwright-in-Residence at the Steppenwolf Theatre in Chicago, produced video series for the global financial media company The Motley Fool, and I once did a three-figure development deal with the *National Lampoon*. Ha ha. No, really. And we came an inch away from selling that TV pitch—about my real-life experience as a rodeo beer vendor—to Comedy Central. I've been represented by some of the biggest agencies in Hollywood. I've studied and worked with the most successful writers, directors, and actors of all time. I've taught Dramatic Writing at Loyola University Chicago and the University of California, San Diego. I founded my own writing studio, Story 27, in Evanston, Illinois. And I hold a Bachelor of Science in Drama Studies from the State University of New York at Purchase and an MFA in Playwriting from Yale.

The bottom line is, I've lived the Writing Life for more than twenty-five years. I've done some really cool things and made some big mistakes. I've learned what's essential and what is not. Though story is art and art is, of course, subjective, I have tried as hard as I could to focus on the principles that are as close to objective truth as possible. If you clash expectation with reality (see Chapter 6 on *Breaking Bad*), mask characters' true selves (see Chapter 16 on *Harry Potter and the Prisoner of Azkaban*), and earn transformations (see Chapter 17 on *Fun Home*), you will write better, smarter, and more authentic stories.

Lastly, before you start, a word of warning. These principles are more interrelated than a Kentucky picnic and all, ultimately, share the same goals—to help you write something essential. You will see the following words repeated throughout: necessary, authentic, inspired, intense, intelligent, emotional, revealing, passionate, essential, critical . . . I think you get the point. This is not the book for people who want to score a quick buck by writing about a cop who partners with a schnauzer. It's for writers who have something important to say; who take story seriously; who dream of writing something meaningful; who feel that if they don't tell the story that's been stuck in their gut like a bullet, they can never be content; who want to write to the very best of their ability and, if the gods are with them, rattle the world.

If this feels like you, welcome to the tribe. Find me on Twitter at @DanJoshuaRubin and let me know how it goes.

"Have confidence that if you
have done a little thing well,
you can do a bigger thing well too."

—DAVID STOREY, Playwright

PART ONE

ESSENTIAL PRINCIPLES of PLOT

In this section you'll learn ten principles to help you craft intelligent, impactful stories that express your unique vision. You'll learn how each part of a well-told story—beginning, middle, and end—works, so you can start strong, generate momentum, and finish in a way that is powerful and resonant. This is old-school, classic dramatic structure.

The focus here is on building true confidence, the confidence you earn by mastering fundamentals—the same fundamentals great writers like James Baldwin used to write *If Beale Street Could Talk* and Mary Shelley used to write *Frankenstein*. I'll break down each part of a story into simple-to-understand concepts you can apply immediately. Once you're confident that you can do something—in this case, finish a well-told story—you'll approach the blank page with a whole different mind-set. And you'll put yourself in position to write something inspired.

1

Drop the hammer.

"Well begun is half done."
—ARISTOTLE, Philosopher

QUICK TAKE

To set up and draw people into your story, introduce your hero and then construct an event that hits their existence like a hammer, something that radically alters their life. It can be as dramatic as a plane crash or subtle as a glance that fuels an obsession. Whatever it is, it is important and meaningful, changes the hero's emotional state, and must be dealt with immediately.

When you drop the hammer, you lay a track for the story to ride on from start to finish. It firmly establishes what kind of story you're telling and what it's about. It helps settle you in when you're writing and, later, helps your audience settle in to experience the story.

The importance of dropping an effective hammer can't be overstated. Countless writers start stories in a blaze of inspiration, but because they fail to set up their story properly, they get lost and quit. That means months, or even years, of wasted time and frustration. By learning how to drop the hammer, you make the process more rewarding and increase your odds of finishing a coherent—and if the gods are with you, *inspired*—story that can be published or produced.

HOW IT WORKS

One key reason writing makes people so anxious is that there are an infinite number of choices—of settings, characters, events, and more. This is particularly true when you're at the very beginning and haven't made a single decision yet. By starting with the construction of the "drop the hammer" event or moment, you give yourself a problem to solve—writing the beginning. We'll work backward, first defining exactly what a hammer drop is, and then exploring how it's set up.

The Drop

When the hammer drops, something profound happens to your hero. The following are the eight essential qualities of an event big enough to launch a story:

1. It is surprising or even shocking—we didn't see it coming and neither did the hero. This puts the hero in a heightened emotional state.
2. It not only heightens the hero's emotional state, it changes their attitude and indicates a shift in fortunes. Note that the hammer can be positive. For example, the hero falls madly in love or wins the lottery.
3. It builds sympathy or empathy for the hero—we know and feel that *this* event, happening to *this* person, at *this* time, profoundly changes their life. After this event we care more about what will happen to the hero.
4. It instills a sense of urgency—your hero must respond immediately to the hammer. It can't be put off. Whether the hammer is as powerful as a tornado destroying a house or as subtle as a woman realizing she's losing her memory, this new reality must be dealt with immediately.
5. It makes clear what kind of story this is in terms of tone and genre—whether it's a comedy, drama, dramedy, tragedy, etc. It doesn't tell us what will happen, but it emotionally prepares us for how the end will feel—heartbreaking, joyful, thrilling, terrifying, etc. It helps to settle in the audience.

6. It establishes an "object of desire"—a person, thing, action, or state of being the hero needs to acquire in order to exist in the new reality. A mother needs to find her missing child, a boy needs to gain his scoutmaster's respect, an athlete needs to break a world record.
7. It provokes a dramatic question in the audience's mind: Will the hero acquire the object of desire? (We'll explore dramatic questions in detail in the next chapter.) For now, note that the simplest definition of storytelling is this: Ask a dramatic question, answer it. By dropping the hammer you provoke the central dramatic question, the one that fuels the story.
8. It projects possible endings. Once the dramatic question is asked, our minds provide answers. If the hammer drops when a wife tells her husband she's no longer sure that she loves him, we picture various endings: the couple getting divorced, renewing their vows, deciding to live in a loveless marriage, etc. While we don't know exactly how the story will end, we know the ballpark and begin to wonder.

If this seems like a lot, that's because it is. It's essential that every moment in your story is well-written, but none more so than this one. We talked earlier about the hammer drop laying down a track for your story to ride on. Each of these elements will help strengthen that track. If you lay down weak tracks, your story will get derailed. You want your tracks made of the highest-quality steel. You want to instill in your audience a deep-seated sense that "this is gonna be good." When you drop the hammer, you tell the audience you're in control. You let them know that this story is going to be entertaining and meaningful, that you won't waste their time.

The Setup

Every story has its own unique needs and every storyteller has their own style, taste, and preferences. Your hero, genre, setting, the length of your story, and the medium you work in all impact the amount of time required to set up the hammer. Some heroes are complex, contradictory characters with elaborate histories, who take a long time to introduce. A story set in 5437 in a distant galaxy on a world no one has seen before needs more setup than a story set in the present day. Therefore, there are no hard and fast rules about when you drop the hammer. Some hammers come down at the very start because they need minimal setup—a loved one dies. Some drop halfway through the story or even later. Many come at roughly the one-third mark. Some stories, like *Finding Nemo* (which we'll explore in the next chapter), drop two hammers; the first is critical to setting up the second. Our goal here is to give you enough information to structure your story but not so much it strangles your creativity. Only you know what your story needs.

It's helpful to think about the effect you want your hammer to have. If it's a comedy, you want your audience to burst out laughing. If it's horror, you want to terrify them. But above all, you want your audience to care about your hero and what will happen. To effectively set up the hammer, focus first on two things:

1. What information is essential to fully understanding the event?
2. What can you do to amplify the impact of the event?

Imagine a story about a man who is paralyzed in an accident. What must we learn in order to care deeply about the accident? What if he's a star athlete or in love with a model who is obsessed with her appearance? What if he's fiercely independent? Or the sole caretaker for five kids and needs to walk to do his job?

If your story is about a single father who must overcome an accident to raise his kids, you need to show him at work. And his job must require physical labor—he's a plumber, telephone line repairman, etc. You're not merely telling us, "This is Ned, he's a fireman." You're setting up your hammer by showing how important his strength and athleticism are to his identity and career. This way when the hammer drops, we're shaken by it.

If it's important to know he has five kids, you might show him struggling to get them all ready for school. Once you establish the necessary information, you can add nuance, depth, and texture—weather, time period, history of the characters, location, etc.—as you see fit.

When you properly set up and then drop the hammer, you're off to the races. When you drop one that's weak—that has no impact, that sparks no action—you're bound to struggle miserably through the writing process and quit before you finish. So, take your time and have fun with it.

HOW A MASTER DID IT

The Tragedy of Hamlet, Prince of Denmark (ca. 1600)
William Shakespeare

When the play starts, two watchmen, Barnardo and Francisco, meet atop a castle in Denmark late at night. The fog rolling off the jet-black sea is so thick they can barely see each other. They're stressed out of their minds. Two nights in a row, a ghost—in the form of the recently deceased King Hamlet—has appeared but said nothing. Barnardo asks if it has come again tonight, but it hasn't. As Francisco heads off, another guard, Marcellus, who's seen the ghost, comes in with Horatio, a scholar and friend of Prince Hamlet. They've brought Horatio in the hopes that he can confirm the ghost's identity, talk to it, and figure out why it's come. Horatio is skeptical of their story.

But sure enough, the ghost appears. Horatio is shocked and terrified. He calls out to the ghost to reveal what or who it is and say why it has come. But the ghost, as if offended, disappears. Pale and trembling, Horatio is shaken to his core. He confirms that the ghost is exactly as they described but adds that it wears the armor King Hamlet wore into battle when he recently defeated the Norwegian army, led by King Fortinbras, to claim the Danish lands. And the ghost at one point frowned just like King Hamlet did before he went into battle. It's clear King Hamlet was revered for his courage and the honor he brought to Denmark.

Marcellus says the whole country's on edge, that cannon-makers and shipbuilders are working on Sundays, and guards have all been put on strict schedules. Horatio says that King Fortinbras's son, also named Fortinbras, is hell-bent on avenging his father's defeat. He's gathering an army of thugs and mercenaries and could ride in to attack the castle at any moment. Horatio notes that before Julius Caesar was assassinated, corpses rose out of the ground to walk the Earth to warn of trouble coming. He's convinced the ghost has come to do the same. The ghost reappears and Horatio pleads with it to speak and help them avoid whatever might be coming. The ghost stays eerily silent. In a panic, Horatio strikes at it with his dagger, but it vanishes once again. They decide to get the dead king's son, Prince Hamlet, certain that the ghost will speak to him.

Scene Two

The newly crowned King Claudius addresses his court, including several lords, his nephew Prince Hamlet, and Hamlet's mother, Queen Gertrude. Claudius assures everyone that he is in control. He has done what all have asked and not only assumed the throne, but married Gertrude who was, only a month ago, the wife of his brother, King Hamlet. He says that Prince Fortinbras demands that he return the Norwegian lands taken from his father, but Claudius tells the court he has no intention of giving in. Young Prince Fortinbras underestimates him. Claudius insists, correctly, that the lands were won fairly in battle and therefore will not be returned.

The king turns his attention to Hamlet, "But now my cousin Hamlet and my son" (cousin back then also meant nephew), and Hamlet mutters an aside, "A little more than kin and less than kind." This is a fully loaded line. He means being a nephew and a son is too many relations, that Claudius is not only unkind as in not nice, but also not the same kind of man as Hamlet, not really from the same bloodline as his nobler father. Claudius and Gertrude plead with Hamlet to stop wearing black and mourning the loss of his father. Claudius says it's unmanly to grieve so bitterly for so long and asks to be welcomed as Hamlet's new father. Gertrude says her dead husband lost his father who lost his father, as do all men. Hamlet agrees this is true. Then, when his mother asks why his loss seems particular to him, he's offended by the word *seems* and states that his weeping and outward signs of sorrow can barely express the depth of his pain. Claudius and Gertrude plead with him not to return to Germany, where he's been attending college in Wittenberg, and Claudius tells him he needs him by his side as his "chiefest courtier," his most important confidante and aid. Hamlet is well-liked, the rightful heir to the throne, and the son of a revered king. To win popular approval, to be seen as legitimate, Claudius needs Hamlet's support. After Hamlet agrees to stay, they're delighted, and Claudius leads his court off to celebrate his kingship and the nation's return to normalcy.

Hamlet is left alone, and Shakespeare lays out his emotional state, his exact thoughts and feelings in explicit detail. He's devastated. He can't fathom that this nightmare is his new reality. He would kill himself if it were not a mortal sin. He says his father loved his mother so much he couldn't bear to let the wind touch her face, that she loved him so much she shrieked in agony at his funeral. He says the shoes that she wore to the funeral were hardly broken in when she wore them barely two months later at her wedding. He is disgusted by his uncle, and states with self-deprecating humor that though his uncle is his father's brother, he is as unlike the fallen king as Hamlet is to Hercules. He is sickened by the thought of his mother having sex with Claudius and considers it incest, every bit as vile and unnatural as a parent sleeping with a child. He is desperate to express his true feelings but can't. He knows that as a prince you must always consider the greater good, that the proper handling of the affairs of the state is more important than his individual feelings.

Horatio, Barnardo, and Marcellus come in to tell Hamlet what they've seen. He grills them until he's certain it was his father that they saw, then makes them promise to keep this secret. He is sure there's been some foul play but has no clue what. He will meet them tonight atop the castle and speak to the ghost—even if Hell itself opens up to stop him.

Scene Three

Polonius, a high-ranking member of the court, and his daughter, Ophelia, meet with his son, Laertes, who is returning to college in France. Polonius gives Laertes a short lecture, packing all the life advice he can into a single farewell monologue. The two then warn Ophelia about spending too much time with Hamlet, who they're convinced doesn't truly love her but only wants to sleep with her. The scene adds emotional and thematic depth in that Polonius and Laertes share the father-son bond that Hamlet has lost. Ophelia, young and naïve, trusts her father and brother and promises to refrain from seeing Hamlet, which only adds to his stress.

Scene Four

Late at night, atop the castle wall, Hamlet and Horatio wait for the ghost to reappear. They hear trumpets and cannon fire. The king and his court are up dancing and drinking. Hamlet notes that this tradition of hard-core partying to celebrate the new king's ascent is in bad taste. He feels Denmark, especially under his father, has had many great accomplishments and this behavior minimizes their stature.

Then the ghost appears. Hamlet terrified, cries out, "Angels and ministers of grace defend us!" He urges the ghost to say if it's good or evil, if it's really his father, to explain what it wants. The ghost drifts off and beckons Hamlet to follow. Horatio and Marcellus beg him not to, fearing it could be a trick to hurl him into the sea. He rejects their pleas. When they try to block his way, he draws his sword and threatens to make ghosts of them. Hamlet goes off. Horatio wonders what this means. Marcellus responds with one of the most famous lines in theater: "Something is rotten in the state of Denmark."

Scene Five

When the ghost is alone with Hamlet, he tells him that he is, in fact, the ghost of his father, and that he is trapped in purgatory, where his days are spent in torment. Since he died unexpectedly before he could fully repent his sins, he could not go to Heaven. But his death was not caused by a snakebite as everyone believes. He was killed by a snake, but the snake was his own brother, who poured poison in his ear while he was sleeping. This led to a gruesome, agonizing death. Though Hamlet had suspected foul play, he is traumatized by the news that his beloved father has endured so much pain. The ghost tells him to avenge his murder, but not to dare take any action against the queen. Hamlet vows he will.

He returns to Horatio and Marcellus excited, teeming with conflicting emotions—fear, rage, outrage, sorrow, even a dark kind of ecstatic joy that his suspicions are confirmed. But above all, he is fiercely determined to avenge his father's murder. He says that the ghost is definitely real. "There are more things in Heaven and Earth, Horatio, than are dreamt of in your philosophy," he says, and cryptically asserts that villains do exist in Denmark. But he doesn't tell them what the ghost said about his uncle. He warns them he may seem mad in the coming days, but not to let on that they know about the ghost. As he orders them to swear to keep this secret, they hesitate. The ghost bellows, "Swear!" which they quickly do. The first act ends with Hamlet's lines, "The time is out of joint. O cursed spite, that ever I was born to set it right. Nay, come. Let's go together."

• • •

Now let's go through each element of a well-struck hammer drop and see how the moment Hamlet learns his father was murdered stacks up.

1. **It's surprising, even shocking.** Though Hamlet suspected something was wrong, it is not only surprising to hear it confirmed by the ghost of his father, but the details of the murder—its wanton cruelty, its fallout, that his father must exist in torment, in purgatory—are shocking.

2. **It changes the hero's fortunes and heightens his emotional state.** In Scene Two, Shakespeare makes it clear that Hamlet is heartbroken and depressed, bordering on suicidal. He must watch helplessly as his uncle, whom he despises, replaces his father as not only the king, but also as his father and his mother's lover. His state changes radically when he moves from being a man with no purpose to one with a sacred mission.

3. **It builds sympathy or empathy for the hero.** Hamlet is morally righteous, loving, sensitive, intelligent, passionate, intense, and funny. He is as fully aware as a character can be. We feel for a young man who learns his uncle is a traitor, his father was murdered and condemned to purgatory, and his mother is committing what he considers to be incest with a villain. That's a heavy load to bear. And note the specificity of how *this* moment affects *this* character at *this* time. Consider how diluted the impact of this moment would be if Hamlet met the ghost two years after his father's murder instead of two months.

4. **It instills a sense of urgency.** Hamlet must deal with this immediately. His father's soul, his honor, his nation, and his mother's body are being desecrated, and the ghost will surely return to punish Hamlet further if he doesn't rise to the occasion.

5. **It makes clear what kind of story this is in terms of tone and genre.** The play is a tragedy. When the hammer drops, a prince meets with the tortured ghost of his dead father, in the middle of the night, by the black, foggy sea. And he's given a

mission—to kill a king who has the full backing of the nation's lords—that is likely to end with the prince's own death.

6. **It establishes the "object of desire."** We know what Hamlet must do to achieve his objective: kill the king.

7. **It provokes a dramatic question in the audience's mind:** Will Hamlet kill the king?

8. **It projects possible endings in the audience's mind.** We know that for this story to end, Hamlet must kill the king, get executed for trying to kill the king, or even quit trying to kill the king. We don't know exactly how this will end, but we can narrow it down to a few credible choices.

Now let's review some of the key choices Shakespeare made in his setup.

Because he is the greatest storyteller who ever lived, he not only brilliantly sets up the start of his story but also the end. The play is a tragedy. We know that Hamlet is going to die. At its heart, the play is an exploration of the nature of life and death, most notably all that is lost when a human being dies: the mind, consciousness, all the thoughts, ideas, personality, emotions, desires, history, relations—all of it, every single thing, comes to an end. Of course, common sense dictates that when you set up a story, you must tell us all of the obvious stuff: where it takes place, who it's about, what kind of story it is, etc. You know this.

But we're hunting bigger game.

This is why we started with Hamlet, one of the most complex characters ever written. What Shakespeare does in Act One, with the setup of his greatest play, is introduce the reader/audience to a character who is spiritually dead, and then construct an event that shatters his hero's state of being. When the ghost reveals he was murdered and instructs Hamlet to avenge the murder, Hamlet springs to life with as much passion, authenticity, and humanity as one can. Just consider for a moment all that is involved in this moment: power, sexuality, family, purgatory, the religious symbolism of brother killing brother in a garden. . . . What Shakespeare sets up is the most alive character he could in order to explore what it means to be alive and what is lost when we die.

HOW YOU DO IT

The following bullet points will help you think through and execute the principle.

- Focus on your objective. You're constructing an event that is powerful enough to get your reader's attention, to hook their interest, and make them want to go on the journey.

- Briefly sketch out a character. For now, keep it simple: for example, a middle-aged, married cop from Brooklyn who loves to cook.

- Establish their basic state of mind. They are happy, unhappy, or just going through the motions. Things are going well, badly, or life is business as usual. Our cop from Brooklyn is profiled in the newspaper or wins an award. He is still young—in his late forties—but has worked hard, saved money, and will retire soon after he puts in his twentieth year, which is a few months away. He loves his wife, who runs the emergency room of an inner-city hospital. Both are a bit burned out and plan to retire to North Carolina. Their dream is to build a little "breakfast shack" so they can work mornings and then golf, sail, fish, and watch the sun set on the ocean.

- Construct an event that impacts your character. It may be the smallest thing in the world (seeing a homeless child, catching a romantic interest's eye) or it may be cataclysmic (an asteroid strike, monster attack, terrorism), but whatever it is, it radically alters your character's state of mind. If they were happy, now they're sad. If they were sad, now they're happy. If they were numb or on cruise control, now they spring to life. The cop who is excited about his upcoming retirement shows up at yet another crime scene to find that the dead body is his only son, who just turned twenty-one. This event shatters life as he knew it.

▶ Define the need that arises as a result of the hammer coming down. The cop needs to catch his son's killer. This need is the object of desire.

▶ Now make it active. Phrase this as a dramatic question. Will the hero acquire their object of desire? Will the cop catch his son's killer?

▶ Once you define how the hammer drops, focus on setting it up so it comes down hard. There's an inherent cruelty in the way writers treat their characters. You're telling the audience, "See this cop? He thinks he's about to retire and enjoy the good life. Watch this." Now, go through what happens before the hammer comes down, and make certain it strengthens the emotional impact of the hammer. If the cop tells his wife that he's taking their son out for dinner, he's been worried about him, this would strengthen the impact of the hammer by showing he loves his boy. If the weather is icy and cold, this might up their desire to get to North Carolina, a dream that's put off after the hammer comes down. The point is that what you're doing here is making your reader care. You want your reader to think, "Oh, man, this event, happening to this character, at this time, is a very big deal."

▶ You're writing the beginning of your story. Have fun. You'll know you've got it when you feel a rush of confidence that comes from knowing you can finish a coherent, inspired story.

MINI FINAL EXAM

Read the following, then answer the question below.

An aging woman takes a long walk in the park. She sees someone who reminds her of a dear friend who passed away. She feeds the birds. She sits on a bench and rubs her foot. It really hurts. On her way home, she shops for tonight's dinner. She drives in heavy traffic. Back in her apartment, her son telephones and as usual rushes through the call as if he is checking it off his to-do list. She considers saying something but lets it go.

She makes tea. She watches the rain fall. She falls asleep watching a political talk show. She looks through some travel brochures, but none interest her. She stares at a collage of photos of her and her husband in happier times—atop a mountain, on the beach, celebrating their anniversary. She checks her phone book, an old one, handwritten. But there's no one she cares to call. There are lines through several names with little crosses that mean they've died. Finally, she heaves a big broken sigh and helplessly watches the sunset.

Which of the following events would drop the strongest hammer in this story?

a) She learns she has skin cancer.
b) Her neighbor asks her to compete in a mahjong tournament.
c) She learns that her dead husband was gay.
d) An anonymous letter arrives, with photos, that says her husband faked his death and now lives in Vienna.
e) Her beautician talks her into wearing a wig that looks fantastic!

CONTINUING ED

In Thomas Hardy's 1891 classic novel *Tess of the D'Urbervilles*, a young teenager, Tess Durbeyfield, is sent off to live with another family, the D'Urbervilles, whom her father believes are wealthy relatives. The hope is that through the D'Urbervilles' connections, Tess, a kind, hardworking, and genuinely lovely gal, will meet a rich husband. At the estate, Tess does attract the interest of a man—but he has no interest in marriage. What does he do to her? How does this incident drop the hammer on Tess and radically alter her life? How does it build empathy for the hero, make readers care what happens to her, and make a political statement about society's treatment of women in the late nineteenth century? Take your time and go through each chapter leading up to this moment. List each thing Hardy does to make the hammer more impactful.

MINI FINAL ANSWER

The best answer is **d) An anonymous letter arrives, with photos, that says her husband faked his death and now lives in Vienna.** This information is impossible to ignore, raises questions, radically alters the hero's state, and provokes her to act.

2

Ask dramatic questions.

"Judge a man by his questions rather than his answers."
—VOLTAIRE, Writer, Philosopher

QUICK TAKE

The simplest definition of story is this: Ask a dramatic question, then answer it. The entire *Lord of the Rings* trilogy is bracketed by the simple dramatic question "Will Frodo destroy the ring?" In the beginning, we learn about the ring, why it is so powerful and must be destroyed. In the end, we learn its fate. This overarching question, the one that fuels an entire story, is called a Central Dramatic Question (CDQ).

Not every Central Dramatic Question must be so overtly asked and cleanly tracked. In some stories, the reader or audience may not be fully aware of what the CDQ is until after the story's finished. Some are more interior, and take place within a character. CDQs can shift and change as new discoveries are made. Though the types of dramatic questions vary, a well-told story is fueled by questions that make people care about what's going to happen.

HOW IT WORKS

There are three kinds of dramatic questions that you can use to propel your narrative forward, keep it engaging throughout, and give it a satisfying resolution:

- **Central Dramatic Questions (CDQ)** give structure to your story as a whole. These are the questions that fuel the main storyline, and are most commonly phrased as "Will the hero obtain their object of desire?" There are four variants: external, internal, shifting, and retrospective.

- **Secondary Dramatic Questions (SDQ)** add nuance, depth, and texture by establishing a second storyline whose core idea and tone complement the main storyline. They also help structure your story.

- **Subordinate Dramatic Questions (Sub DQ)** give shape to smaller sections of your story as well as add nuance, depth, and texture.

The basic structure of dramatic questions works like this: Set up, Ask, Build, Answer. You set up the question by making the hero's emotional state clear. You drop the hammer, which changes the hero's state and provokes the dramatic question. You build tension by raising the stakes and making your audience guess how the question will be answered. Then you answer the question. Here is a simple story to illustrate the basic idea. Again, in training, we always start out as simple as possible and then add in complexity as we go.

- **Setup:** Our hero, a successful businessman, meets his girlfriend for dinner. He's had a long, hard week and is excited to finally relax and enjoy a nice, low-key meal. His girlfriend shows up and hugs him, but she's got a strange look in her eye. He asks her about it, but she only smiles.

▶ **Ask:** He wonders if something's wrong. Then, to his shock, she gets down on one knee and takes out a ring. This drops the hammer, and provokes the dramatic question: Will he say yes?

▶ **Build:** The entire dining room turns to watch his response. He tells her that they should discuss this in private. She says she needs to know now—she's either leaving with her new fiancé, the man she loves, or she's leaving as a single woman. Enough's enough. It's time.

▶ **Answer:** He looks deep into her eyes; even he doesn't know what he's going to say. Then, to the joy of all, he says yes. The entire restaurant bursts into applause. This answers the question.

How you ultimately construct your narratives and manage dramatic questions is impacted by what you're writing and your personal style. Your story may not end with a definitive, climactic answer. Scenes or chapters may build and release the tension several times before building up again. There's room to play with these principles and exercises. For now, think of mastering dramatic questions like putting together the edge of a jigsaw puzzle. There's still a lot of work to do but you get a jolt of excitement from knowing that the narrative has a shape. This gives you the sense that your hard work will ultimately be rewarded with a coherent—and, hopefully, inspired—final product that deserves to be published or produced.

Central Dramatic Question (CDQ)

Central Dramatic Questions fuel the main storyline. They help you, as the writer, structure the overall arc of your story and give your audience something to focus on throughout. There are four variants: external, internal, shifting, and retrospective. They are not mutually exclusive. A single story may be propelled at various points by each kind of question.

An **external CDQ** is one that deals with the hero's attempt to acquire an object of desire that is physical, or external. They need to find a missing person or buried treasure or win a race. These are the most common types of CDQs. For example, this is why there are so many shows set in police stations, hospitals, and law offices. It's easy to track whether the cop will catch the criminal, the doctor will save the patient, or the lawyer will win the case.

An **internal CDQ** is one that deals with the hero's attempt to acquire an object of desire that deals with the character's quest to achieve greater peace of mind. Will the hero learn to love himself and let go of guilt? This type of dramatic question is more commonly explored in fiction because it's the easiest medium for going inside a character's mind.

Many stories have both external and internal CDQs that are so closely related, they're essentially one question. For example, in the film *Gravity*, an astronaut, grieving the loss of her daughter, is stranded in space after an accident. The external CDQ is "Will she make it back to Earth?" The internal CDQ is "Will she rediscover her love of life?"

A **shifting CDQ** shifts from one question to another. For example, in Alfred Hitchcock's classic 1960 horror film *Psycho*, the film shifts CDQs as it moves from "Will Marion get away with stealing money from her boss?" to "Will Norman dispose of Marion's body?" to "Will her family discover what Norman's done?" This works particularly well because the subject is a man with a split personality, and the disorienting nature of the shifting questions relates to the story's subject matter.

A **retrospective CDQ** is one that's only clear to the reader or audience in hindsight, after they've finished the story. In Anton Chekhov's 1891 novella *The Duel*, the story arcs on the evolution of the main character, Laevsky, from an immature, anxiety-ridden narcissist to a more responsible, authentic adult. But while you're reading it you would never think the CDQ is "Will Laevsky grow up?" You get caught up in external questions regarding Laevsky's romance with his free-spirited girlfriend, Natasha, and his looming duel with a German zoologist, Von

Koren, who is so disgusted by Laevsky's lifestyle that he feels entitled to kill him.

• • •

Again, we want these precepts to offer you enough structure to feel confident that you can finish a satisfying story, but not so much that it stifles the spontaneity and joy of writing. That said, should you desire a little more hand-holding, here is a very simple way to outline a story. Think up a hero. Drop the hammer and provoke the CDQ. For example: A woman returns from a vacation with her mother to find her husband's been kidnapped. The CDQ is, Will she find her husband? Now imagine your story as a train ride that can go to one of three destinations:

1. The hero acquires the object of desire (she finds her husband).
2. The hero fails to acquire the object of desire (she will never find him).
3. The hero partially acquires the object of desire (she finds him, but he's changed so fundamentally that he is no longer recognizable as his former self).

The train metaphor works well because it gives your audience the sense that the story is moving in a meaningful direction without revealing where. This is important because if you want to get your work published or produced, a tight, coherent narrative—one that makes it easy to see what kind of story you're telling and what it's about—is much simpler to edit, punch up, and improve. It also makes it much simpler for you to make creative decisions based on whether the story is on or off track. Every scene must relate to the CDQ as tightly as possible. For example, let's say the woman seeking her kidnapped husband has a complex relationship with her hypercritical mother. The two having an intense argument about money could, regardless of the plot, add depth to the hero's character. But the scene is far more likely to be engaging if she needs her mother to put up fifty thousand dollars to rescue her husband.

Secondary Dramatic Questions (SDQ)

In television, the Secondary Dramatic Question is called the "B-Story" (the CDQ is the "A-Story"). The SDQ is important, but not as important as the CDQ, and it takes up less time. There is only one reason to include an SDQ: It adds nuance and depth to the idea you're exploring. Let's say you're writing a story about an aging tennis star who competes, for the last time, at Wimbledon. Though she's had a fantastic career, she never won that tournament and fears it has tarnished her legacy. Hypercompetitive, she can't bear the thought that she's not considered the greatest of all time. The CDQ is simple: "Will she win Wimbledon?"

Now, let's say you're interested in exploring the nature of competition and want to add a second storyline that complements the first. So, you give the hero a seventeen-year-old daughter who is a rising tennis star. The kid not only makes Wimbledon, but she's a real contender to win. In the SDQ we track, "Will the daughter win Wimbledon?" While mom is a hard-ass who trains longer and more brutally than any player in history, her daughter is a party girl who relies on her natural talent and believes there's more to life than winning. Her mother loves her but also bitterly resents her for what she feels is disrespect for her talent. By exploring two unique personalities and how they handle competition, we gain greater insight. The story's rhythm, texture, and style will shift in interesting ways as we move from one storyline to the other.

Subordinate Dramatic Questions (Sub DQ)

Subordinate Dramatic Questions relate directly to the CDQ or SDQ but take up less time, and they too add texture, nuance, and depth to the story's main idea. A Sub DQ might be resolved in a sequence, scene, or even just a part of a scene. To stick with our mother and daughter tennis players, let's say the mother knows she must get her serve up to 100 miles per hour to win. The

Sub Dramatic Question, is, of course, "Will mom nail a 100 mph serve?" We may see her working with the world's most expensive, demanding coach, attacking serve after serve. We may see her barely able to lift her tortured arm at the end of practice. This dramatic question is subordinate but directly related to the CDQ: "Will she win Wimbledon?" When you hear people talk about being on the edge of their seats, what they mean is that they're riveted by the way one dramatic question provokes another and another as your story builds momentum, raises stakes, deepens character, and moves toward its conclusion.

HOW A MASTER DID IT

Finding Nemo (2003)
Andrew Stanton, Bob Peterson, and David Reynolds

In the animated Pixar film *Finding Nemo*, Marlin is a tiny orange clownfish who has just scored a beautiful new home with a gorgeous view of the open ocean at a place called "the drop-off." The neighborhood is bursting with brightly colored fish. His wife, Coral, is delighted. What a perfect place to raise their hundreds of soon-to-hatch babies who sleep soundly in their eggs. Marlin worries that the babies won't like him. Coral says there are so many, one will surely like him. As Marlin playfully chases Coral, he stops cold. The neighborhood that was just bursting with life is suddenly deserted. Where did everyone go? He turns to see Coral staring down a barracuda who lurks outside the drop-off. This sets up the hammer.

Marlin pleads with Coral to take shelter, but she darts below to protect her babies. The barracuda speeds toward her, teeth snapping. Marlin shoots in front of it, but is knocked unconscious. He wakes later that night and desperately searches for Coral. But she is gone. And so are all their children. They've been devoured by the barracuda. Alone, Marlin cries. This drops the hammer.

He then spots something orange glowing below. He glides to it and finds one baby still alive, sleeping soundly in his little egg. He names him Coral's favorite baby name, Nemo, and promises not to let anything happen to him. With the CDQ "Will Marlin protect Nemo?" made explicitly clear, the opening credits roll.

Since this hammer dropped so early, just a few minutes in, the storytellers immediately begin setting up another one. Nemo, now a little fish kid, wakes Marlin with joyful cries of "First day of school! First day of school!" Marlin, still traumatized, is not ready to let Nemo go. He tries to talk him out of it, but Nemo is determined. Before they can set off, Marlin makes him exit and return three times to make sure it's safe to go outside. He relentlessly drives home the point that the ocean is a dangerous place.

Marlin brings Nemo to school but is overprotective and embarrasses him in front of the other kids. The local dads are surprised to see Marlin finally leave his anemone home, a smaller one far from the drop-off. A large blue stingray, the teacher Mr. Ray, shows up singing about the joys of adventuring and all of the kids hop on his back. Marlin is a nervous wreck as Nemo rides off into the wild blue yonder. When he finds out the kids' field trip is to the drop-off, he panics and races after them.

Riding on Mr. Ray's back, Nemo marvels at the awesome sights and creatures passing by. They get to the drop-off and, while Mr. Ray lectures, Nemo and three little friends sneak over to the drop-off. They dare each other to go out farther and farther. High overhead, a small boat bobs on the surface. Marlin races in shrieking, "Nemo!" and humiliates his son in front of all his new friends. He tells Nemo, "You think you can do these things, but you can't!" Nemo has one healthy and one "lucky"—or deformed—fin, which gives Marlin additional doubts about Nemo's abilities. When Marlin tells Nemo he must come home, Nemo says, "I hate you." Marlin is stung. His fear of not being loved by his child has come true.

Nemo swims up toward the boat. Marlin warns him not to touch the boat. Nemo makes it all the way up and defiantly slaps the bottom. As Nemo swims down to face his dad's wrath, a scuba diver appears and captures him. Marlin feverishly tries to save the boy but is blinded by the flash of another diver's underwater camera. He gets his sight back just in time to see the boat speeding off and desperately follows the trail. But after several miles, the trail fades. Marlin pops his head above the water and sees nothing but a vast expanse of ocean. His son is lost. This drops the second hammer.

As gut-wrenching as the first hammer is, the second one is even worse. Marlin's attempt to protect his son, his only surviving family member, has caused the boy to hate him, to be kidnapped, and taken away to God knows what kind of torment and possibly murder. However terrible the grief of losing his wife and kids to the barracuda attack was, at least his conscience was clean. This time, it's his fault. And he must live with the guilt *and* terror of not knowing where his small child is or what's happening to him.

The CDQ shifts from "Will Marlin protect Nemo?" to "Will Marlin find Nemo?" Notice how simple it is to state these dramatic questions. Both need just four words. Yet we're exploring one of the most profoundly important human questions: How do parents keep children safe? These questions were particularly poignant when *Finding Nemo* was released in 2003, not long after the terrorist attacks on September 11, 2001, which killed thousands of innocent people, including children. The long, silver barracuda bears an unmistakable resemblance to an airplane.

On a personal note, I was a young father with a four-year-old when the film came out and I was shocked when Coral and the other babies were murdered in the first five minutes. A mother I was with had to carry her screaming child out of the theater. My little girl was rattled. I remember thinking, "These bastards better know what they're doing." With that intense reaction in mind, let's see how the writers managed dramatic questions to craft the story.

After the boat disappears, the Sub DQ is "Will Marlin figure out where the boat went?" It's "sub" because it's subordinate to the CDQ "Will Marlin find Nemo?" So, it works like this: "Will Marlin figure out where the boat went, so he can find Nemo?" Now let's go quickly through the beginning of Act Two to see how the writers ask and answer dramatic questions to propel the story:

▶ A blue fish tells Marlin to follow her. She knows which way the boat went. He does. Then she turns on him and tells him to quit following her. *What's wrong with her?*

▶ She has short-term memory loss. But she's his only hope. Then a great white shark shows up, flashing horrific rows of teeth. He insists they come with him. *Who is he? What does he want? Where is he taking them?*

▶ They glide through mines laid around an abandoned submarine. *Will they explode?*

▶ The great white takes them into a room where there are other sharks who each have smaller fish beside them. The great white's name is Bruce and he's part of a twelve-step–type group that helps fish quit eating other fish. Tonight, members had to bring new fish as guests to increase their membership. The little guests are terrified—*will they be eaten*?

▶ Marlin spots the scuba mask dropped by the diver who took Nemo. It has fallen onto a rock jutting out nearby. An address is written on it. But Marlin can't read "human." Dory says she can, *but can she*?

▶ Dory and Marlin both grab the mask and get in a tug-of-war. It snaps, striking Dory in the nose, and blood seeps out. It drifts into Bruce's nostrils and drives him mad with desire. The other sharks shout, "Fish are friends, not food!" Marlin and Dory race off in the mask with Bruce hot on their heels. *Will he eat them?*

▶ After Bruce traps them in a torpedo shaft, he accidentally launches a rusty old torpedo that not only explodes—it sets off all the mines! *Were Marlin and Dory killed?*

▶ We cut to Nemo dropping into a scary-looking fish tank. It turns out he was captured by a scuba-diving dentist and now lives in a tank full of quirky fish driven to anxiety and depression by their limited surroundings. This sets up the Secondary Dramatic Question, *Will Nemo escape the tank?*

Notice the rhythm of the story: Question asked, question answered. The film runs on two tracks, fueled by related questions, "Will Marlin find Nemo?" and "Will Nemo escape the tank?" The SDQ adds depth as Nemo's new father figure, Gill, builds up Nemo's confidence by teaching him to confront risk. Gil has the faith in Nemo that Marlin lacks.

As Marlin battles to get to Nemo and Nemo battles to escape the tank, their struggles reveal internal questions. For Marlin, it's "Will he learn to accept risk?" For Nemo, it's "Will he learn to trust himself?" His confidence has been shattered by his neurotic father, who taught him he can't do things, that he's sure to be killed by the dangerous world.

The writers are in complete control of *all* their dramatic questions. If you've seen *Finding Nemo*, I'll bet you can remember every scene. You remember the surfer dude turtles, the fish ritually chanting "Shark Bait hoo-ha-ha," and the seagulls barking "Mine." Why is that? It's because each scene is a perfectly told short story, fueled by a clearly asked and intelligently answered dramatic question. In hindsight, knowing the film is one of the most beloved and highest-grossing of all time, it's easy to forget the risk they took by opening with such a violent scene. But it worked, and parents like me who were initially taken aback came to realize that the writers knew exactly what they were doing.

This is an important point about mastering the craft. No one finishes watching *Finding Nemo* and thinks, "Gosh, what a well-structured story." You leave thinking about the nature of risk, and what it takes to become a whole person and a loving parent. You leave feeling how fragile and beautiful life is. You leave feeling grateful to the storytellers for having the courage to ask the most challenging questions, for helping you live a more fulfilling, courageous, and dignified life. It's the writers' commitment to craft, their ability to operate the heavy machinery of story, that provokes these heightened states and teaches us how to live.

HOW YOU DO IT

The following bullet points will help you think through and execute the principle.

▶ In the first chapter, you shaped a dramatic question that is provoked by the hammer coming down. This is your Central Dramatic Question. Its basic format is simply "Will the protagonist acquire their object of desire?" For example, "Will the cop catch his son's killer?" When you write out your dramatic question, keep it as simple and clear as you can. "Will Marlin find Nemo?" is succinct and active.

▶ As you craft your CDQ, consider your story's subject matter, medium (novel, screenplay, video game, etc.), and main idea. For example, if you're writing a novel about twenty-four hours in the life of a shopkeeper and you're interested in the way each day is a metaphor for a lifetime, your story is fueled by an *internal* dramatic question. It might be "Can a man find contentment?" This is laid out as follows:

- ▷ **CDQ:** Will a shopkeeper find contentment?
- ▷ **Type of CDQ:** Internal
- ▷ **Medium:** Novel
- ▷ **Main Idea:** How each day encompasses a lifetime

Make sure that your CDQ, medium, and main idea align. A novel feels right for this, but a video game about a day in the life of a shopkeeper would probably not work.

▸ A strong dramatic question makes it easy to envision lots of promising Sub Dramatic Questions. In the story about the cop looking for his son's killer, it's easy to imagine him hunting for evidence, interviewing witnesses, chasing leads, etc.

▸ Add a Secondary Dramatic Question if you need one. For example, in *Finding Nemo*, there are two questions:

- ▹ **CDQ:** Will Marlin find Nemo?
- ▹ **SDQ:** Will Nemo escape the tank?

In the tank, Nemo meets a father figure, Gill, who teaches him he's strong enough to take risks. This allows the writers to explore the nature of parenting and risk from different angles. Gill is a very different father than Marlin.

▸ If you have an external CDQ, you can run an internal one concurrently. For example, in *Finding Nemo* you have:

- ▹ Will Marlin find Nemo?
- ▹ Will Marlin learn to accept risk?

If your story has an external CDQ, consider adding an internal one to add depth and offer insight into your protagonist.

▸ Practice the setup/ask/build/answer dynamic of dramatic questions. Create a dramatic question. Set it up, build tension by raising the stakes, then answer the question. It works like this:

- ▹ **Setup:** A saleswoman is lonely. She spends night after night solo—on the road, in hotels, airports, and planes, and comes home to an empty condo.
- ▹ **Ask:** A client shoots her a look that seems suggestive.
- ▹ **Build:** She falls madly in love with him and, despite her independent spirit, can't eat or sleep until she wins his heart.

▷ **Answer:** They go on a date that is so magical they elope that night and live happily ever after. Sometimes fairy tales do come true.

▶ As you craft your narrative, keep track of all of your dramatic questions: Central, Secondary, and Sub-Dramatic Questions. As you list them, stick to the basics: Make sure they're clearly asked, explore interesting ideas, build tension, and make you want to tell your story.

MINI FINAL EXAM

Read the following, then answer the question below.

Our hero, Shmuel Finkelbein, is the leader of the Magnificent Klezmer Boys, the first klezmer band to break into the mainstream with their hit album *Never Mind the Meshuggaas, This Is the Magnificent Klezmer Boys*. But in the studio, while recording their second album, things are not going well. The pressure is becoming unbearable. Drummer Yuval "Yukkel" Goldfarb can't keep the beat, equipment's malfunctioning left and right, and Morty Borkowsky refuses to play the hammered dulcimer. He won't even play it on the tune Shmuel wrote specifically for the hammered dulcimer! Tension runs high. Shmuel calls time-out and asks the band to gather round.

You're writing the last moment of the scene. All the following lines express emotion, but which asks a question and provokes the most curiosity about the next scene? Shmuel says:

a) "What's happened to us!? We were musical revolutionaries, absolute geniuses, and now we're bubkes! Bubkes! I'm going home. You guys . . . do whatever you want."

b) "Morty, you hurt my feelings. You know how important the hammered dulcimer is to me. And yet now—now—you won't play it? This is spite. And it's shameful."

c) "Now you see my clarinet?!" Then he smashes it to pieces and cries, "Now you don't!" and storms off.
d) "We're going to take a break, then come back and play 'Yiddish Nights.' If it's not inspired, I'm going to fire one of your asses—on the spot."
e) "You know what? Clearly, I don't have what it takes to lead this band. Let's just all go get some sandwiches and a nice big bowl of soup."

CONTINUING ED

In the opening shot of the Netflix series *Russian Doll*, Nadia Vulvokov attends her own birthday party in New York City. She's a street-smart computer programmer, a tough woman with a head of wild red hair, and a chain-smoker. She doesn't suffer fools easily and won't hesitate to let people know if she thinks they're full of shit. She also seems profoundly unsettled in her personal life. After she develops an attraction to a man at the party, the two head out for a romantic encounter, but when she crosses the street, she's run over by a speeding taxicab. What happens to her next? Why did it happen? What does it mean? How does it make you feel more empathy for Nadia and care what happens next in not only the episode, but the entire series?

MINI FINAL ANSWER

The correct answer is **d) "We're going to take a break, then come back and play 'Yiddish Nights.' If it's not inspired, I'm going to fire one of your asses—on the spot."** This makes it explicitly clear what will happen next, raises the stakes, builds tension, and asks a clear dramatic question, Will the band nail the next take? And if they don't, who will get fired? It's the best choice for making your reader want to turn the page and see what happens next.

3

Explore all endings.

"A narrative is like a room on whose walls a number of false doors have been painted; while within the narrative, we have many apparent choices of exit, but when the author leads us to one particular door, we know it is the right one because it opens."
—JOHN UPDIKE, Author

QUICK TAKE

When someone tells you a story, the first thing you wonder is "Does this have a point?" The end of your story answers that question—it expresses your theme, or main idea, the one the entire narrative is crafted to convey. It's revealed by simple analysis. If two brothers struggle to forgive each other's sins and, in the final moment, embrace, the theme is that resentment can be overcome.

The end of your story is where we determine whether the journey was worth our time. A great ending fuses both logic and emotion. Stories are not op-ed columns. They're not essays. They're designed to make us feel intense feelings—to recoil in horror, cry our eyes out, want to kill someone, laugh hysterically, or feel connected to forces bigger than ourselves.

You always—*always*—want to end strong.

This principle is about discipline and grit. It's about taking the time to, within reason, explore all endings, so that you fulfill the promise of your stories. Whether it's to terrify, enlighten, shock, move, or inspire—whatever it is, you want to take your audience to the limit. This means writing endings that are meaningful, inevitable, surprising, just, emotional, and authentic. We'll explore all of these qualities in detail below.

HOW IT WORKS

Some writers feel the entire point of writing is to discover what they believe through the process of telling their story. Others start with an ending in mind because they have an idea to express and want to lead audiences to the same conclusion. Regardless of when you decide on your ending, you want to make sure it's the most impactful and insightful it can be. To do this, carefully consider your setup, what your audience expects to happen, and then look for ways to exceed their expectations.

If a waiter carries a tall stack of dishes toward spilled milk, and he wipes out, it might be funny, but that's exactly what's expected. You will never make your mark by giving publishers and producers exactly what's expected. (We'll dig into this more in Chapter 6, "Clash expectation with reality.") But if the waiter pirouettes, does a somersault, and catches every dish, or tumbles onto a stovetop and bursts into flames, or if he wipes out but responds in an unexpected way—laughs hysterically, then sobs uncontrollably—you might be in business.

For every setup—bits of dialogue and action, scenes, chapters, and whole stories alike—elite writers identify the obvious conclusion, and rule it out. The bad news is this will make your job harder. But as the writer Thomas Mann said, "A writer is someone for whom writing is more difficult than it is for other people." The good news is this will lead you to the full realization of your unique talent and help you discover the truth of how you see the world. How you deal with that dish-carrying waiter's battle with the spilled milk reveals who you are. The writer who has the waiter break all the dishes, crack his head open, and get fired is a different person with a different worldview than the one who has the waiter's colleagues—the cooks, busboys, and other waiters—rallying to catch all the dishes before they hit the floor and then hugging it out as a team.

In order to select the best possible ending, you need criteria to define what "best" means. Here are six qualities of a great ending: meaningful, inevitable, surprising, just, emotional, and authentic.

Meaningful

The sequence of events leads to a logical conclusion. Because A and B happen, it means C. In the movie *Jaws*, Chief Brody moves to the small town of Amity because in New York City, one man can't make a difference. When he kills the shark, this tells us that one man *can* make a difference. A man who could not make a difference moves to a town where he can make a difference—and he does. Therefore, it means one man can make a difference.

Inevitable

Given the nature of your protagonist, antagonist, story events, and the world you create, you can't fathom the story ending any other way. Every loose end is tied up and there are no logical flaws. Master storytellers include lines of dialogue and/or conjure images that help create this feeling of inevitability. This is called "foreshadowing," where you subtly hint to the audience what will happen. The foreshadowing must be impactful enough for your audience to notice it, but not so heavy-handed that it gives the ending away. For example, in *The Lord of the Rings*, when they begin their adventure, Gandalf tells Frodo that he senses Gollum has a role to play in the destruction of the ring. And he does. Gollum does something at Frodo's moment of truth that saves the world.

When you finish a story, your mind races back through it to make sure everything checks out. When Gollum takes his final action, you recall Gandalf's line, and it helps create the feeling that this final moment was inevitable.

Surprising

Have you ever listened to someone tell you a story where you could see the ending coming a mile away? It's excruciating. The challenge is in writing a scene that feels both inevitable *and* surprising. You can't just spring a cheap surprise on your audience. "It was all a dream!" is a cop-out.

There are two ways to make your ending surprising without relying on pranks or gimmicks. You can trick your audience into thinking something else will happen. Or you can surprise them with how it happens. Again, go back to our dish-carrying waiter walking toward spilled milk. What happens to him or how he responds can make the end surprising.

Just

Your ending is *just*—it's fair within the context of the story. This doesn't mean what happens to the characters is necessarily fair. Of course, life is not always fair. It's full of injustice. But story justice is different from traditional justice. It's more nuanced. It deals with what happens to the character *and* the reader or viewer. Consider this Saturday morning cartoon on a family-friendly channel. Mother is making Thanksgiving dinner alone in the kitchen. An impish kitten romps with a ball of yarn by her feet. She tickles his belly. He smells the turkey on her fingers, looks up, and sees the magnificent bird, just out of the oven. She warns him, "Not for you, kitty." He nods politely that he understands. She calls him a sweet little guy, then leaves the room. He leaps onto the counter but can barely make it and hangs there by his little paws. He finally pulls himself up and nibbles some turkey. Its sheer deliciousness intoxicates him. As he goes in for another nibble, his head is blown to smithereens and blood spatters the walls. Mom enters carrying an AR-15 and coldly tosses him into the trash.

This is unjust on three levels. First, the cartoon is on Saturday morning on a family-friendly channel. This implies that it will be appropriate for all ages and not contain graphic violence. Second, there was nothing in the story to lead us to believe this woman is stressed out enough to kill the kitten over a minor offense. And third, the kitten doesn't deserve the death penalty for doing what comes instinctually to him. Again, the writer might argue, "But that's life. Bad things happen." This is wrong because it breaks your promise. When you tell a story, you promise to give your audience insight into *why* things happen. Anyone can pick up the newspaper and see random, senseless violence.

Emotional

Think of any story, in any medium, that you love—love with all your heart. Now try to remember how it made you feel at the end. You likely had intense feelings of joy, sorrow, rage, shock, hurt, wonder, relief, or delight. You did not walk out of the theater, close the book, or shut the game console and do a Mr. Spock impersonation, coldly reciting your take on the story's meaning. You felt it deep in your guts. As a writer, you want to deliver a major jolt of emotion in the very final moment, to give your audience or reader something to help make the experience last.

Authentic

Authenticity is like an electric current—it adds credibility and a life force to a story. Authenticity comes from an alignment between the writer, characters, and the time it's written. Above all, you must believe what your ending says about life. If you love light comedies, have a sunny disposition, and feel every day is a gift, it is highly unlikely you could write a gangster film in which everyone gets slaughtered. Take a second to consider your favorite writer/director and the story you consider their best. You will find a tight connection between who they are, what's happened to them, how they view or need to view life, and the ending of their story.

Toward the end of Elizabeth Strout's short story "A Little Burst," a mother, Olive Kitteridge, whose feelings have been wounded by her new daughter-in-law, enters the woman's room, pulls out a sweater, draws a line on it with a magic marker, and neatly refolds it, because, "It helps some to know that at least there will be moments when Suzanne will doubt herself." It's poignant, comedic, and tragic. The story ends with Olive clutching her handbag, leaving the wedding reception, and picturing her heart as a "big red muscle, banging away beneath her flowered dress." This moment is so intense and layered, it had to come from a real place.

HOW A MASTER DID IT

The Night Of (2016)
Richard Price and Steve Zallian

In HBO's eight-episode TV series *The Night Of*, Nasir "Naz" Khan is a high school senior from Jackson Heights, Queens. He's Muslim American, the son of working-class Pakistani immigrants. His mom works in a clothing shop. His dad drives a cab that he co-owns with two friends. Naz came of age during the terrorist attacks of 9/11 and was viciously bullied at school as a "terrorist." He has huge sad brown eyes, a nerdy side part, and is a good student. He tutors one of the coolest kids in school, a handsome African American basketball player who invites Naz and his buddy to a party in Manhattan. This is a big deal to them. It will seriously up their status and give them a real shot to finally, for once in their lives, hook up with beautiful girls.

At dinner, Naz's parents give him a hard time about going to the party, leery of him getting into trouble. Later, he waits for his buddy to pick him up. He nervously practices introducing himself to the girls he's about to meet. But his friend calls and backs out. Naz, desperate to go, steals his father's cab and heads into the city. People try to hail the cab and curse him for passing them by. He pulls over to find the "Off Duty" light. As he does, a young woman hops into the back seat. He explains he's off duty, but when he sees she's a beautiful, black-haired girl with a mysterious allure, he's intrigued. Her name's Andrea and she asks him to take her to a beach on the Upper West Side. As they drive, we see shots of the cab through surveillance cameras. Andrea asks Naz about himself and figures out that he chose her over going to a party. She's flattered. She leans through the little window, her head beside him in the front seat. He's smitten.

They find the beach and sit beneath the George Washington Bridge. Its lights glow in the ripples of the Hudson River beneath a full moon. She asks about his life and his family and listens to his answers. She tells him about the father she's lost. He talks about the pressure of always feeling like you have to do what everybody else wants. They are falling for each other hard. She takes a hit of ecstasy and hands him one. He hesitates. Raised Muslim, he doesn't do drugs. But taken in by the moment, he pops the pill. She tells him she can't be alone. We'll learn later she's being stalked by a shady guy who managed her late father's estate.

Naz, glassy-eyed and grinning, drives her to Brooklyn. As they walk toward her brownstone, two men call him "Mustafa" and he stops, unsure what they said. They make racist jokes about him having bombs. His silly grin could be a sign of disrespect. One guy glares at him with malice as Naz follows Andrea into her place. This world is filled with threat and menace.

Her place is gorgeous and huge—four stories—and she lives there alone. It feels dark and lonely. She plays music, pours them shots of tequila, and then takes out a knife. She spreads her fingers on the table and violently stabs down between them in a game of "five finger filet." She tells Naz to do it. He does. She tells him to do it again—to her hand. He does. But this time he stabs her. Blood flows. She is aroused and kisses him passionately. They rush upstairs to her bedroom and make love.

Later, Naz wakes alone in the kitchen in a T-shirt and boxers. The fridge door is open beside him. Half-asleep, he drifts up to the darkened bedroom, sits on the bed, and tells her he has to go. She doesn't answer. He moves around the bed and turns on the light. His eyes fill with fear. We pull back to see Andrea's naked, blood-soaked body *slaughtered*. Blood is everywhere. She's been stabbed countless times. Naz, panicked, races downstairs, pulls his coat on, and grabs the bloody knife they played with earlier. He flies out the door and it locks behind him as he rushes toward his dad's cab. But he forgot the keys. He runs back to the brownstone, breaks a window on the door—and is spotted by a neighbor staring out his window. He opens the door, finds his keys, runs back out, and drives off in the cab.

Terrified, still reeling from the drugs, he makes an illegal turn and gets pulled over by the police. He denies drinking, but the officer smells tequila on his breath. She is in no mood for his lies and tells him to get out and place his hands on the car. He does and smears blood on the roof. He covers it with a slight move of his hand. Just then, a call comes in—about a murder nearby. The cop puts Naz in the back seat and drives off to investigate. Naz will just have to wait to get processed for drunk driving.

Naz's eyes go wide when they pull up to Andrea's brownstone. It's crawling with cops. After an eternity watching them work, Naz is brought to the police precinct. The place is bustling with activity. Even in hardened New York City, the savage murder of a wealthy white girl is still big news. Naz adjusts himself repeatedly to make sure the knife hidden inside his jacket doesn't stick out. Finally, it comes time to process him. The arresting officer is in a foul mood from being forced to work long past her shift. She pats down every inch of him and, to the shock of all, pulls out the bloody knife. He screams and runs but he's tackled, arrested, and processed. Homicide Detective Dennis Box, a veteran and good enough guy, explains to him that they have his DNA on the knife, his DNA on the body, his DNA at the crime scene, and the victim's DNA on him. He tells Naz to confess, that it will be for the best. Naz insists that he didn't do it. But he's not convincing.

Even he's not sure. Box tells him he is charged with first-degree murder. This drops the hammer and asks the Central Dramatic Question of the series, "Will Naz be found guilty?"

Now, we're going to take our time and explore various endings, the one they chose and why it worked. The two most likely endings are, of course, that Naz is found either guilty or not guilty by the jury. These could play out as follows:

Guilty:

- A jury finds Naz guilty because he is proven guilty.
- A jury finds Naz guilty, but he might not be guilty.
- A jury finds Naz guilty, but he's not guilty.

Not Guilty:

- A jury finds Naz not guilty because he is proven not guilty.
- A jury finds Naz not guilty, though he might be guilty.
- Naz is found not guilty, but he is guilty.

Now let's look at some less predictable endings:

- There's a hung jury and Naz will be retried.
- There's a hung jury and Naz won't be retried.
- Awaiting trial, Naz is killed in prison.
- Naz escapes prison, runs off, and assumes a new identity.
- The case is thrown out due to police/prosecutorial misconduct.
- It was all a dream caused by Naz being on drugs.

Now let's look at what the writers did and see why it works. They chose:

- There's a hung jury and Naz won't be retried.

At first glance, this choice might seem underwhelming. But after we go through the criteria for great endings you'll see why their choice is a strong one.

Meaningful

At its heart, the series is about the dehumanizing effect our criminal justice system has on people. This is exactly what happens. A bright young man is accused of a crime, goes through the criminal justice system, and comes out a hardened, tattooed drug addict with a shaved head who is unrecognizable to his own mother. In one of the harrowing final scenes, Naz sits alone in a store and sees an old friend—who testified against him. The once doe-eyed Naz stares him down with a murderous gaze. He has been profoundly and irreversibly changed.

Inevitable

The writers make this ending feel inevitable for three reasons. The first is that the evidence is so overwhelming against Naz that it seems like he must be guilty. But late in the series, he takes the stand, looks the jury in the eye, and admits that it is possible that he did it. He was on drugs. And he has no memory of the incident. But he liked Andrea, a lot. He had no conceivable motivation to kill her. He seems convincing when he says he doesn't believe he did it.

The second is that there are other suspects, one of whom was far more motivated than Naz to kill Andrea. This man had romantic interest in her and was after her money.

The third is that, although the case against him is exceptionally strong, there is reasonable doubt. The DA is a world-weary realist. She goes after him in the first trial with all she's got. But her doubts about his guilt grow throughout. After the jury becomes deadlocked, she must make a decision to invest limited resources in retrying Naz or to drop the case against him. If she couldn't put him away this time, she won't have better luck next time. So, she lets him go. The logic of this choice is flawless, giving it a feeling of inevitability in hindsight.

Surprising

It's surprising because you expect a straight up guilty or not guilty verdict.

Just

The Night Of is neo-noir, but it's also a coming-of-age story. It's on HBO, so you expect it to be dark and edgy. It's co-written by Richard Price, who's known for writing neo-noir detective stories, and Steve Zallian, who wrote the jet-black films *Hannibal* and *The Girl with the Dragon Tattoo*. The title, *The Night Of*—as in "Where were you on the night of the murder?"—makes it clear this is a crime drama. The network, writers, and title all tell us this show will explore the dark side of human nature.

A key tenet of noir is that the hero, a seemingly decent man, is pulled into a lurid world of sin, not just by a cruel twist of fate, but by something lurking deep within. Andrea is a classic femme fatale, alluring and deadly. Another character—one without the repressed rage that comes from being an outsider, teased and bullied during 9/11—would have sensed the inherent danger in Andrea and not gotten involved with her.

On the night she's killed, Naz makes a series of mistakes. He steals his father's cab. He hooks up with a girl who is both in danger and dangerous. He takes a drug without knowing what it is. He plays "five finger filet" with the knife and cuts her. He races out without the keys to the cab. He breaks back into the home. He makes a wrong turn, gets pulled over, and lies to the cops. After he found the body, he should have called the cops and immediately told the truth. Though it's easy to see why he didn't, the fact is he makes one bad decision after another.

The story feels just because the writers keep their promise to give us insight into the dark side of human nature, through a neo-noir about the criminal justice system. The writers ask a dramatic question in the first episode, track it through the entire series, and then deliver a meaningful answer in the series finale. They make a promise and they deliver on it.

Emotional

The last time we see Naz, he is a shell of his former self. He is hopelessly alienated from his family. He smokes heroin from a pipe. And he is haunted by memories of Andrea. He sits alone at the beach by the bridge, exactly where he sat with her on their first and last night together. He imagines her appearing beside him. The camera moves to a wide shot where Naz looks tiny, seated alone by the water beneath the bridge. The naïve child he was, the promising student, the loving and dedicated son, are all long gone. He will forever be under suspicion, and the future looks grim.

Authentic

In a Spring 1996 *Paris Review* interview, co-writer Richard Price said that he often thinks about the saying, "If God hates your guts, he grants your deepest wish." Before Naz met Andrea, his deepest wish was to hook up with a beautiful girl. His wish is granted, and it destroys his life. That's a key reason this ending works so well. It's in perfect alignment with the writer's vision. The idea expressed by this story has been in his mind for more than twenty years. If you watch interviews with both writers, Price and Zallian, who won the Oscar for writing the screenplay to *Schindler's List*, you can feel that these men carry themselves with a heavy energy. Determining what is or isn't authentic is far more art than science, but I think it's fair to say, these two particular men are comfortable exploring the dark side, and better off writing neo-noir than light comedy.

HOW YOU DO IT

The following bullet points will help you think through and execute the principle.

- Your objective is to find an inspired ending. Focus on these six essential qualities: meaningful, inevitable, surprising, just, emotional, and authentic. A truly inspired ending meets all six. The surprise may only be in how the ending happens. For example, in Junot Diaz's novel *The Brief Wondrous Life of Oscar Wao*, he tells you in the title that the hero's going to die. So he had to orchestrate the death in a way that's unexpected.

▶ Write out your CDQ in as few words as you can. Will the cop catch his son's killer? Will Marlin find Nemo? Will the lovers end up together? As you generate ideas for endings—or answers to the CDQ—start by keeping it reductively simple. There are three very basic ways your story can end: happy, sad, or mixed. Your hero acquires their object of desire (happy), fails to acquire their object of desire (sad), or your hero acquires their object of desire but pays a high price or fails to acquire their object of desire but learns a valuable lesson (mixed).

▶ Brainstorm possible endings. Aim for quantity. Let it rip without judgment. There is no downside to exploring "bad" ideas. Go big and keep in mind what Bruce Springsteen says: The line between your very worst idea and your very best idea is paper thin. It's this simple: The more ideas you consider, the more likely you are to find *the* one.

- ▷ Riff on ways your story can end happily.
- ▷ Riff on ways your story can end sadly.
- ▷ Riff on ways your story can end mixed.

▶ Read through your list of possible endings and trust your gut. Consider who you are at your core. (We'll dig into this in more detail in Chapter 24, "Hunt big game.") Which ideas stir something deep inside you? Which feel not just authentic, but necessary for you to explore or confront? If none meet the criteria, keep going. You want the idea that rattles you, that makes you feel vaguely euphoric, the one that could not possibly work . . . or could it?

▶ Once you think you've got it, take a breath and work through the checklist. Is it meaningful, inevitable, surprising, just, emotional, and authentic? In plain English, does the idea knock your socks off? If not, which of the criteria does it fail to meet? Work with it until it does.

MINI FINAL EXAM

Read the following, then answer the question below.

You're writing a melodramatic movie—a tale of religious inspiration—aimed squarely at a mainstream heartland American family audience. A single, working mother nervously checks her toddler's temperature. It's 102. Her intuition screams that something is seriously wrong. The little guy has not been himself for a week and he's got a glassy look in his eyes. His skin seems unusually tender. She calls her pediatrician, who insists it's just a cold. A devout woman, she prays fervently over the child. But nothing helps. He cries and writhes through his restless sleep.

Unable to bear it any longer, she wraps him up, puts him in his car seat, and drives to the emergency room. The doctor on call runs a battery of tests and ultimately learns that the boy has a disease that could be fatal. He sends her to experts who unanimously agree—it will be a miracle if the boy lives to see his next birthday. She pleads with them to find a cure, but they insist there is none. Some kids, somehow, beat this illness—but fewer than 1 percent. She could not endure the loss of her child. After the last doctor offers yet another lame apology, she vows to save her boy herself.

Based on this setup, and the six criteria, which of the following endings is the most effective?

a) Once she realizes all hope is lost, she takes the child to a river, fills her pockets with stones, and walks in so they drown together.
b) After the child passes, she comforts herself by having a destination wedding—with one of the boy's doctors who is an absolute hunk.
c) The child passes and the mother becomes a bitter alcoholic who spends the rest of her life cursing the heavens.
d) After DNA tests reveal the boy is not her child, she abandons him at an orphanage.
e) As she senses the little guy's light fading, she prays with a fervor unlike anything she's ever experienced. The color returns to the boy's face, the light to his eyes. She brings him back to the hospital and even the most skeptical doctor is amazed to find the boy is truly cured.

CONTINUING ED

In the 2008 film *The Hurt Locker*, written by Mark Boal and directed by Kathryn Bigelow, an American soldier, Sgt. William James, serves a tour of duty in Iraq. His job is to defuse bombs. The guy who had the job in his unit before he got there was blown to smithereens. When Sgt. James does it, he's completely consumed by his work and seems to relish being at the edge of death. In fact, he goes out of his way to court danger and put himself, and at times his unit, in harm's way. The film starts with a quote, "War is a drug."

At the end of the film, James makes a decision that the vast majority of human beings would not make. What does he decide to do—and how does his decision relate to the quote at the beginning of the film? How is his decision inspired by the moment he spends at a supermarket staring down the cereal aisle? After you watch the film, carefully walk the ending through the six criteria for an effective and hopefully inspired ending: meaningful, inevitable, surprising, just, emotional, and authentic.

MINI FINAL ANSWER

The correct answer is e) **As she senses the little guy's life fading, she prays with a fervor unlike anything she's ever experienced. The color returns to the boy's face, the light to his eyes. She brings him back to the hospital and even the most skeptical doctor is amazed to find the boy is truly cured**. The story is meaningful in that it espouses the power of prayer. It feels inevitable—though this is more art than science—in that the woman is so committed from the start. It is surprising that her final burst of prayer would pull the kid out of it. It's just that this is a "tale of inspiration" and this innocent child deserves to live. It's emotional in that a small child suffers and is brought to the edge of death. And, though it's hard to determine authenticity here, the woman's conviction makes it convincing.

4

Connect with "therefore," not "and."

"If you transition scenes with 'and,' you're fucked."
—TREY PARKER, Writer

QUICK TAKE

This principle is about leveraging the power of cause and effect to tell purposeful and coherent stories that build momentum and drive toward meaningful conclusions. Picture wires connected to a stack of dynamite. For our purposes, the dynamite is the ending. It could be the end of a conversation, scene, chapter, or the whole story. The electric charge must flow directly to the dynamite to set off the explosion. If a wire is frayed or there are wires that have weak or loose connections, the charge will fizzle out and the dynamite will fail to detonate. In a story, this means scenes and chapters will fail to resonate and the ending will feel anticlimactic.

When you link bits of dialogue in a conversation, chapters in a novel, or scenes in a film or play with a tight chain of cause and effect, they crackle with life and drive more deeply into the heart of your ideas. By "tight chain," we mean A directly causes

B, which directly causes C. A man reminds his friend that he owes him money, which causes the friend to get insulted and vow never to borrow a cent again, which causes the lender to insult him, which causes the two to trade blows. A happens *therefore* B happens *therefore* C happens. Now compare this to the loosely connected stories that little kids tell. They connect events with "and." They'll say, "And this happened, and that happened, and this happened." It's adorable, but the longer it goes on, the more bewildering it gets.

HOW IT WORKS

When you connect events using "therefore" instead of "and," your options decrease. If you say Joe punches Doug and connect the next action with "and," then literally anything can happen. Joe punches Doug and Mongol hordes invade Kentucky. If you connect with "therefore" you have to work within a logical frame. Joe punches Doug *therefore* Doug 1) ignores him; 2) scolds him; 3) hits him back; 4) storms off; 5) apologizes for upsetting him; 6) falls down unconscious. You still have many options, but all are much more likely to result in a meaningful conclusion.

This gives you room to explore ideas and discover the true nature of your characters as you think through what each choice means. But, even more importantly, in doing this work, you discover who *you* are. For example, let's say that you have always considered yourself an angry, aggressive person. But as you explore this interaction between Joe and Doug, you are moved by the idea that Doug responds to Joe's violence with compassion. You love the idea that Doug not only takes a punch, but apologizes for upsetting his friend. This tells you who Doug is, helps you understand what you value or long for, and says something meaningful about the nature of compassion.

To give yourself some flexibility, you can transition dialogue and actions with "but" or "meanwhile." For example, Joe punches at Doug *but* Doug inexplicably vanishes. To transition events that move between storylines, you use "meanwhile." Joe punches Doug therefore Doug apologizes for upsetting him, *meanwhile* Mary tells Jane about a fight she saw in the street. You want to keep the action flowing smoothly, without the transition to the second storyline feeling too jarring. Here, we tied the two scenes together by alluding to a fight. That's called "connective tissue." By adding some connective tissue, our minds stay engaged as we register the fact that we're still exploring the same idea from storyline to storyline. And that smooths out the transition. *Finding Nemo* handles this with expert precision, seamlessly moving from the Marlin storyline to the Nemo storyline and back.

As you build your outline, don't get hung up on perfectly defining every transition. That's letting the tail wag the dog. The point here is to leverage the power of cause and effect to keep your story focused, build momentum, reveal character, and explore ideas in greater depth.

HOW A MASTER DID IT

South Park
"Breast Cancer Show Ever" (2008)
Trey Parker

In the *South Park* episode "Breast Cancer Show Ever," Wendy Testaburger vows to kick the shit out of her fourth-grade classmate Eric Cartman after he ridicules her presentation on breast cancer. This is the ninth episode of the twelfth season and, by this point, Cartman has been racist, sexist, traitorous, and rabidly anti-Semitic. He is a narcissistic maniac. He once took vengeance on a bully by tricking him into eating *his own dismembered parents.* Due to the staggering number of wicked acts he's perpetrated, Cartman is arguably the vilest character in history. That's impressive for a chubby little ten-year-old boy.

In stark contrast to Cartman, Wendy is a goody two-shoes who plays by the rules. An outspoken feminist and social activist, she is the hero of this episode. Her objective is to finally put Cartman in his place and stop his evil from spreading. Cartman is the antagonist. His objective is to stop Wendy from kicking his ass and ruining his reputation as the cool kid. He is, of course, only the cool kid in his own mind. But he's convinced of his status and will do anything to keep it. On top of this, he can't stand to have any rules or limits placed on him. He reacts bitterly and often violently to any attempt to restrain him, whether it's by his single mother, teachers, politicians, friends, *anyone*—he will not be stopped.

In the following, we'll go through a basic outline of the story to see how the writer connects events with "therefore" to tell a tightly focused, effective, insightful story.

Fade in:

- Wendy begins a presentation to her fourth grade class about breast cancer awareness. *Therefore,*

- Cartman interrupts her with immature jokes. *Therefore,*

- Wendy pleads with their teacher to do something about Cartman's awful behavior. *Therefore,*

- The teacher weakly admonishes Cartman to stop. *Therefore,*

- Cartman realizes he can act with impunity and makes even more offensive jokes that crack the class up. *Therefore,*

- Wendy, enraged by his disrespect and unchecked aggression, tells him she's going to kick his ass after school. *Therefore,*

- Cartman laughs and says, "It's on, bitch!" *Therefore,*

- Word spreads far and wide that Cartman and Wendy will fight. *Therefore,*

▶ Cartman realizes he's made a terrible mistake. He can't fight. He'll be humiliated in front of the entire school when he's beaten up by a girl. *Therefore,*

▶ Cartman secretly apologizes to Wendy and pleads with her to let him out of the fight. *But,*

▶ She insists that he apologize to her in public. *But,*

▶ He refuses, as that would make him look like the chicken he really is. *Therefore,*

▶ Angrier than ever, Wendy vows to thrash him the minute the school day ends.

Do you feel how tension builds and the stakes are raised? Notice how clean it is, how free from tangents and wasted time. There are no frayed wires—the charge flows powerfully through the wire—cause-effect-cause-effect. Wendy insists on a public apology, which Cartman refuses, which makes Wendy angrier, which makes Cartman more panicked. This entire single-storyline episode builds this chain from start to finish. And this leads to two very important scenes, one in the middle and one at the end.

As the final seconds of the day tick off, Cartman is so desperate to get out of the fight, he waddles up to the front of class, leaps onto the teacher's desk, and literally poops on it! This gets him sent to detention where he kicks back, delighted, feeling like a genius. But his little buddies show up at the library where Cartman serves detention and tell him everyone says he's a chicken and only pooped on teacher's desk to get out of the fight. Cartman assures them he's just a rebel and still totally wants to fight Wendy. The boys are delighted and tell him they rescheduled the fight for the next morning. Wendy knocks on the library window and barks furiously, "Tomorrow morning, you're fucking dead!"

That night, Cartman shows up at Wendy's house, pretending to be a bullied nerd. He cries and whines and pleads with her parents to make her promise not to beat him up. Mr. and Mrs. Testaburger fall for Cartman's shtick and sanctimoniously lecture her about how wrong it is to respond to words with violence. When she tries to explain who Cartman is, her dad cuts her off. "If there is any word of you fighting at school, it is over for you, missy!" Wendy says, "Yes, sir," and promises not to fight. Cartman, behind her parents' backs, sticks out his tongue and flashes her double middle fingers.

This scene is important because it drives to the heart of what *South Park* is—a satire of modern culture. Writer Trey Parker leans heavily libertarian in his politics and is repulsed by what he considers to be Hollywood's phony liberalism. Here, he's ridiculing the ignorance and hypocrisy of the clueless adults, particularly Wendy's dad. He not only treats his own daughter with disrespect—he doesn't even bother to ask why she's so uncharacteristically angry at Cartman—but his language, "It's over for you!" is violent. So, the tight chain of cause and effect pushes the characters, particularly Cartman, to dig deeper, do more, and expand the story to include other characters. This drives the narrative into the dead center of what Parker believes, and allows him to fulfill the potential of his genre—satire. But, as so often happens with master writers, he goes further and penetrates deeper.

The story should be over here. The Central Dramatic Question has been answered. Cartman will not get beaten up by Wendy. But, drunk on his own evil genius and unchecked power, he gets to school early the next day—where every kid is gathered to see the big fight—and waits for Wendy. When she shows up and refuses to fight, he clucks like a chicken, "Bok be bok be bok!" She tells everyone what Cartman did—cried like a little baby with his mommy—but he denies it, and no one believes her. She is not only defeated but humiliated.

But Cartman's *still* not finished. Later, in class, Wendy, broken, rests her head on her desk. Cartman, emboldened by his unchecked power, gets up in class and does a presentation . . . on breast cancer. Except it's really just a low-rent comedy routine where he cracks cheap jokes about making breast cancer a "distant mammory." Wendy is stunned and breathlessly exclaims, "You unbelievable bastard! You beat me and you still won't stop." She charges Cartman and shakes him, demanding he stop—and is sent to the principal's office.

As the chain of story events grows, the tension continues to build and the story drives to the heart of its main idea. At the principal's office, Wendy is stunned to learn that Principal Victoria will not punish her. She tells Wendy that she's seen her posters around school and is herself a breast cancer survivor. She explains to Wendy that cancer is a "fat little lump" and regardless of the cost, even if it means disobeying your parents, you must fight cancer, because if you don't, it will take everything from you. Wendy knows full well that Principal Victoria is telling her to fight Cartman. *He* is a cancer. Whether you win or lose doesn't matter, what matters is you can't let evil people make you feel powerless. You have to fight.

This causes Wendy to storm out of the principal's office to the playground at recess to challenge Cartman before the entire school. He pitifully reminds her that she will get in trouble, but she doesn't care. The two then throw down and Wendy beats him to a pulp, repeatedly smashing his face into the monkey bars, sending teeth flying. Exhausted, spent, knowing she will be seriously punished, Wendy sadly declares, "I'm finished" and stumbles off. Cartman—battered and bruised—sobs hysterically. He knows that everyone thinks he's uncool now and that his reputation is ruined. His friends assure him that the fight has not changed anything. They never had any respect for him. In fact, they could not possibly think any less of him. Cartman convinces himself that they are only saying this to make him feel better. And he takes this to mean that they still think he's cool even though he got beaten up by a girl. In other words, he is so cool that nothing he can ever do can make him uncool! The episode ends with Cartman literally jumping for joy.

Because Trey Parker builds his narrative on an airtight chain of cause and effect, he turns a twenty-two–minute animation into the perfect expression of a critically important idea. You can never change evil people. You can't reason with them. You can't make peace with them. You can't win them over with kindness. No matter what you do, they will always spin things to their advantage. And they will keep coming—and take over everything, unless they're stopped with force. The best you can hope for is to feel a little less powerless.

HOW YOU DO IT

The following bullet points will help you think through and execute the principle.

▸ Your objective is to generate action and to keep your narrative tightly focused and on track from start to finish.

▸ Go back to your character's dramatic need: What is their object of desire? Why do they need to acquire it? Get clear on this and be specific. In our example, the cop (let's give him a name, Bill McGreavy), a boisterous Irishman from Bay Ridge, Brooklyn, needs to catch—and maybe even kill—whoever murdered his son.

▸ Get into the dead center of your character's being. *Become* them. Method act. In other words, think of what you want most—to land a job, find true love, get into college, etc.—and instill these feelings into your character. You're writing your story, not your grocery list—get into it. It's no accident that many great writers—Shakespeare, Quentin Tarantino, Tracy Letts—began their careers as actors. They know how to access emotion.

▸ Now that you are firm and clear on what your character needs, identify what stands in their way. Your objective is to start with a very small action your hero can take to acquire their object of desire, and take it all the way to acquiring or definitively failing to acquire it. Start by simply stating, "This happens therefore . . ." Then add what happens. You're building a chain of cause and effect. See if you can write at least twenty. And, again, put some *feeling* into it.

Make it hard for the hero. Push them to their limits. Challenge them physically, mentally, and spiritually. Test your own ability to—in character—meet these challenges. Surprise yourself.

▸ If you are fully committed when you do this, you will be amazed by how naturally your story falls into place. Trust your gut. When you nail it, you won't just know it, you'll feel it. But be sure that there really is a direct, or tight, connection between cause and effect. And have fun.

MINI FINAL EXAM

The following is an outline for a chapter in a thriller. Cut the two weakest plot points, the ones that interrupt the story's flow.

1. Bill and Mary are coworkers who fall for each other. *But,*
2. Mary is married to a marine. *Therefore,*
3. She considers the necessity of patriotism. *Therefore,*
4. She tells Bill they can't get together. *Therefore,*
5. Bill writes her intense love letters. *Therefore,*
6. Mary meets him at a motel. *But,*
7. They run into Vince, a friend of Mary's husband. *Therefore,*
8. Vince asks them to go in on a robbery. *Therefore,*
9. Mary pleads with him to keep her secret. *Therefore,*
10. Vince tells her he'd like to, but times are tough. *Therefore,*
11. Bill gives Vince $500. *Therefore,*
12. They head home, fearing Vince will still rat them out.

CONTINUING ED

Watch the first scene of the 1992 *Seinfeld* episode "The Contest." It begins with George Costanza telling Elaine, Jerry, and Kramer a story about something that happened with his mother. George's story includes a tightly linked chain of events. List each one. After his story, he makes a declaration that provokes a response from the others, which leads to all four agreeing to take part in a contest. Work through exactly how the scene travels from George's declaration to the start of the contest. And look at how each cause provokes a comedic effect.

MINI FINAL ANSWER

The correct answer is to **cut numbers 3 and 8.** We don't care about Mary's contemplation of patriotism or Vince's desire to pull a robbery. The story points below flow seamlessly from start to finish.

1. Bill and Mary are coworkers who fall for each other. *But,*
2. Mary is married to a marine. *Therefore,*
3. She tells Bill they can't get together. *Therefore,*
4. Bill writes her intense love letters. *Therefore,*
5. Mary meets him at a motel. *But,*
6. They run into Vince, a friend of Mary's husband. *Therefore,*
7. Mary pleads with him to keep her secret. *Therefore,*
8. Vince tells her he'd like to, but times are tough. *Therefore,*
9. Bill gives Vince $500. *Therefore,*
10. They head home, fearing Vince will still rat them out.

5

Escalate risk.

"It seems to be a law of nature, inflexible and inexorable, that those who will not risk cannot win."
—JOHN PAUL JONES, Naval Commander

QUICK TAKE

When you craft plot points that force your protagonist to take greater and greater risks to achieve their objective, you reveal more of who they are and build momentum as the stakes are raised and tension increases. If you think about your own life or people you know, consider the risks one takes or refuses—in relation to their character. For example, if you're walking down the street and someone urgently asks for help because they're being followed, and you see a large scary man walking toward you, the risk you take in this moment—or refuse to take—says a lot about who you are.

But this principle goes beyond the risk of physical harm. I mean risk in the broadest sense of the word. When you take an action that could result in loss of any kind—to your status, job, wealth, pride, body—you take on risk. A daughter risks being judged when she shares a secret with her mother. A grad student risks being seen as a lightweight when he presents a paper to the chairman of his department. A man who hates his body takes a risk when he takes off his shirt at the beach.

The key point here is that you want to keep escalating the risks your hero takes, because if one risk is followed by a lesser risk, the story drags. At the end of the film *Ordinary People*, a father finally confronts his wife about the fact that she doesn't love their son. This puts their marriage and family at maximum risk. This is the secret that no one dares to speak. It comes at the very end of the film because anything that comes after that would be lessened in contrast and fall flat.

HOW IT WORKS

Human beings evolved over tens of thousands of years in hunter-gatherer societies, which has impacted our psychological development in two ways that are important here. One is that we are predisposed to conserve energy. In his bestselling book *The Personal MBA*, author Josh Kaufman writes,

> Here's a universal truth of human nature: People are generally lazy. The critical insight is that being lazy is a feature, not a bug. Think what would happen if one of your ancient ancestors ran around all day for no good reason until they collapsed from exhaustion? If a predator or enemy appeared, they'd have no reserves left to respond to the threat—a very bad situation. As a result, we've evolved to avoid expending energy unless absolutely necessary. . . .

So, we try to get things done while conserving energy and avoiding risk. Ten thousand years ago, if you could get water from a stream right outside your campsite, that's where you'd get it. You wouldn't trek across the plains, where weather, wild animals, and injuries could be fatal. If you had anything—a pelt for warmth, herbs for medicine, status in the tribe—you guarded it with your life. There was no margin of error. If you were lost, got sick and couldn't heal, or your tribe cast you out, you were dead. We're hardwired to project strength and protect our status. This is why so many people fear public speaking and work so hard to make themselves look good on social media. We hate to lose. Consider how you feel when:

- Your boss criticizes you in front of the team.
- Your doctor says you could have a serious illness.
- Someone breaks up with you.

You feel bad, right? Really bad. Even losses that seem trivial in hindsight feel much worse when they happen. For example:

- You get a speeding ticket.
- Your favorite team loses the big game.
- You say something foolish in an important meeting.

Now, let's look at how energy conservation, loss aversion, and risk escalation work in story. A man goes to his cabin in the woods for the weekend. It's a long drive through the snowy mountains. He gets there and he's famished. He unpacks groceries and considers two options for dinner. He can make a sandwich or beef stew. The sandwich will take two minutes. The stew will take much longer, but he's really in the mood for stew. Is forty-five minutes of prep and an hour of cooking time worth the reward of having stew? If he slaps together bread and cheese, that says one thing about his character. If he meticulously follows a recipe for stew, that says something else.

The next day there's a blizzard, and high winds knock out the power. There's no internet and his phone runs out of charge. After he polishes off the stew and the sandwich fixings, there's not much left to eat. The general store is seven miles away. He looks out the window and sees ten-foot snow drifts. A jolt of nerves. The cabin is freezing. Should he trek to his neighbors' house a mile away? What if they're not home? And they're not that friendly. He'll look like an idiot. Two days pass and the power's still out, the roads impassable. He's out of food and hungry. With snow still falling hard, the wind whips his face as he treks to his neighbor. He now risks physical injury and the shame of feeling like a beggar. He gets to his neighbors' house, but no one answers. He walks around, clears a window with his hand, and looks in. Should he break in? They must be away. They'd understand. He'll pay for any damage.

He kicks the door. Again. More violently. And again. Wood splinters. The door flies open and he recoils in horror when he sees the owner, a bearded Goliath, pointing a shotgun at him. "I-t-it-it-it's not what you think," he stammers. Goliath fires. The blast rattles the world. But, incredibly, the bullet ricochets and strikes the Goliath in the forehead, killing him instantly. What should our hero do?

Look at how the risks escalate. He starts by risking time (sandwich or stew), then bodily harm (trekking through the blizzard) plus the embarrassment of "begging" for food, then possible consequences from breaking into a home, and now, with a dead body lying on the floor, caused by his illegal entry, he risks life in prison or even execution. The clean progression of the risks he takes is essential to keeping the story engaging.

In this story, the character is aware of the risks he's taking and the escalation is easy to quantify. But that's not always the case. In *Finding Nemo*, when Marlin shouts at Nemo, "You think you can do these things, but you can't!" he doesn't realize he's risking his son's love. And, when Marlin risks his life to protect his wife and many babies in the first scene, it may seem like a bigger risk than the one he takes later to protect Nemo from the scuba diver who captures his son. Technically speaking, risking your life to save your spouse and many babies is a bigger risk than risking your life to save one child. But the risk Marlin takes to save Nemo *feels* bigger. Nemo is the only family Marlin has left. He made a vow to protect him. And whereas we never met the babies who were killed in their eggs, we know Nemo, so we feel closer to him. The barracuda attack was not Marlin's fault.

But this time, his actions drove Nemo to swim up to touch the boat—and get caught. So, when the risk is more emotional, operates on more levels, and is more personal to the audience, it feels like an escalation.

HOW A MASTER DID IT

Pulp Fiction (1994)
"Son of a Preacher Man" Sequence
Quentin Tarantino and Roger Avary

Vincent Vega is a supercool hit man who works for a vicious crime boss, Marcellus Wallace. Rumor has it that Wallace is insanely protective of his wife, Mia. Vince heard that Wallace once threw an associate, Tony Rocky Horror, out of a fourth-story window, just for giving Mia a foot rub. Wallace has asked Vince to take Mia out for a night, to keep her company while he's out of town. Vince's objective is to play the perfect gentleman, show Mia a nice time, and leave without incident. But this is a high-risk situation. It's odd that his boss would do this, and he suspects it is to test his loyalty.

Vincent, played by John Travolta, is an unfairly handsome, ultra-charismatic, and dangerous man. Mia, played by Uma Thurman, is gorgeous, interesting, intelligent, and edgy enough to handle being married to a major-league crime boss. Vince knows full well that agreeing to take Mia out is a massive risk. He could say the wrong thing. He could be tempted to have sex with her. She could fall for him and put him in a very bad spot. The situation is fraught. But saying no to the boss is an even bigger risk. A more cowardly, less self-assured henchman might have talked his way out of this assignment. Vince is sure he can handle it. Maybe too sure.

Dressed in a slick black suit with a Texas tie, Vince starts the night by stopping at his dealer's place to pick up a bag of heroin. He injects himself, pockets the rest, and cruises the

Los Angeles streets in his red 1964 Chevy Malibu. A warm grin crosses his face as the drug kicks in. Right out of the gate he's put his judgment at risk. He arrives at the Wallaces' home and finds a note on the door from Mia that says she's getting dressed and he should make himself a drink. He's amused by the note, enters, and carefully chooses a bottle of Scotch. He can handle his drugs and alcohol, no doubt. But still, adding hard liquor to heroin further clouds his judgment.

Meanwhile, Mia watches him on a monitor while doing lines of coke. She talks to him through the intercom as we stay close on her bright red glossy lips. They're both wasted, gorgeous, supercool, all dolled up, and alone together on a Saturday night.

Vince drives her in his Chevy. The two have obvious chemistry as they pull up to one of Mia's favorite places, Jack Rabbit Slim's. It's a brightly colored diner where the staff are legendary Hollywood lookalikes including Ed Sullivan, Buddy Holly, and Marilyn Monroe. Every little detail that fuels their connection escalates Vince's risk of making a catastrophically bad decision. I'll put a + next to each bit that adds to Vince's risk.

In their booth, she notes he's back from Amsterdam and asks how long he spent there. He says three years. She tells him she spends a month there each year to chill out. He's impressed. + *They share a connection that's deeper than most people they associate with, which ever-so-slightly increases the odds of these two flirtatious, attractive people becoming intimate.* He asks about the TV pilot he heard she once acted in. She tells him it was called *Foxforce Five* and she was one of the foxes. Her character got to tell a joke in each episode, but she won't tell it to Vince because she's embarrassed. It was dumb. There is a moment of silence and she tells him, you know you've found someone special "when you can just shut the fuck up for a minute and comfortably share silence." He says, "Well, I don't think we're quite there yet, but don't feel bad, we just met each other." + *Sharing silence breeds intimacy, which in this case is dangerous.*

He then asks to try her expensive milkshake to see if it's worth the money. He moves her straw aside, but she tells him to use it. He hesitates. She assures him she doesn't have cooties. He sucks the shake through her straw and agrees the milkshake is exceptional. She's pleased. + *They're literally swapping spit.*

She goes to the bathroom to "powder her nose," and tells him to think of something interesting to say. He says he will and watches her long, slender legs walk to the ladies' room. He turns to see the Marilyn Monroe impersonator's skirt blow up naughtily toward her waist. + *He's attracted to Mia and this place, pulsing with life and legendary starlets, fuels his desire.*

In the ladies' room, Mia powders her nose—with yet another great big line of coke. + *This further clouds her judgment, escalating Vince's risk, despite his ignorance of it.* She returns and he, through mischievous giggles, asks her about the incident with Tony Rocky Horror. She asks if he thinks she had sex with Tony, and he tells her, grinning, about the foot rub. She denies it and teases him about being a gossiper. + *By asking her about a possible infidelity, he's also probing to see if she cheats on her husband, if she's open for business.*

The Ed Sullivan impersonator announces a dance contest. Mia tells Vince that she wants them to enter and she wants to win. He has no choice. + *He either risks offending her and alienating his boss or he dances.* Later, the two get on stage, take off their shoes, and dance together. Of note, Travolta (who also starred in *Saturday Night Fever* and *Grease*) is one of the great dancers in movie history. They dance slowly, undulating before each other. + *The sexual energy between them is palpable.*

They return to her house, Mia wearing his trench coat, and playfully dance their way into the home. They are wasted, giggling, and holding a trophy (we'll learn later they didn't win it, just stole it). + *They are high, not just on drugs, but on life. They're two outlaws who get each other completely.* They stop dancing, make eye contact, and fall silent. He asks her if that's what you call an "uncomfortable silence." + *In other words, he's asking if they've each found someone special.* She says, "I don't know what you call that." + *The sexual tension rises yet again.*

She breaks the tension by calling for more drinks and music. He says he needs to take a piss and goes to the bathroom. On the big-money, reel-to-reel sound system, she plays Urge Overkill's cover of Neil Diamond's sexually suggestive "Girl, You'll Be a Woman Soon." As the song fills the room, she plays air guitar and dances languidly, eyes closed, her movements bordering on erotic. + *Listen to the song she chose, then try to imagine one that does more to stir anticipatory hormones and thoughts of hot forbidden sex.*

In the bathroom, he doesn't just need to take a leak. He needs to tame his lust and extract himself from this now ultra-high-risk situation. He must choose between the risk of having sex with her, which would threaten both their lives if Marcellus found out, or making her feel rejected, which could piss her off and cause her to falsely accuse him of making a pass at her.

He lectures himself in the mirror about the importance of loyalty. This is intercut with Mia's dancing reaching an ecstatic frenzy before she plops on the couch and smokes a gigantic blunt, lighting it with Vince's silver flamethrower lighter that she finds in his pocket. + *She's aroused by the song and more wasted than ever.* He warns his reflection, "You're gonna say goodnight, go home, jerkoff, and that's all you gonna do!" Mia also finds the bag of heroin in his pocket and, thinking it's coke, snorts a great big line. It hurts her head. She recoils in pain. Blood pours out of her nostrils and white fluid oozes from her mouth. + + + *This catapults Vince's risk level to thermonuclear.* Determined to do the right thing, Vince returns to tell her he has to leave. But he's shocked and terrified to find her passed out. He can't wake her up. But he can't take her to a hospital; if he does Marcellus will surely find out and slaughter him.

We cut to Vince in his Chevy speeding down the street with Mia out cold in the passenger seat. He desperately tries to reach his dealer, Lance, on his cell phone. Busy watching cartoons and eating "Fruit Brute" cereal, Lance ignores the incessant phone ringing. He finally answers and warns Vince not to dare bring some "poo butt" to his house—just as Vince's red '64 Malibu screeches across his lawn and crashes into the house. Vince assures him that Lance is a dead man if he doesn't help save Marcellus Wallace's wife. After a comedy of errors with his angry, screeching wife, Lance finds a medical textbook. He tells Vincent the only way to save her life is by impaling her breast with a needle full of adrenaline shot directly into her heart. If it works, she should be okay. If not, she's dead. Lance refuses to be the one to inject Mia and sets Vince up with a tremendous needle. Vince lifts the needle high in the air. Petrified, he gathers the strength and courage to strike the blow. + *Vince could literally kill her right now.* He slams down the needle through Mia's breast into her heart. She springs to life, stunned, but, thank God, alive and able to speak. It worked.

Vince and Mia return to her house, traumatized and spent. They pause by the front door to discuss how to handle this. Vince says, "I'm of the opinion, that if Marcellus Wallace lived his whole life, he don't need to know nothing about this incident." Mia agrees. After a tender moment, when she tells him the joke from the pilot of *Foxforce Five*, they part ways.

• • •

From start to finish, every thing they do escalates the risk: the drugs, booze, flirtation, talk of being together in silence, the discussion of her alleged affair with Tony Rocky Horror, the Marilyn impersonator's raw sexuality fueling his desire, more drugs, the dance contest, stealing the trophy, her wearing his coat, dancing their way home, giggling and wasted, late at night, playing a naughty song, more drinks, a big fat joint, more drugs. With each interaction, the writers crank Vince's risk level higher and higher. After she overdoses, he must take her to the hospital and risk Marcellus's wrath when he finds out. Or risk letting her die due to inadequate treatment. And if all this is not enough, he must slam down a giant needle into her heart and risk killing her outright. The writers flawlessly escalated Vince's risks so that when he says "I'm going home to have a heart attack" at the end of the evening, it rings true.

HOW YOU DO IT

The following bullet points will help you think through and execute the principle.

- At this point, you know what your hero needs. Now let's focus on what your hero stands to lose if they fail to acquire their object of desire. The cop, McGreavy, who discovers his son's dead body is willing to risk everything—his pension, marriage, house, savings, life—to get the bastard who killed his son.

- Identify the types of risks your hero is willing to take. For example, if you're writing a romance, the hero might risk humiliation and their self-esteem.

- What kind of risks is this particular character willing to take that others might not? And conversely, what kind of risks are they unwilling to take or would really struggle to take? In Spielberg films, the hero often risks facing his deepest fear. Indiana Jones hates snakes but ends up in a pit filled with them to find the Ark of the Covenant.

- Again, story is fueled by emotion. To make the risks your characters take seem compelling, you, as the character, need to be *forced* to take the risk. We would much rather conserve energy and avoid loss of any kind: of our money, time, status, friendships, loved ones, or our lives. Make sure to feel each one.

- List risks your hero might take to achieve their objective. Go for quantity. Think up at least ten, but the more the merrier.

- Put the risks in order from lowest to highest. A character who hears a noise late at night risks losing a little sleep when he gets up to see what's what. He risks accidentally firing a bullet when he grabs his gun. He risks his life and freedom when he fires at the shadow coming toward him.

▸ As the risks escalate, stack them. By "stack," I mean make the risks take place on multiple levels. When a woman goes parachuting, she risks her life. When she brings along her daughter, who idolizes her for her courage, she risks letting her daughter down if she chickens out.

MINI FINAL EXAM

Read the following, then answer the question below.

A successful middle-aged executive reads the *New York Times* on the train to work. She's struck by a photo of war orphans crowded into a dangerous refugee camp in a far-off part of the world. One particular little girl's frightened look moves her deeply. She thinks about the girl for weeks.

Finally, the executive decides to find her and, if possible, adopt her. This will mean a setback to her career, confronting her intense fear of flying, and trekking through a war-torn country with little chance of success. She contacts local humanitarian organizations and locates a few camps the child might be in. She flies for twenty-three hours across the world. In full body armor, she travels with a bodyguard through a mountain town where fighting is heavy. She moves into a refugee camp that's wracked by desperation, violence, and disease. She finds and befriends the girl. She pays a bribe to a corrupt official to stamp the paperwork to adopt the girl. But before she formally asks the girl to become her daughter, she suffers a terrible anxiety attack when the full weight of becoming a mother hits her. And what if the girl rejects her?

After days of torment, she summons the courage to ask, and the girl, with a hint of distrust and resignation beyond her years, says yes. The two take a white-knuckle jeep ride through an intense gun battle back to the airport, then fly through extreme turbulence in a wicked storm. Not wanting to start their relationship with a lie, the mom lets the girl see her fear. The girl, unfazed, holds her trembling hand until the plane finds smoother skies. The two share a smile. Tears fall from the woman's eyes. She's a mother now, and she's capable of anything.

Which is correct?

a) The risks she takes are in the right order.
b) The last risk she takes must be to formally ask the girl to call her "mother."
c) The biggest risk is always the risk of death, so the mother should collapse and almost die on the flight home.
d) The mom needs a romantic love interest to risk her heart on another level.
e) The story doesn't work because the little girl takes no risks.

CONTINUING ED

In director Rob Reiner's and screenwriter William Goldman's 1990 film adaptation of Stephen King's novel *Misery*, Paul Sheldon is a famous romance novelist who is imprisoned by Annie Wilkes, his "number-one" fan, after she rescues him from a car accident. Annie is a strong, ruggedly built woman who has worked as a nurse and on the surface appears to be cheerful and friendly. But she's a serial killer with a long track record of murders she's gotten away with. She is obsessed with Paul's romance novels, which feature a heroine named Misery Chastain.

At the start of the film, what risk is Paul taking with his career and writing? And how does this risk affect Annie's opinion of him and his work? Carefully list each thing Paul does to escape the situation, and what he endures as a result of each one. Note how the risks he takes escalate, and on what levels these risks take place—physical, mental, and spiritual. In the final moments of the film, what risk does Paul take, and what does it say about the trade-offs and nature of fame?

MINI FINAL ANSWER

The correct answer is **a) The risks she takes are in the right order**. This story moves toward a resonant climax, where the mother's final risk—allowing the child to see her vulnerability and fear during extreme turbulence—feels right. Here the woman is not just risking her life on a turbulent flight, she's risking rejection—or discovering the girl is coldhearted, and the whole thing was a terrible mistake. Imagine how awful it would be if the kid gave her a nasty look while she was trembling with fear. So, to reveal her vulnerability before the child is a very big risk and works as the final one.

6

Clash expectation with reality.

"If you want to make God laugh, tell him your plans."
—WOODY ALLEN, Filmmaker

QUICK TAKE

Imagine that you're a chef, that cooking is your greatest love—it defines you as a person. You meet someone you fall for and invite them for dinner. Deep in your gut you feel that this person is the one. You spend days studying recipes, shopping for ingredients, buying candles, picking out music. You want to share everything you are and have to give.

The big night comes. The table looks perfect and the fragrances from your culinary masterpiece fill the air. After a nice glass of wine, the moment comes. Your date slides into their seat, loads up a forkful of the casserole you spent six hours crafting, and puts it into their mouth. Silence. Their face contorts, repulsed. They almost gag as they swallow. Think of this moment, when your expectation clashes with reality, as entering a heightened state of consciousness. What happens next is full of meaning. How you respond defines who you are and will shed light on your relationship. If you calmly tell the person they need to leave, you're different from someone who finds the situation funny and, with good humor, orders food in.

You've no doubt heard the term *plot twist*. This clash between expectation and reality is what we mean by a plot twist. In 1609 the Spanish playwright Lope de Vega wrote a short treatise entitled *The New Art of Writing Plays*. In it he said, "Always trick expectancy; and hence it may come to pass that something quite far from what is promised is left to the understanding."

You tell stories to give insight into the meaning of life. Clashing expectation with reality is an effective way to make your stories substantive and meaningful. We find out who we are when life doesn't go as planned.

HOW IT WORKS

A fascinating thing happens when you read or watch a story. You move in and out of literally becoming the characters, usually the protagonist. Sometimes you're so fully enveloped in the story that, along with the characters, you respond to the clash between expectation and reality as if it happened to you. As a character approaches what looks like a garden hose but turns out to be a snake that bares its fangs, your heart races, and if the snake springs at the character, you scream. You might literally throw the book or bucket of popcorn. Other times, there's a distance between you and the character. In a comedy it is fun to watch a character with a flaw or blind spot—greed, lust, gluttony—get into trouble that you see coming but they can't.

How many twists you write and the types you create are dictated by your taste and the genre you're working in. Sometimes the twists are subtle and appear in bits of dialogue or even just the thoughts of a character who comes to a realization. The old Road Runner vs. Wile E. Coyote cartoons are nothing but twists—Wile E. Coyote expects to kill the roadrunner and his evil schemes backfire, harming only the perpetrator. The clashes between expectation and reality are frequent, sudden, and explosive. In a family drama there may be just a single twist that reveals itself slowly over the course of the entire story. But good twists are always meaningful. Silly as Wile E. Coyote may seem, he represents the absurdity of fanaticism. Whenever you see a character or story last so long—he was created in 1949 and is still in the cultural consciousness—it's because there's a deeper meaning.

In Sophocles' tragedy *Oedipus Rex*, written in 430 BC, when King Oedipus realizes that the reason his land suffers from plague is because he inadvertently killed his father and married his mother, the shock is so great it resonates more than 2,400 years later. This intense degree of shock is necessary to express the horror of the idea. Imagine how different the story would be if, early in the telling, King Oedipus muttered, "Man, I hope this plague is not due to this whole married-to-my-own-mom thing."

In the biblical story of Adam and Eve, the first man and woman live in the beautiful Garden of Eden, naked as jaybirds and fully at peace with God. Then one day, God tells them about the Tree of Knowledge and warns them not to eat fruit from it. There are plenty of other trees to eat from, so it's no big deal to avoid this one. But God goes off and a serpent appears. He talks Eve into disobeying God's commandment, and Eve talks Adam into joining her. But after they eat an apple from the Tree of Knowledge, they realize they're naked. And when God returns, they're ashamed. God realizes what they've done and tells them that they must leave the Garden of Eden. He kicks them out and when they try to return, the way is blocked by angels with flaming swords. The story expresses what countless people, for thousands of years, believe represents humankind's desperate desire to reconnect with our creator.

Consider how different the vibe of this story is from that of Oedipus. Here, the twist leaves us with a sense of mystery. Why did Adam and Eve disobey God? Did God expect them to follow his commandment? If so, did he make a mistake? How could God make a mistake if he is all-knowing? Why can't human beings handle eating fruit from the Tree of Knowledge? Why didn't God explain what would happen? The story would lose all its power and we would never ponder these questions if there was no clash between expectation and reality. If it began with God saying "I know you two knuckleheads won't listen, but I'm gonna throw a Hail Mary pass here and hope you will—do not, I repeat, do *not* eat from that tree over there or I will kick you out of Eden and you will know pain unlike any you can imagine. And whatever you do—do not listen to the talking serpent. He is not cool." If this were the case, if what happens is exactly what the characters and audience expected to happen, the story would lose its mystery and power.

Here's how it breaks down:

1. The characters' expectation is established. It might be flawed due to the characters' biases or shortcomings, but it is reasonable given who they are.
2. The clash is believable and surprising. Any half-wit can prank an audience with a cheap surprise or bore them with something merely believable. Writing story events that are believable and surprising is essential.
3. The clash reveals character. When Oedipus plucks out his eyes and wanders off, it reveals a man who admits his sin and accepts responsibility.
4. The clash is substantive and meaningful. If your hero opens her lunch and finds out she has a tuna sandwich when she expected ham and cheese, and she likes tuna just the same, who cares? Make the clash count.
5. The clash—the degree of shock/surprise—is appropriate for the type of story you're telling and ideas you're exploring.

Again, as always, we want to avoid rigid, creativity-stifling rules. The key point here is twofold: that when expectation—of the viewer/reader or characters or both—clashes with reality, it is meaningful and, of course, entertaining. Whether the surprise is terrifying, hilarious, or stunning, is spontaneous or comes about slowly, it gives us what we came for—a heightened and insightful experience.

HOW A MASTER DID IT

Breaking Bad, "Dead Freight" (2012)
George Mastras, Vince Gilligan

In the television series *Breaking Bad*, Walter White is a middle-aged high school chemistry teacher. He has a special needs teenage son and an unemployed wife who is far along in an unplanned pregnancy. He's exhausted, maybe even full-on depressed. The first time we meet him, he is exercising on what has to be the saddest piece of fitness equipment ever built—some sort of tiny elliptical trainer a foot from the wall. It's a powerful visual symbol of a man who is going nowhere—slowly. The kids in his class, for the most part, could not care less about chemistry, and more than a few are outright disrespectful.

Walter is a brilliant chemist who once contributed research to a team of scientists that won the Nobel Prize. He then cofounded a company called Gray Matter with his friend Elliot and his then-girlfriend Gretchen. Something happened with Walter that caused him to break up with Gretchen and leave the company. He sold his shares for a pittance to Elliot, who went on to marry Gretchen, and the two built Gray Matter into a multibillion-dollar public company. The shares Walt sold for a few thousand dollars are now worth hundreds of millions. Walter lives with regret and repressed rage. He is convinced that Elliot and Gretchen unfairly stole his research and cheated him out of his millions.

In the pilot episode, he collapses while working a second job at a car wash after school and learns that he has terminal lung cancer. He not only faces death but also the prospect of leaving his family in dire financial straits. Determined to provide for his wife and kids, he teams up with a former-student-turned-drug-dealer, Jesse Pinkman, to manufacture methamphetamine, aka crystal meth. As Walter's expertise grows, and he confronts rival drug dealers—and the law—it turns out he has a gift for criminality. He creates an alter ego, Heisenberg, whose ambition, cunning, and ruthlessness know no bounds. What starts out as a plan to merely provide for his family builds into a lust for power and respect. He has a desperate need to prove his greatness to himself and the world, to build an empire.

Walter is arguably the greatest antihero in the history of television. His greatness is revealed by the massive effort he puts into plans and the countless times his expectations clash with reality. Throughout all six seasons, Walter spends an inordinate amount of time in a heightened state, pushed to the limits, where his intellect, morality, courage, talent, pride, weakness, pettiness, vindictiveness, and cruelty are revealed.

• • •

In the episode "Dead Freight," Walter's crew learns that the FBI is tracking the barrels of methylamine (a chemical required to make crystal meth) they have been stealing from a warehouse in Germany. In large quantities, it's worth millions. Without it they're out of business. Now that they're cut off from their source, they must score another one fast.

The episode begins, as all *Breaking Bad* episodes do, with a flash forward—a brief scene that will be relevant later. A kid, about twelve, races his dirt bike through the desert. He tears through the brush, leaps over hills, and skids to a stop. Something has caught his eye. He takes off his helmet and kneels by a tarantula. He puts out his bare hand and it creeps into his palm and up his arm. He takes a jar out of his jacket pocket, unscrews the top, and drops the hairy spider in. He stares into the distance. We hear the whistle of a passing train, and the kid rides off.

The theme music plays and the opening credits roll.

Lydia, the woman who has arranged their methylamine shipments, tells Walter that before the methylamine is placed in barrels and shipped to Germany, it's transported by rail from a plant in Long Beach, California, to one just outside Flagstaff, Arizona. Passing through a stretch of rural New Mexico, it enters a "dark territory" where the train loses all communication. Lydia has the train's schedule and knows which car the chemical is in. It's an "ocean" of methylamine, worth tens if not hundreds of millions.

Trembling with greed, Walter plots to steal it. But how? He gathers his partners, Jesse Pinkman and an aging cop, Mike Ehrmantraut, to plot the heist. They assume they'll have to hit the train hard and kill the conductor and engineer to take out any witnesses and give them time to get the stuff. But Jesse pitches an alternate plan to avoid spilling blood. They'll bury two 1,000-gallon plastic tanks by the tracks, one filled with water. They'll block the train with a truck at a crossing and distract the crew. While the train is stopped, they'll bust open the car carrying the methylamine and suck it into the empty tank. Then, they'll refill the tank with water to replace the methylamine, so as not to trip any alarms as the car's weight changes. Impressed with Jesse's thoroughness, Walter agrees to execute the plan. To pull it off they'll need another body, so they bring along a soft-spoken young man, Todd. He pulled another job with them and was reliable.

The day arrives. It's on.

Mike drives a stolen dump truck onto the tracks and pretends to stall. The train comes to a stop. Heart-pounding music plays as the thieves spring into action. Walter mans the hoses attached to the plastic tanks buried underground. Jesse climbs under the train and connects a hose to suck out the chemical. Todd leaps on top of the train to fill the tank with water. All is going perfectly, until a good Samaritan shows up and offers to use his truck to push the "stalled" dump truck past the tracks. This radically reduces the time left to pull the job. Mike calls Walt on their burner phones and yells at him to hurry. Walter insists they suck up every single drop. Mike screams at him to finish. The train starts to roll on and picks up speed. Todd jumps for his life off the top. But as Jesse finishes disconnecting his hose, he's trapped below. He lies still and flat between the train's steel wheels and miraculously avoids being crushed to death. The train goes off and it's over. They made it. They just scored a fortune! The crew erupts in celebration.

Then the little boy on the dirt bike pulls up. He takes off his helmet, smiles, and waves hello. The men exchange looks. Todd smiles and waves hello back—then takes out his gun and blows the kid away. The glass jar with the tarantula trapped inside clinks out onto the desert sand. Jesse, who loves kids, gasps in horror, and the episode ends.

• • •

Though some critics felt the train heist was implausible, the sequence is widely considered one of the series' best scenes. It's two minutes of pure adrenaline. And even if one feels the heist strains credibility, the craftsmanship of the storytelling is undeniable. Let's break down why the twist works.

The expectation is made clear. They will block the train, suck out the chemical, refill the tank with water, and get out of there. It will go down in one of three ways: 1) they will successfully steal the chemical without alerting the crew; 2) they'll alert the crew and have to escape, possibly using violence; or 3) they'll get busted.

Their plan is ingenious. They've made every effort to dot all the i's and cross all the t's, and they even manage to handle the unexpected arrival of the good Samaritan. This causes the audience to let its guard down further.

When the kid shows up and Todd kills him, it is believable. He was set up in the flash forward. But it's still surprising as, caught up in the adrenaline of the heist, we have forgotten him. The heroes never expect some kid to pull up on a dirt bike in the middle of the desert at the worst possible moment. That Todd—a seemingly mild-mannered young man—shoots him is shocking but also believable. The truth is, we don't know Todd and, after all, he's no choirboy. The kid is a witness. He can get them all put away for life.

The clash reveals character. The fallout from this takes place in the next episode when Walter, Mike, and Jesse must decide what to do with Todd and the body. We learn that Jesse and Mike still have souls. Killing innocent kids goes way too far for them. Jesse punches Todd in the face and insists they execute him. Mike thinks executing Todd is Walt's decision, but he wants to cash out and be done. Walt insists he is tormented by the murder but his real concern is their business. He convinces Mike and Jesse they need Todd, who is a reliable member of the team now. Todd also vaguely threatens them by telling them he has a powerful uncle in prison. Walt says they can't afford to reflect on the morality of the operation now. They are close to making a fortune. He wants it. After that, they can all get out and tend to their souls. In one of the most disturbing scenes in the series, after discussing this with Jesse, Walt returns to work and, not realizing Jesse is still there, whistles while he works. He could not care less about the dead boy. He is evil, more evil than Jesse ever imagined.

The clash is meaningful. When you sup with the devil, you'd best have a long spoon.

HOW YOU DO IT

The following bullet points will help you think through and execute the principle.

- The first step, of course, is establishing the expectation. It may be as small as a busy gal settling in for a comfy night of uninterrupted sleep or as big as a religious man arriving at the Pearly Gates and expecting Almighty God to welcome him with open arms. Whatever it is, you make it explicitly clear—ideally by showing, not telling—what the character expects. When a loving couple expect to share a naughty interlude, they behave very differently from when they expect to discuss an infidelity.

▶ Make it clear that your character is entirely reasonable for expecting what they expect. For example, a man who is stricken by food poisoning from eating sushi at his favorite place had every reason to anticipate a healthy meal. If he gets sick from eating sushi at a filthy dump with health code violation notices taped to the door, he's dismissible. We could see the incident coming a mile away.

▶ Pack the cannon. In other words, make us care about what happens. In the *Breaking Bad* example, Walter and his crew put a great deal of time and effort into their plan, which makes us root for them to succeed. Because we're fully invested, we feel the clash deep in our gut. (We'll discuss this further in Chapter 15, "Write characters to the top of their intelligence.")

▶ Use misdirection to hide the coming clash. Let's say a wife gets a call from her husband at work telling her that he just landed a huge new account. She is absolutely thrilled—she buys flowers to bring him and has made all the arrangements for an expensive vacation in Hawaii. She pulls up to the parking space at the back of his design studio with her bouquet and sees an attractive, black-clad woman slink out, straighten her dress, scurry into a car, and drive off. That bastard! She throws down the flowers and marches into his studio to find him lying on the couch. . . . with a bullet in his head.

▶ Foreshadow with integrity. Everything must be believable upon review. Once the clash between expectation and reality hits, your readers become juries. They review all of the previous action to see if the twist was fairly set up. For example, the woman we see leaving the office must be entirely believable as someone who just committed murder. She can't have a light energy, filled with the playful vibe of someone who just had a frolic. That would be pranking the audience and pranking is never cool.

▶ As always, trust your gut. If you think it would be a great moment to experience, it's working. If not, tweak it until it is. Unless it is the very end of your story, a great clash is both the end of one event and the beginning of another. The dramatic question shifts from "Will the husband appreciate the good news?"—she bought tickets to Hawaii!—to "Who was that evil woman and why did she kill the husband?"

▶ Above all, have fun with this. In the last chapter we talked about the scene from *Pulp Fiction*, where Quentin Tarantino sets up the horrific clash between expectation and reality when Vince prepares to say goodnight to Mia, fearing she'll be insulted—but finds her overdosed on heroin. And in the famous scene where Vince lectures himself about loyalty in the bathroom mirror, you can feel Tarantino's sheer delight in crafting the clash to come. Have fun with this. It's among the supreme joys of telling stories.

MINI FINAL EXAM

Read the following, then answer the question below.

A little boy, about nine years old, lives alone with his loving mother in a small apartment in Chicago. His father ran off almost a year ago and last they heard was living with a teenage girl in Florida. His mother, a strong, independent woman, teaches middle school in Rogers Park. But the grind of managing pubescent tweens and teens on top of the shock of losing her husband is taking its toll. The little boy is worried about her.

With Valentine's Day coming up, he wants to do something special for her. So every chance he gets at school, he works on building a big bouquet of flowers out of construction and crepe paper. He puts many hours into crafting each flower—roses, tulips and his mom's favorite, daffodils. The big day arrives, and he gathers up his flowers and walks the nine long city blocks home, back to their apartment building. The elevator takes forever to get to the top floor, but finally makes it. He sprints out, runs full speed down the hall, then carefully places the bouquet behind his back. He rings the bell and hears his mom come to the door. She opens it. He thrusts out the bouquet and shouts, "Surprise! Happy Valentine's Day, Mommy!"

Which of the following is the most effective way to clash expectation with reality?

a) Mom smiles joyfully and hugs her magical little man.
b) Mom bursts into tears, but they're tears of joy.
c) Mom's face lights up but the boy's heart sinks when he sees that, behind her, the apartment is covered with bouquets of expensive roses. Mom has a new beau.
d Mom is unimpressed with the flowers. When the boy's lip trembles, she tells him to knock it off and quit acting like a damn little sissy.
e) Mom is so shocked by his gesture, she suffers a massive heart attack and dies.

CONTINUING ED

In the 1999 suspense film *The Sixth Sense*, Bruce Willis plays psychiatrist Malcolm Crowe. One night, after returning from an award ceremony recognizing Malcolm's work as a child psychologist, Malcom and his wife share a glass of wine and prepare for a romantic interlude, when they suddenly notice the bedroom window's been shattered. Someone has broken in and this person is in their bathroom. He's a former patient, wearing nothing but underpants, who is enraged by his belief that long ago, when he was brought to Malcolm as a troubled child, Malcolm failed him. Malcolm tries to comfort him, but the man suddenly pulls out a gun, shoots him in the stomach, and then kills himself.

Time passes. Malcolm has, we assume, healed from the gunshot. But his marriage, which seemed so warm in the first scene, has grown cold and distant. He works on another case, helping a troubled young boy, Cole, who oddly claims that he can see dead people. Though Malcolm thinks this is a delusion, over time, he comes to believe that the boy is telling the truth and counsels him to try to talk to the dead people who have been visiting—and terrorizing—him. Cole does, and it slowly helps him integrate his special ability into his life. This is the lesson Malcolm teaches Cole. What does Cole teach Malcolm? Why does this work as a clash between expectation and reality, and what does it say about the nature of death and our ability, or inability, to accept it?

MINI FINAL ANSWER

The correct answer is **c) Mom's face lights up but the boy's heart sinks when he sees that, behind her, the apartment is covered with bouquets of expensive roses. Mom has a new beau.** It is surprising, believable, and meaningful. This is a pivotal moment in the kid's life. The first two answers are believable but not surprising. The last two answers are surprising but not believable.

7

Max out the middle.

"Play it fuckin' loud."
—BOB DYLAN, Musician

QUICK TAKE

All parts of your story are difficult to write. There are infinite possibilities for every choice—where to set the scene, what the characters say, what happens, and how everyone responds. None of it is easy. But generally speaking, it is simpler to craft the narrative for your beginning and ending than the middle, because its purpose is not as simple to define. In the beginning you set up and ask the Central Dramatic Question (CDQ). In the end, you answer it. But what do you do in the middle?

You give your readers an experience. You give them the purest form of the experience that you promised. If your story is a drama, you tear their hearts out. If it's a comedy, you make them burst out laughing. If it's horror, you terrify them. You amplify emotion and crank up spectacle. Your audience didn't come for a lecture; they came to feel. It's here, in the dead center of your story, that you hit them hard. This will keep it from dragging and give them what they came for.

HOW IT WORKS

When Bruce Springsteen made his breakthrough album, *Born to Run*, he knew he had to produce a hit record or his career was finished. His first two albums, *Greetings from Asbury Park, N.J.* and *The Wild, the Innocent & the E Street Shuffle*, were critically acclaimed but made no money. Columbia Records would not give him a fourth chance. He needed to go big. And big and bombastic he went, with soaring, hyperemotional tracks like "Thunder Road," "Backstreets," and "Jungleland."

In his autobiography, *Born to Run*, he talks about his fear of releasing the album, how he forced his band and producers to rework it countless times. He didn't let it go, until he had a deep conversation with a close friend and coproducer, Jon Landau, who explained the mysterious nature of art, and how "what makes something great may also be one of its weaknesses."

During the Jewish holiday Purim, revelers are encouraged to whip themselves into such a frenzy, they don't know the difference between cursed and blessed. This is the ballpark we're in when we say "max out" the middle. It's about pushing the limits of what you can get away with. It's about challenging yourself to go bigger, badder, wilder, crazier, more intense than you thought possible.

If there is one place you get to break free from all constraints of narrative and focus exclusively on generating raw emotional power, it's here in the middle. Go big, especially in early drafts. You can always pull it back. If you've properly set up your CDQ, and built empathy between the hero and your reader/viewer, you've earned their trust and can just let it rip.

Blow shit up, leap off cliffs, race at high speeds down mountains and through alleys. Storm the fort, jump out of the plane, push the button. If it's a love story, rip the lovers apart—or thrash them together in a primal, dirty, wrong-just-wrong sex scene. It may just be about the intensity of the emotion. If it's a quiet drama of an introverted scientist, hopelessly alone and trapped by his theories and thoughts, isolate him to a degree he never dreamt possible.

That covers the feelings you're going for here. Now, let's talk about some hard, structural choices you might consider. I'm saying "consider" because, again, you don't want to be forced to paint by numbers, to strangle your creativity and stifle your originality. Every story is unique, and you need to stay as free as you can.

But two classic tricks, or tools, that often work well include the following:

- Midpoint Climax—this refers to a climactic action, a high point of emotion that is a plot twist, or "reversal," as in an event that changes the hero's fortune from good to bad or bad to good. We discussed this in the previous chapter, "Clash expectation with reality."

- Fake Victory/Fake Defeat—the idea here is that you trick the audience into thinking the story will end one way, when it really will end another way. If your story will end on a positive note, you put the "all hope is lost" moment here. If your story will end in tragedy, you put the most hopeful moment here.

No generation in history has consumed more stories than those of us living in this age of mobile phones, streaming movies, print-on-demand, podcasts, and video games. So, you might wonder how the hell the same tricks or misdirections can still work. Sophisticated audiences surely know that if the hero is trapped in the jaws of death and the story's only halfway through, it's probably going to work out well in the end. But these structural choices work for this reason: If a story is well written—the characters are well-drawn, the situations believable, and the events structured to reveal personality, explore ideas, and stir emotions—then the reader or audience is drawn in, captivated by the quality of the storytelling, and only able to focus on what you as the storyteller want them to focus on.

In *The Return of the King*, the final installment in the Lord of the Rings trilogy, the middle is bleak. Frodo is rolled up in a giant spider's web, about to be eaten. He's been stung and he's paralyzed. His skin turns blue, his eyes roll back in his head, and on top of this he is exhausted from the hell he's been put through in the first two books. You're fully invested in him, you know what's at stake—the fate of the world—and you know, instinctively, how awful it would be to be eaten by a giant spider. At that moment, it's impossible to simultaneously think about the ending or dramatic structure or anything but the spider.

As always, how you approach this depends on your temperament, personality, the story you're telling, and the ideas and vision you need to express. Stay free. But not too free.

HOW A MASTER DID IT

If Beale Street Could Talk (1974)
James Baldwin

In this short novel that flies like a bullet without chapter breaks straight through for two hundred pages, young lovers Tish and Fonny and their families struggle against a corrupt, vicious system that has wrongly imprisoned Fonny for a rape he didn't commit. He is a twenty-one-year-old sculptor, a sensitive soul trapped in a violent, nightmarish prison. Tish, the story's eighteen-year-old narrator, is shattered by his imprisonment, but determined to fight it as best she can. The two are childhood sweethearts who are truly in love. They get each other on every level. But they live in New York City of the 1970s, and the cops and district attorneys are crooked and have it in for any black kid who happens to look at them sideways, refuses to kowtow, or is just in the wrong place at the wrong time. The police rip Fonny from his tiny studio apartment one night after a rape, haul him into a lineup—where he is the only black man included—and he's picked out by the traumatized victim. If this isn't bad enough, Tish is pregnant.

Disastrously, the families have little money, few meaningful connections, and no real strings to pull. The entire action is fueled by a simple Central Dramatic Question: "Will the family rescue Fonny from the system?" He's stuck in a tiny cell with a filthy toilet that overflows, surrounded by predators, and the clock is ticking. He's kept from the general population, but the longer he's kept in prison, the greater the odds of him eventually being assaulted, his mind going, or both. He has to get out.

Throughout the novel, you feel a weight crushing down on all these people. It's hard to make ends meet. It's hard to find good work, a nice place to live, and a way to control the rage they feel when the deck is stacked against them in every way. Tish, whose real name is Clementine, has loving parents: Joe, a tough, streetwise man, and Sharon, a world-weary but very much spiritually alive woman who had her two girls young and is now in her early forties. Tish has an older sister, Ernestine, who loves her dearly and is a scrappy child advocate, committed to the struggle against the system.

Fonny's mother, Mrs. Hunt, is a deeply religious woman but ignorant, judgmental, and terrified. She never could relate to Fonny, and only wants him to accept Jesus. Her daughters, Adrienne and Sheila, are not much better, though Adrienne has a trace of humanity. The only hope the families have is that Ernestine was able to help Fonny get a passable attorney, a young white lawyer, Arnold Hayward. He genuinely cares, but he's got little money to work with and the case against Fonny is all but airtight—the victim says it was him. The victim has moved to Puerto Rico and the only hope they have is to get to her and explain that Fonny was with Tish and their friend, Daniel, the night of the rape, and that he is a good kid—about to become a father—and pray she'll take back her statement against him. There are really two stories provoked by the CDQ: One is external, "Will the families rescue Fonny?" The other is internal, "Will the stress and pressure break the characters, destroy their hope, and turn them against each other?"

What we're focused on here is what the author, James Baldwin, does in the middle. He infuses it with raw emotion: rage, tears of joy and sorrow, violence, desperation, fear, and true friendship and familial love. And all this emotion keeps the middle fully engaging, if it is at times hard to read, because the rage and pain expressed are so intense.

In one scene, Tish's parents, Joe and Sharon, joined by her sister, Ernestine, invite Fonny's family, Frank and Mrs. Hunt (Baldwin hardly mentions her first name), and their daughters, Sheila and Adrienne, over to their apartment to break the news of the pregnancy. (I'm repeating names because a group is hard to track.) Tish makes a pittance at a cosmetics counter in a department store and very well might end up a single teen mother.

The way Sharon and Joe see it, Tish and Fonny's baby will make them all one big family and they want to unite forces to get the young man out. They hope that Mrs. Hunt will rally. But Tish has her doubts. The women in Fonny's family never really loved him, never understood his quirky personality and artistic soul, and have barely gone to visit him in prison, or "The Tombs" as it's called. Frank is the only one who truly loves his son and is devastated by his imprisonment and his own inability to do anything about it. When the Hunts arrive, Tish's mom and sister serve cocktails, soda, and ice cream. Though the men, Joe and Frank, get along fine, the tension between the women is palpable. Mrs. Hunt and her daughters are arrogant and look down on Tish's family, whom they consider inferior.

Adrienne wants to get to the point—so she can get the hell out of there. Tish insults her for not visiting Fonny and then breaks the news that she's pregnant. The news rattles Frank, who is moved, and would normally be joyful, but this only exacerbates his sense of utter helplessness. Then, incredibly, Mrs. Hunt lashes out at Tish, "I guess you call your lustful action love . . . I don't. I always knew that you would be the destruction of my son. You have a demon in you—I always knew it. My God caused me to know it many a year ago. The Holy Ghost will cause that child to shrivel in your womb. But my son will be forgiven. My prayers will save him." All are stunned that the woman could say such a hateful thing and curse her own grandchild. Frank is so disgusted, he cracks her with a backhand and knocks her to the floor. Joe leads him out so the two can talk privately at a local bar.

The Hunt women make it clear they want nothing to do with the child and will not help in any way. Sharon is stunned. Tish calls Adrienne filthy names, but Adrienne stands her ground. Baldwin writes, "Real hatred choked off the air." Ernestine then rips into Adrienne, threatens to cut her throat, and throws the Hunt women out of the apartment. She follows them down the hallway, unleashing blistering riffs of profanity at Mrs. Hunt. "Blessed be the next fruit of thy womb. I hope it turns out to be uterine cancer. And I mean that." She vows never to let them near the child and threatens to kill them if they ever cross her path again. When the elevator finally opens and Mrs. Hunt and her daughters get in, Ernestine spits in Mrs. Hunt's face and she rages at them through the elevator shaft, "That's your flesh and blood you were cursing, you sick, filthy dried up cunt! And you carry that message to the Holy Ghost and if He don't like it you tell Him I said He's a faggot and He better not come nowhere near me." She then returns to the apartment with tears streaming down her face.

Baldwin, as Tish, writes, "Sharon, in all this, had said nothing. Ernestine had delivered me to her, but Sharon had not, in fact, touched me. She had done something far more tremendous; which was, mightily, to hold me and keep me still; without touching me."

It's hard to imagine anything more despicable than a woman, in the name of a loving God, cursing a desperate, pregnant teenage girl whose childhood best friend, the father of her unborn child, and the woman's own son, faces life in prison. Not just prison, but a dirty, filthy, violent prison that will, without question, destroy him. This is how Baldwin kicks off the middle part of his story. And he doesn't let up. In the next part, Tish recalls the night she and Fonny first made love. It's a tender, graphic, riveting encounter that fully captures the pain, fear, wonder, awe, and beauty of having sex with someone you're in love with. The scene is for the first time emotionally complex, as we experience it knowing Fonny will be arrested a short time later.

Following that, Tish recalls a night when, after she moved into Fonny's tiny apartment, he had a friend, Daniel, come over. The two were thrilled to reconnect and Tish felt real love for Daniel, if only because Daniel is one of the few people who she'd seen make Fonny so happy. Daniel was a big black kid who got busted for having marijuana (grass, as they called it back then) on him, and the cops, with purely evil intention, hit him with another charge of stealing a car. Daniel, a good-natured young man, went away for two years. And that night, he couldn't stop crying. Fonny and Tish took turns holding him. He couldn't bring himself to say what happened but it was obvious, and will be confirmed later, that he was sexually assaulted and, beyond that, witnessed another young prisoner get raped by nine guys.

This too is an emotionally layered, almost-too-painful-to-read scene. You have three people—essentially children—three good souls struggling mightily to care for each other, and you experience this tender, loving scene, this flashback, knowing that in the present moment, Fonny is in prison. James Baldwin, like so many great writers, doesn't hold back. Not every story, of course, has to be this intense, but he had a mission: to express the pain, suffering, joy, creativity, love, and full humanity of his characters. And he unleashed it all in the middle.

HOW YOU DO IT

The following bullet points will help you think through and execute the principle.

- Identify the primary emotion at the center of your story. There will, of course, be many emotions, but one is front and center. Get clear on what it is. When you tell this story, you are making a promise to your readers to stir this specific feeling in them.

▶ Riff on ideas for chapters, scenes, or moments that express the feeling you need to express. As always, here, the more the merrier. But stay focused on your hero and their object of desire. What's the most intense thing they can do to get what they need? Or what's the biggest mess they can get in?

▶ Read through your list of ideas and trust your gut. Which ones make you feel the most intensely? Take these ideas and think of ways to crank up the volume on them. Push yourself to dig deeper and feel even more.

▶ In the previous chapter, we discussed clashing expectation with reality. See if you can leverage that principle to engineer a scene in which the hero experiences a shock that triggers an explosion of feeling.

▶ Go big. Create a spectacle. Obviously, you must stay within the constraints of your story—its physics, rules, tone, etc.—but that said, what is the absolutely loudest, biggest, craziest, most intense scene you can think of? In the 1995 heist film *Heat*, Robert DeNiro's crew of machine-gun–wielding bank robbers get into an all-out war with the cops on the streets of downtown Los Angeles. What's the most outrageous, spectacular, emotionally intense scene you can create, within the context of your story's genre?

▶ Challenge yourself as a writer, as a person, to *feel* here more than you're comfortable feeling. (Of note, this right here could be the biggest cause of writer's block. What if it's not a block but a fear of feeling?) Go to the places you've never gone before, and feel things weaker writers are too afraid, uptight, or hung up to feel. Why not swing for the fences? By making bold choices you risk making a fool of yourself. But by not making them, you risk irrelevance. So, either way, you're taking a big risk. And remember, you can always pull it back if it's really off the mark.

MINI FINAL EXAM

Read the following, then answer the question below.

You're writing a comic novel about a group of automotive assembly line workers—Little Jack, Big Jack (the behemoth), Super Jane, and Jan Van Hamm—who are fanatic hockey fans. Their fictional team, the Edge City Dragons, has made it to game seven of the Stanley Cup Finals. They are dying to go, but they can't afford tickets. At lunch, the factory owner's son, Drake, mocks their poverty. He got himself two front row seats. He paid $7,000 and he doesn't even like hockey. He asks if one of them wants to go. They recoil; what's the catch? He hid the other ticket somewhere in the city.

Why? He wants them to kill each other hunting for it. "If one of you finds it, I'll see you at the game. If not, I couldn't care less." They insult him. He giggles. "Well, if you change your mind, it's taped to the yellow dog." They agree to watch the game together at the bar. No one knows what "the yellow dog" even means. Then it hits Big Jack. There's that little park near the arena . . . with a statue of a yellow dog! They exchange looks. Super Jane says she needs to use the restroom and walks—then runs—out the front door. The other three spring after her, shoving, tripping, and tackling each other. It's game on!

Which of the following is *least* likely to max out the middle?

a) As Little Jack and Jane race toward the yellow dog in a temporary alliance, the passion that's been building up between them for the past two years finally erupts, and the two turn into an alley to go for each other with unbridled passion.

b) The four provoke a massive accident with buses, cars, a motorcycle, and a truck that's transporting chimps to the Edge City zoo. As the chimps run wild, Little Jack nearly chokes Big Jack to death in the wreckage. Super Jane is pinned in her Prius—that catches fire. And Jan Van Hamm vows to kill Drake.

c) All four get to the yellow dog at the same time and erupt into a brutal battle. Big Jack wins, only to find a note that reads "My bad, I left the ticket on my desk." Jan Van Hamm bursts into tears. They sadly agree they're just four pathetic losers.

d) As Jane speeds up to the yellow dog on a stolen motorcycle, Big and Little Jack commandeer a helicopter that spins wildly out of control overhead. Jan Van Hamm, sure he's about to miss out, shouts "He's got a gun!" and provokes mayhem.

e) As all four pull up to the same intersection in different vehicles, they see the giant statue of the yellow dog being hauled away on a flatbed. They each spot the large white envelope taped to its back leg. They U-turn, zigzag, and speed through the intersection to follow the flatbed, causing a massive pileup that wrecks Big Jack's beloved '66 Camaro. He tells Super Jane—who started this—that she is no longer his friend. All agree their friendship is over.

CONTINUING ED

The 2004 screwball comedy *Anchorman: The Legend of Ron Burgundy* revolves around Ron, a pompous anchorman who is a big fish in the relatively small pond of San Diego news in the 1970s. His best friends include a wannabe ladies' man, reporter Brian Fantana; a crude sports reporter, Champ Kind; and a clueless weatherman, Brick Tamland. The plot centers on the tumult caused by the addition to their team of a woman, Veronica Corningstone, with whom Ron falls madly in love, despite his appalling chauvinism. Rattled by the stressful situation at work,

Ron's team takes a long walk to buy some new clothes. They wander into a deserted industrial space where they're accosted by Wes Mantooth and his rival news team. When does this scene occur? What, if anything, does it have to do with the story? How far does it escalate? And how does this brawl relate to the genre of "screwball" comedy—as opposed to say, satire or light comedy?

MINI FINAL ANSWER

The correct answer is **a) As Little Jack and Jane race toward the yellow dog in a temporary alliance, the passion that's been building up between them for the past two years finally erupts, and the two turn into an alley to get after each other with unbridled passion**. This one is the *least* likely to work as "maxing out" the middle. It lacks the degree of spectacle and emotion necessary to execute the principle. It may be a hot love scene, but what we need here is over-the-top comedy.

8

Begin the end with a critical decision.

"The event that occurs at the second act curtain triggers the end of the movie."
—BILLY WILDER, Screenwriter, Director

QUICK TAKE

In theater, film, and television, stories are often broken up into "acts," which are simply units of action that end with a climactic moment—a burst of violence, a sudden kiss, or the arrival of an unexpected character, etc. The classic three-act structure is really just another term for beginning, middle, and end. In the quote above, Billy Wilder refers to the second act "curtain" because back in the old days a curtain literally dropped two times at the theater—once at the end of Act One and again at the end of Act Two. These "act breaks," or intermissions, gave the audience a chance to take a leak and stretch their legs. In order to keep the audience engaged—so they wouldn't go home during the breaks—playwrights put a shocking revelation, a big fat plot twist, a stunning effect, or maybe all three just before the "curtain." But the key thing here, according to Wilder, is that what happens at the second act curtain forces the story to a conclusion.

To personalize this, consider the moment when someone who has been getting on your nerves for a long time finally goes too far. You ask them a thoughtful question and they insult you in front of other people. You can take no more and essentially say, "I've had enough." Everybody watching knows the battle's about to start. There's a two-step quality to the critical decision. Something big happens to end the middle section, or Act Two. It's often a wicked clash between what the hero expected and what actually happens. And now, because of this, the hero consciously decides to risk it all and wrap things up.

HOW IT WORKS

The moment when you pivot from the middle into your ending is vitally important. Here, you give your reader/audience a chance to take a breath and gear up for the finale. It's a similar moment to the one just after the hammer drops. It instills a strong sense in your reader/viewer of "this is gonna be good."

One time I was flying home with my wife from a vacation. A hurricane had recently hit Florida. At around four in the morning the pilot woke us up to let us know that he was not going to divert the flight to Atlanta, as he had told us he might. He said that we were going to land in Miami as scheduled. His exact words were, "We're going to miss most of the hurricane, but not all of it. I'm not going to lie to you. It's going to be rough." He instructed the stewardesses to take their seats. He made it clear we would not get breakfast. And he warned us to stay in our seats with our seat belts fastened low and tight across our laps so that "no one's head gets splattered on the ceiling." Cold silence fell over the cabin as the bumps got rougher. Dark clouds and driving rain whipped past the window. Lightning flashed. A grown man sobbed and puked into the little paper bag. (I swear it wasn't me. I just clutched my armrests and squeezed my eyes shut so hard it's a miracle they ever opened again.)

You can look at a flight as a story. The CDQ is "Will the pilot safely land the plane?" The moment the pilot makes the critical decision to fly through the tail end of a hurricane is the beginning of the end of the story. The pilot, the hero, took an action to end the story. The rocking was so horrendous, the shaking so dreadful, I could not tell that we had landed, but landed we had. This answered the CDQ and ended the story. This is a good metaphor for storytellers. Like the pilot, let your audience know that you're not just going to end your story, you're going to give them an experience.

This principle is called "Begin the end with a *critical* decision." Merriam-Webster's definition of the word "critical" includes the following: "Exercising or involving careful judgment or judicious evaluation"—as in critical thinking. And "of, relating to, or being a turning point or specially important juncture"—as in a critical phase.

Your protagonist must be the one who makes the critical decision. It can't be a chance occurrence, and the decision can't be made by anyone else. A protagonist is a substantive being moving through a meaningful experience. At this point, which usually occurs about two-thirds of the way through the story, they know what's at stake. They realize what it all means, and they have exhausted other options. This story must come to an end—starting now.

This moment can be in the midst of a massive spectacle—your hero decides to put her starfighter into warp speed and attack the bad guy's lair in a blaze of glory. Or it could be a quiet, interior moment. An elderly widower decides to end his life rather than face dementia alone. And there's no taking this moment back. Once this action is taken, to walk it back would reveal something essential about the hero. The 1976 film *Rocky* is elevated by this moment. The night before the big fight, Rocky tells his girlfriend, Adrian, that he can't beat Apollo Creed. He's not good enough. But he makes a critical decision—that he'll be the first boxer ever to go the distance with Creed, who's the greatest boxer of all time. If Rocky can do this, if he's still standing when the final bell rings, he'll be redeemed, he'll know that he's not "just another bum from the neighborhood." He is fully aware of what's at stake—his own redemption. Though he can still quit at any time—no one is forcing him to enter the ring—it's a no-turning-back point because if he quits after making this declaration, it'll change the meaning of his life. He will forever be just another bum from the neighborhood.

It's important to foreshadow with integrity—to suggest whether the story will end happily, sadly, or a bit of each—without giving away what happens. *Rocky* is about redemption. The film makes you fall in love with this boxer who is good to everyone he meets, but wasted his chance of building a professional career because he took easy money collecting debts for a local mobster. He chose to become a nobody, and now he has one more shot to become someone special. Instinctively you know that Rocky will go the distance—if not, it would be the cruelest film ever written. This no-turning-back moment is often quiet, for obvious reasons—it's not easy to fully realize the magnitude of an event in the midst of chaos. It's slotted between the midpoint, which is fueled by intense emotion and spectacular theatrics, and the ending, which is often deeply impactful because it answers the Central Dramatic Question.

In terms of character, it's about showing the reader/audience that the protagonist understands the gravity of the moment. In terms of story design, it tells the audience to prepare for the grand finale.

HOW A MASTER DID IT

Frankenstein, or _The Modern Prometheus_ (1818)
Mary Shelley

Victor Frankenstein is a young medical student recovering from the shock of losing his mother. To escape his grief—and perhaps psychologically fight back against the cause of his grief, death—he buries himself in his work. He's had a lifelong fascination with discovering how nature works, and learns how to reanimate dead tissue. He then commits to doing the unthinkable—creating a sentient being by reanimating dead body parts. His creation will be a large, athletic being. He will convert death and decay into strength, vitality, and beauty. Alone in his apartment, he cuts himself off from the world and falls into a mania as he works day and night to discover the secret of giving life. He fantasizes about creating a "new species" who owe their lives to him and bless him as God.

One night, he finishes his work and the being comes to life. But it's not beautiful. Its eyes are watery and dead and its skin is yellowy and translucent. It has pearly white teeth that stand in contrast to its black lips and hair. Its limbs twitch and convulse as it groans in pain. Horrified by this "catastrophe," Victor can't bear to look at it and races out of the room. The creature escapes and vanishes.

Exhausted, hysterical, sickened by the experience, Victor becomes deathly ill. It takes four months to get back on his feet. Meanwhile, the creature wanders the world and is shunned and violently attacked by everyone he meets. He hides in a forest, scavenges for food, and finds a house with a close-knit family that he watches and studies for weeks. He steals a book from them and over time teaches himself to read and speak. He's intelligent and longs for connection, to be loved. One day, he sees his reflection in the water and is horrified by how hideous he looks. Still, he decides to do all he can to connect with the family he's been watching. He leaves them gifts. He does chores for them while they're out. The grandfather is warm-hearted and blind. If anyone can accept and welcome the creature, it is surely this kind old man. The creature introduces himself to the man, who welcomes him, but when the rest of the family returns, they shun him, crying out in terror and chasing him off. To the creature's horror, the family is so traumatized by his presence, they sell the home and move away, leaving him hopelessly alone.

Enraged, he sets off to take revenge on Victor. He finds Victor's childhood home and stalks the family. When he finds Victor's little brother playing alone in the woods, he strangles him and steals his necklace. Later he finds the family's loving nurse, Justine, asleep in the woods. She had joined the search to find the missing boy and fallen asleep in the forest. The creature plants the necklace on Justine. She can't account for her whereabouts at the time of the murder, and after she's discovered to be in possession of the necklace, she is arrested, tried, and hanged.

The creature finds and confronts Victor, who is not only disgusted by the sight of him, but also detests his evil soul. The monster explains what he's been through—the loneliness, anguish, and rejection that drove his rage. Victor is guilt-ridden and moved. The creature pleads with him to create another being, a female who will end his loneliness. They will escape into the desolate jungles of South America and never bother Victor again. Victor wants no part of creating another life. But the creature vows to make him suffer as he himself has suffered. He will kill all of Victor's friends and family and bring him to ruin. Terrified and desperate, Victor agrees to create a mate for the creature, who vows to watch Victor's ass—and does.

Tracked by the creature, Victor goes off to a remote island and starts to construct the mate. But the closer he gets to completion, the more his disgust grows. He is repulsed by the work itself, and this time considers all possible outcomes. What if this process creates inherently evil beings? What if the female he creates is horrified by the creature? Or he can't stand her, and her creation only exacerbates his rage? What if she is as cunning and evil as the creature and they mate? These ghoulish beasts could build a race of beings that torment humankind. He fears that his work could one day destroy the human race, and all for his own ego, selfishness, and arrogance.

As Victor contemplates these nightmarish scenarios and stands mired in his own regrets, he senses that he's being watched. He looks up and sees the creature's face gazing at him through the window, his lips curled into a malicious grin in the moonlight. Victor trembles with passion bordering on madness, and tears the female creature to pieces. The creature howls in agony at the sight of his only hope for happiness and companionship destroyed, then wanders off.

Later that night, Victor returns to the home he's rented by the water. He stands guard, terrified, certain the creature will return. He hears someone paddling toward his home in a boat, but he can't see them. His heart pounds as he hears footsteps coming closer. The creature opens the door and enters. He reminds Victor of the promise he's made to him and pleads with him to reconsider. The creature has suffered unimaginable torments and traveled massive distances to see his mate. Victor refuses to help him. The monster is enraged, declares himself Victor's true master, and orders him to start over and create his companion. But, again, Victor refuses. The two exchange threats—the creature assures him that he has nothing to live for and therefore can inflict immense suffering on his creator. "I will watch with the wiliness of a snake, that I may sting with its venom. Man, you shall repent of the injuries you inflict."

Victor fires back, "Devil, cease; and do not poison the air with these sounds of malice. I have declared my resolution to you, and am no coward to bend beneath words. Leave me; I am inexorable."

The creature knows that Victor plans to return home to marry his sweetheart, Elizabeth, and says, "It is well. I go; but remember, I will be with you on your wedding night."

Victor stares him down, and says, "Villain, before you sign my death-warrant, be sure you yourself are safe."

It's on.

Victor is ready to throw down right there, but the creature runs out, gets into his boat, and shoots across the moonlit waters with an "arrowy swiftness." Victor paces the floor, terrified of the horrors the creature will inflict on the world, and realizes that he is virtually certain to be killed. But he bursts into tears when he thinks of Elizabeth finding her "lover so barbarously snatched from her." And he makes a second critical decision: to fight. "I resolved not to fall before my enemy without a bitter struggle."

The protagonist and antagonist have both made the same critical decision, they each plan to kill the other. This is the beginning of the end. This is also a slick piece of misdirection. Victor just tore the creature's "woman" to shreds. If the creature kills Victor, he will destroy any last vestige of hope of ever having a mate. So, what the creature does on Victor's wedding night is not kill Victor—he murders Elizabeth, his wife. By focusing our attention on Victor's death, and doing it so intensely, Shelley pulls focus away from what actually happens.

The next day Victor is so exhausted he falls into a deep sleep and wakes feeling as if a "film had been taken from before my eyes." He feels "as if I belonged to a race of human beings like myself." He then makes another critical decision. "I had resolved in my own mind, that to create another like the fiend I had first made would be an act of the basest and most atrocious selfishness; and I banished from my mind every thought that could lead to a different conclusion." This sets up the final confrontation. It is between an enraged monster, hell-bent on vengeance, and a fully human being who wishes only to love his woman, serve humankind, and live in peace.

Shelly writes both characters to the top of their intelligence, but consumed by conflict. She lets you know the end is near, and tricks you into thinking that Victor or the creature will die, when in fact Elizabeth does. Shelley masterfully crafts her narrative. Greatness is never an accident.

HOW YOU DO IT

The following bullet points will help you think through and execute the principle.

- The beginning of the end is the moment when your protagonist *consciously* decides that they will resolve the Central

Dramatic Question once and for all. The weather may be terrible, the plane might have a busted wing, there might be no visibility, but here the pilot decides they're going to try to land. In a sports story, this is when the hero enters the arena for the championship game. In a love story, this is when the lovers go away for the weekend, knowing full well that by Sunday evening they will either be engaged or broken up. In a Western, this is when the good sheriff realizes that no townsfolk will fight by his side, and he's going to have to face down the bad guys alone.

▶ Get clear on the specific action your hero must take to acquire their object of desire and resolve the story's CDQ. And make sure it's the most intelligent decision this hero, in this specific situation, can make.

▶ To write this well requires getting into the appropriate mindset. Think of something you dreaded doing for ages. Maybe it was confessing your guilt, breaking up with someone, sharing a secret, or quitting a job. Something happened that finally made you realize, "I must put an end to this once and for all." This is the mindset you need to write this scene.

▶ Identify the specific reason your hero must act *now*. Why can't they put off this decision another minute? It could be that the plane is low on fuel, bad guys have just arrived in town, or it's the night of the big game. It could be they can't live without their loved one another second longer. Why must your character resolve their situation right now?

▶ Make sure that your character realizes the implications of what's about to happen. Heroes are not oblivious. They don't meander into their fate. They don't necessarily need to blatantly express it—"this one's for all the marbles"—it may just show in their actions. In the cop story we've discussed, McGreavy decides that he knows who killed his son. He's been told by his superiors to back off, that he's too close to the case. But he's got to act on what he knows, and he tells his wife that he is going to take the murderers out. She is a devout Catholic who is against this, but he tempts her soul to the dark side—they must do this for their dead son. She not only blesses his decision, she decides to help.

▶ Try hard to put yourself in your reader/viewer's shoes. What would it take to fully engage them, to get complete buy-in, to make them really care about your hero, the event that's about to go down, and what it all means?

MINI FINAL EXAM

Read the following, then answer the question below.

In the viral video "Leeroy Jenkins," we see a close-up of a computer screen featuring characters from the massive multiplayer video game *World of Warcraft* huddling just outside an underground labyrinth known as the Rookery. Dressed in armor, each character is played by a different person, but the group works together as a team. Since all the characters have the same object of desire—to succeed in their mission—they are a group protagonist. Their goal is to help one of the players, Leeroy, obtain special armor. The guy playing Leeroy has stepped out and is not involved in the planning. The group comes off as lovable nerds, who meticulously plot their strategy. They'll use powerful spells like Intimidating Shout and Divine Intervention among other things.

After much planning, they calculate their odds of success as a 32.3 percent chance of survival. They clearly wish the odds were better, and contemplate whether or not to go in. Just then, the guy playing Leeroy returns and says, "Alright, chums, I'm back. Let's do this." Then he cries out, "Leeeeeeeeerooooooyy Jenkins!" and rushes in. The group has no choice but to follow. They are immediately set upon by winged creatures. They struggle valiantly, but it's no use. As Leeroy runs wildly through the maze, the guys drop like flies. One guy calls for another to "Rez us! Rez us!" (as in cast a spell to resurrect them), and another uses something called a "Soulstone." But nothing works. They are disgusted with Leeroy and insult him bitterly as all of their hard work goes to crap. The mission is officially dead when Leeroy himself is killed. One guy calls him stupid, to which Leeroy replies, infamously, "At least I have chicken." Apparently, he was fixing himself some chicken while the group worked so hard to develop a strategy on his behalf.

At which moment in the story is the critical decision made?

a) When the guys calculate their odds of success and realize it's only 32.3 percent.
b) When one guy tries to use a "Soulstone."
c) When they gather at the mouth of the Rookery in support of Leeroy.
d) When Leeroy says that he decided to make chicken.
e) When Leeroy shouts his name and races into the Rookery, forcing all to follow.

CONTINUING ED

In the Food Network cooking show *Chopped*, on every episode four professional chefs compete in a contest. There are three rounds. For each round, contestants are given a "mystery" bag filled with different, often unusual, food stuffs. In round one they make an appetizer, round two an entrée, and round three a dessert. After each round, a contestant is "chopped," or cut, by a panel of three celebrity chef–judges. For the last round, the two remaining contestants make dessert.

What is the energy like as the two remaining contestants complete their last task of making dessert? (Hint: It often ends with the judges counting down the final ten seconds they have to finish making their elaborate confections.) Afterward, the two finalists sit together in a room as the judges debate their final decision. How do these conversations realize the principle of beginning the end with a critical decision? How critical is this decision to the contestants? How does the tone of this moment contrast with the tone of the contestants' ultimate dessert-creating moments? And lastly, how does the discussion between the judges increase viewers' desire to see the show's resolution? (As a bonus, consider the way the show also executes the next principle, "Confirm the decision," since these two principles are tightly paired.)

MINI FINAL ANSWER

The correct answer is **e) When Leeroy shouts his name and races into the Rookery, forcing all to follow**. This is the action that forces the story to its conclusion in which the Central Dramatic Question is answered—the team will not be successful in their mission.

9

Confirm the decision.

"The maddening thing for someone with a Western scientific turn of mind is that it's not what's in your pack that separates the quick from the dead. It's not even what's in your mind. Corny as it sounds, it's what's in your heart."
—LAURENCE GONZALES, Author

QUICK TAKE

After your protagonist makes the critical decision—to slay the dragon, stand up to the bully, land the burning plane, break free from an abusive relationship, accept God into their heart—whatever it is, they are not finished. The first decision begins the end of your story. But then, they must make a *second* decision that confirms their commitment. Again, heroes don't half-ass important decisions—if they do, those decisions lack meaning. So, here, at the very end of your story, as the hero is about to take their final action, the one that answers the Central Dramatic Question, another final, almighty hammer drops. It's as if the universe itself needs to stare into the hero's eyes and check their guts like a maniacal drill sergeant: "Are you *really* gonna do this? Are you *sure*, motherfucker?" And what the hero decides to do, the final action they take, will forever define the essence of their character—and end your story.

HOW IT WORKS

In the last chapter, "Begin the end with a critical decision," we discussed the moment in the film *Rocky* when Rocky makes the critical decision to go the distance because it will prove that he's not "just another bum from the neighborhood." But that doesn't just lead to a simple montage in which he gives the fight his all. That would be a vapid cliché, a lie that says all you need to do in life is make a decision and voila!—your dreams come true. Instead he fights the fight of his life, but in the fourteenth round he takes a spectacular beating and goes down.

The beating is so savage, his own manager screams at him, "Stay down, Rock!" But he struggles to his feet and battles on. The round ends—only one more to go. He staggers to his corner. His eyes are swollen shut. He can't fight if he can't see. They'll have to throw in the towel. But Rocky growls, "You stop this fight, I'll kill ya." He tells them to cut one eye open so he can see. The trainer slices Rocky's eyelid. Blood shoots out. He's prepared to risk death, blindness, or brain damage—anything—to finish the fight. And off this confirmation of his decision, he battles through the fifteenth and final round—and goes the distance.

In the Kazuo Ishiguro novel *The Remains of the Day*, Mr. Stevens, a butler who has dedicated the entirety of his life to serving his ultra-wealthy employers, makes the critical decision to visit the woman he has always been in love with, Ms. Kenton. She is a former coworker who was madly in love with him, but whom he rejected and let get away long ago. In an exchange of letters, he learns that she separated from her husband and would love to see him, and he decides to visit her. It's a long trip through the English countryside. He hopes she'll return with him to the estate where they worked together so many years earlier. His dream is to make up for lost time and bring meaning to his life.

The two meet in the afternoon. They are older now, world-weary but still very much in love. They share a pleasant meal. Toward the end, she tells him that her daughter is pregnant, and she will need to help out with the baby. She mentions that her husband is helpless without her and she must return to him. Mr. Stevens's heart is shattered. In this moment, he makes a second decision—to say nothing, to let her go. He fails to confirm the decision.

These two moments—Rocky demanding to have his eye cut open, Mr. Stevens sitting quietly and saying nothing—are wildly different in tone. But they're the same moment in terms of dramatic structure. They're a final test. They give the hero one last chance to prove their mettle, to reveal their true nature, by making a second and final decision. This second decision answers or leads directly to the moment the Central Dramatic Question is answered and ends the story. Rocky confirms his decision to go the distance and proves that he is not just another bum from the neighborhood. Mr. Stevens fails to confirm the decision to win back Ms. Kenton, and accepts that he has wasted his life.

Think of these moments—dropping hammers, critical decisions, etc.—as beads on a string. You can rearrange them, slide them around, to shape your story in your own unique way. For example, Ishiguro has Mr. Stevens make the decision to visit Ms. Kenton early in the story, but he actually visits her later. Much of their relationship is told in flashbacks in between. You have tremendous flexibility to play with these principles as you see fit.

The first critical decision usually begins the ending at around the two-thirds to three-quarters mark. This sparks a chain of actions that leads to a second decision that gives the hero a chance to confirm (or deny) the first one. These are conscious decisions. The hero knows exactly what is happening and what it means. To avoid repetition, you want to vary the setting and/or tone. In *Rocky*, he makes the critical decision to go the distance quietly late at night in bed in a broken-down room, alone with his girl. He confirms the decision covered in blood before twenty-five thousand screaming fans under extreme pressure to call it quits, inches from his goal.

• • •

In Chapter 3, "Explore all endings," we emphasized how important the end of your story is. Let's take a step back here and hit this key point again. The ending reveals the meaning of your story. Even if you got everything else right—dropped the hammer, built a tight link of cause and effect, wrote characters to the top of their intelligence—it all comes to nothing if you mess up your ending. If it's trite, not backed up by logic and all the previous action, your story will be forgotten. Your audience will leave feeling disappointed. Your book will be tossed. Your video game deleted. By zeroing in hard on the moment your hero confirms or denies this momentous decision, you, as the writer, take responsibility for your ending. Your protagonist makes this decision *consciously*, whatever the fallout may be. This is where you reveal who they truly are or what they've become. And you accept whatever meaning one may reasonably infer from studying this final action.

HOW A MASTER DID IT

The Godfather, Part II (1974)
Mario Puzo, Francis Ford Coppola

In 2017, Francis Ford Coppola released *The Godfather Notebook*, a reprint of Mario Puzo's original novel that includes notes Coppola wrote on every page. It gives deep insight into his thoughts on the story. In a quote on the cover he says, "Upon the second reading, much of the book fell away in my mind, revealing a story that was a metaphor for American capitalism in the tale of a great king with three sons: the oldest was given his passion and aggressiveness; the second his sweet nature and childlike qualities; and the third, his intelligence, cunning, and coldness."

There are two important points in here. The first is that Coppola saw the story of *The Godfather* as a metaphor for capitalism. The book came out in the early 1970s when America was mired in the Vietnam War—a war that killed millions of

Vietnamese and more than 50,000 American soldiers, the vast majority of whom were under twenty years old. The national mood was grim, and there was a pervasive sense, especially among young people, that America was no longer living up to its ideals. The second important point is that Coppola saw one of the great king's sons as sweet-natured and childlike and another as cold and cunning. These are the key ingredients he would use to tell this story. The great king is Don Vito Corleone. The sweet son is his middle son, Fredo. And the cold and cunning son is the youngest, Michael. (The other son, his oldest, is Sonny, who is gunned down in the first film.) The decision that will be confirmed at the end of *The Godfather, Part II* is Michael's decision to kill his own brother, Fredo. In other words, Vito's legacy will be that his cold, cunning son murders his sweet, childlike son. This is a metaphor for America, and an indictment of the excessive and corrupting nature of capitalism.

In order to show how this principle, "Confirm the decision," works in *The Godfather, Part II*, we need to start at the beginning and work our way back up to the moment Michael decides to kill Fredo.

In the first film, the Central Dramatic Question is "Will the Corleone family retain power?" We care about the Corleones because although Vito is a criminal, capable of theft and murder, he's not sadistic or bloodthirsty like the other bosses. He simply sees himself as a businessman who provides services—gambling and prostitution—that people want and that, in his mind, are victimless crimes. He also runs some legitimate import/export businesses. He is Sicilian and devoted to his two families—the Corleones, the most powerful crime syndicate in America, and his wife and five children, Sonny, Fredo, Michael, their baby sister Connie, and adopted son Tom Hagen. Family is *everything* to Vito and they are all extremely close. If he has one rule, one commandment, it is that you never—*never*—take sides against your own family.

The hammer drops on Vito when he rejects a deal to go into narcotics with the other crime families. They want to leverage his connections to politicians and the police. But Vito feels drugs are a dirty business, and fears his high-powered connections will turn on him if he deals drugs. Enraged by his decision, the other bosses put a hit on him. He takes five bullets but incredibly survives. The story tracks the transition of power from the aging Vito to Michael, who is named acting don after Sonny is murdered and Fredo—who is too weak to be the boss—is sent off to Vegas to learn the casino business. Vito recovers from his injuries, but later dies of a heart attack. Michael acts quickly and decisively while the Corleone family is still strong. He has all the other bosses executed and is named Godfather.

This coronation is particularly tragic as Vito saw Michael as his best hope to realize his dream of making the family business legitimate. Vito never meant to become a criminal—it was simply the only real option a poor immigrant had to control his own fate, to be the one who pulls the puppet strings rather the one forced to dance on them at the whim of other men. His ultimate dream was to help Michael become Senator or Governor Corleone. The last thing Michael ever says to his father is, "We'll get there, Pop. We'll get there." Michael is a metaphor for America at the time—young and full of promise but losing its soul.

The Godfather, Part II picks up the story in the late 1950s. Michael has relocated the family to Reno, Nevada, where they have moved heavily into the casino industry. They live together in multiple houses on a gorgeous estate overlooking Lake Tahoe. Michael and his wife, the New England WASP Kay, have a young son and a daughter, and she pushes him daily to keep his promise to become legitimate.

In another storyline, we simultaneously track Vito's original rise to power so that we can watch both men, side by side, father and son, as they struggle to take care of their families at the same age. We're not going to talk about the Vito storyline here other than to say that America, at the turn of the twentieth century, was a simpler, less ruthless place. True to his values, Vito spends a great deal of time with his family. In one moving scene, young Vito watches baby Fredo, feverish and howling in pain, get held down by his mother as another woman applies leeches. Vito is so empathetic that he seems to be in even worse pain than poor Fredo. Throughout the film, his devotion to his family is contrasted with Michael's descent and estrangement from his.

Michael works on a huge deal with another heavyweight criminal, an old associate of Vito's, named Hyman Roth. On the surface, Roth wears the mask of an old Jewish retiree. He lives in a modest home in Florida and watches baseball. He pretends to care for Michael out of respect for his father. But beneath the mask, Roth is a sociopath whose lust for power knows no bounds. He has many congressmen and multinational business leaders in his pocket. Roth is working with the Cuban government to arrange a deal to run all the casinos on the island. The kind of money this can safely generate is the motherlode of criminal enterprise. To pull off this deal, though, Roth needs Michael to put in millions. The Corleones know the casino industry, are worth a fortune and, of course, reliably corrupt. Michael's plan is to get this deal done with Roth, then finally, once and for all, take the Corleones into the legitimate "hotel and leisure" industry. Roth's goal is to use the money to install a president in the White House and expand his empire even further.

Throughout the film, Michael is under unimaginable pressure. The stress of dealing with someone of Roth's stature is immense. To say these two arch-criminals operate at the top of their intelligence is a gross understatement. It's a life-or-death chess match and neither can trust a word the other says. At one point, Roth orders a hit on Michael by having two hit men attack him in his bedroom. This attack violates any semblance of decency, as it could have killed Michael's wife and kids. Though the hit fails, what's worrisome is that the hit men could get so close—that means they were tippped off by a traitor within the Corleone family.

The Godfather, Part II CDQ starts out as "Will Michael make the Corleones legitimate?" but shifts to "Will Michael save his soul?" when it becomes clear that in this world, there's no such thing as legitimacy. Everyone is corrupt. And, the pressure on Michael mounts.

His sister, Connie, once a loving young woman, has become a bitter floozy who drinks to excess, ignores her own kids, and never misses a chance to insult Michael by comparing him unfavorably to their father. His wife, Kay, has a miscarriage—and the unborn child was another boy, which Michael desperately wanted. On top of all this, the US Department of Justice is holding nationally televised hearings on organized crime and has flipped Frank Pentangeli (Franky Five Angels), a capo in the Corleone family. A loyal capo in the Corleone family flipping was once unthinkable. That someone Michael truly loved and was good to would rat him out, would desecrate the family name on national television, is beyond words. As the film progresses, Michael's pain—his anger and his hurt—build exponentially. In one scene, he presses a warm washcloth to his eyes, and you can feel how hard he must work to hold it together. In fact, the stress was so intense, Al Pacino, who played Michael, had to be hospitalized, and filming shut down for days until he recovered.

But the hardest shot he takes is yet to come. Kay's contempt hits new heights after Michael's machinations defeat the government's case against him. Her Ivy League–educated marine has become everything he swore he'd never be and worse. In a fit of helpless rage, she tells him that she didn't have a miscarriage, she had an abortion. He slaps her across the face and casts her out of the family. In his mind, his own wife hates him so much she murdered their baby son. One can't imagine a bigger perversion of Vito's ideal of family than this act. Michael is getting attacked by the federal government, corrupt local politicians, Hyman Roth, his own capos, his sister, and his wife. Think of each of these things as cuts that bleed out his humanity.

And this brings us to the storyline that ultimately damns Michael's soul: the murder of Fredo. In the middle of the film, Michael and Fredo are in Cuba doing business with Roth. Fredo's been brought along to entertain the congressmen who are there to get a piece of the action. At a live sex show, Michael overhears Fredo say that he's friends with one of Roth's henchman, Johnny Ola—a man he had just pretended not to know. Michael realizes that the traitor within his organization is Fredo. We never learn exactly what Fredo did, but he was most likely a patsy tricked into giving information about the compound—information that almost got Michael, Kay, and their kids killed. In in a famous scene, as all hell breaks loose in Cuba when communist revolutionaries overthrow the government on New Year's Eve, Michael clutches Fredo's face and tells him, "I know it was you, Fredo. You broke my heart." This terrifies Fredo, who runs off, and Michael must flee the crumbling nation without him. (Of note, this chaotic, extremely emotional scene happens right in the middle of the story, as we discussed in Chapter 7, "Max out the middle.")

Michael gets word to Fredo that he is not going to hurt his own brother, and the film's ending begins with the two having a conversation at the Nevada family estate. They talk in a cold room—you can see Michael's breath—with floor-to-ceiling windows overlooking a world whited out by ice and snow. This scene takes place at the two-thirds mark of the film. Fredo sits awkwardly in a chair that lies way back as Michael enters the room. He can't look at Michael, who needs to know not only what caused the betrayal, but what, if anything, Fredo can do to help him defeat Roth. Fredo confesses he gave Roth's crew information, but swears he didn't know it would be used for a hit. He pitifully cries that there was something in it for him and rages about all the hurt he's felt at being treated like a dummy, at being passed over by his kid brother. He then tells Michael all he knows about Roth. It's enough to show that he was in tight with Michael's archenemy, but not enough to help Michael win. Michael tells him that he's no longer a brother to him, no longer a friend, no longer anything, and walks out. Michael then enters a dark room where his hit man, Al Neri, sits alone, waiting, and says, "I don't want anything to happen to him while our mother is alive." His real meaning is clear: Kill Fredo as soon as their mother dies. This is the critical decision at the conclusion of act two that will lead directly to the end of the film.

Later, with about half an hour left in the film, Fredo weeps over their mother's open coffin. (Of note, the scene that dissolves into this one wraps up young Vito's storyline. In its final moment, he holds Michael and waves his little hand out a train window, telling him, "Say goodbye, Michael," as the family leaves Italy.) Connie embraces Fredo, who can barely stand. He asks Tom if he can speak with Michael, but Tom adamantly refuses. Connie is mortified and goes to talk to Michael. It is a profoundly moving scene. Michael is spiritually dead inside—in one interview, Coppola describes him as a "living corpse." He has cracked under all the pressure and can barely move. She kneels before him, apologizes, and admits that she's hated him. But she now understands how hard he's worked to be strong for the family. She pleads with Michael to forgive Fredo, who is so sad and lost without him. He holds her hand and silently rises, then drifts across the room where their mother lies, and finds Fredo seated at a table. He stands coldly before him. Fredo looks up into his eyes, a lost child, and throws his arms around Michael's waist. As orchestral music crescendos, Michael slowly lifts his eyes to look at Al Neri. Even Neri, a hit man, seems ashamed. Michael gives the slightest nod yes. And, in this silent exchange, Michael confirms the decision to kill his own brother.

The magnitude of this sin can't be overstated. Michael not only has Fredo murdered, but he watches it take place. He violates his father's most sacred code. But what's important here, in this chapter, is that when Connie pleads with him to forgive Fredo, you can practically hear the storyteller asking, "Michael, are you sure you want to kill your own brother?" And he does. Heroes, or in this case, antiheroes, don't take their final action in a fit of emotion. The CDQ is always answered consciously, with the hero fully aware of what they are doing. Michael makes a decision to kill Fredo, and then confirms it, in the coldest blood. He chooses to damn his soul and seal his fate.

HOW YOU DO IT

The following bullet points will help you think through and execute the principle.

▶ Write out your Central Dramatic Question. As an example, we'll work through this with our story of the cop looking to catch his son's killer. The CDQ is "Will the cop catch his son's killer?"

▶ Identify the moment the hero makes the critical decision. The cop decides that he knows who did it—and he's going to kill him. The audience/reader must know why the hero thinks that taking this action will resolve the CDQ. Be specific and clear. If the cop kills the man who did it, he will have acquired his object of desire and this will provide a satisfying end to the story.

▶ Up the pressure on your hero. What would make it as hard as humanly possible to confirm their decision? The important thing here is that when your hero confirms the decision, they make a conscious decision to seal their fate. The cop's wife pleads with him not to damn his soul. But he convinces her that he can't live with himself if he doesn't avenge his son's death. He'd rather go to Hell. And she agrees.

▶ Contrast the tone of when the decision is made and when it's confirmed. You want to keep these two moments from feeling repetitive and to make each moment as compelling as possible. For example, one moment takes place in chaos, one in contemplation. Use tone, colors, music, volume, setting, etc., to create each moment as its own unique experience.

▶ When the hero confirms the decision, they must do it in a way that is surprising. Either what happens or how it happens is not what we expected when they made the decision. In the story of the cop, we don't expect him to lure his wife into helping him.

▶ Is it authentic? Do you believe that this protagonist would take this action?

▶ Make sure the decision is meaningful and resonant. You'll know you have it if it conveys a core truth of how you see the world. The cop killing the wrong guy expresses an idea—that false narratives get people killed. This feels like a relevant message.

MINI FINAL EXAM

Read the following, then answer the question below.

You sketch out a treatment. It's for a story about a high school senior who is sweet as can be by nature, but as he enters twelfth grade he's plagued with thoughts of suicide. His parents are going through a bitter divorce. His older sister takes her frustrations out on him. And he's madly in love with a girl who doesn't know he exists. He smokes weed every chance he gets, plays countless hours of video games, and has trouble sleeping.

At school, a teacher notices his grades are slipping, and that he looks awful, and asks him to stay after class to talk. But the kid won't engage. He really doesn't know what he's feeling. The teacher asks about cut marks on his forearm and the kid swears it's just from playing with his dog. The teacher says he'd like to talk with his parents, but the kid begs him not to call them. The teacher promises not to if the kid will promise to call him if he feels bad. The kid promises that he will. The teacher gives the boy his cell phone number and tells him he will leave it on because he's worried about him. That night the kid suffers a terrible anxiety attack. He looks at the clock. It's only 9:45 p.m. His mom and sister are out, and he has no clue where they went. He can't fathom making it through the night. But he makes the critical decision that he wants to live.

Which answer best exemplifies the principle of forcing the protagonist to confirm (or deny) the critical decision?

a) Having made the decision to live, he confirms it by baking and decorating an elaborate cake to surprise his mom and sister with. He now wants to celebrate life.
b) The kid calls the teacher, who doesn't answer his phone, provoking an even more intense anxiety attack. Then, with tears in his eyes, he grinds up every pill in the house in the sink disposal, empties the bullets in his mom's gun and tosses them, and plays his guitar for all he's worth until the anxiety fades.
c) The teacher shows up, unannounced, having sensed the boy was in trouble, and takes him to a psychiatrist. The two hug it out—the teacher is a true friend.
d) The girl he's in love with texts him to ask for a date and his confidence rises. Now, he's got someone to live for.
e) The kid attempts suicide and his mother finds him unconscious. She screams and cries and pleads for him to please wake up.

CONTINUING ED

In the 1953 Western film *Shane*, the title character is a mysterious stranger, a gunslinger who rides into a small town in a valley in the Wyoming territory around 1890. He's a handsome man who wears a jacket with buckskin fringe that gives him a bit of flamboyant style that the rugged cattle ranchers in these parts snicker at. He befriends a rancher, Joe Starrett, and takes a job as a farmhand on Joe's ranch. Joe lives with his young son, Joey, and his wife, Marian. They get along well, and Shane clearly has great affection for both Joe and his wife. Joey idolizes Shane. When Joe faces harassment from a local cattle baron, Rufus Ryker—who tries to run Joe off the ranch—Shane gets involved.

There are two storylines fueled by the following dramatic questions. Will Shane save Joe's family's ranch? And will Shane find a home in town? Ultimately, Shane makes a very emotional decision about whether or not to stay. How does little Joey force Shane to confirm his decision in one of the most powerful final moments in film?

MINI FINAL ANSWER

The correct answer is **b) The kid calls the teacher, who doesn't answer his phone, provoking an even more intense anxiety attack. Then, with tears in his eyes, he grinds up every pill in the house in the sink disposal, empties the bullets in his mom's gun and tosses them, and plays his guitar for all he's worth until the anxiety fades.** Having the teacher unavailable and upping his anxiety as he feels abandoned forces him to dig deep to escape his demons. This series of actions confirms his conscious decision to live.

10

Wrap up fast.

"You enter strong and you exit strong and you're going to be okay."
—CHRIS FARLEY, Comedian

QUICK TAKE

After the Central Dramatic Question is answered, tie up any loose ends and get out as quickly as possible. If you linger too long, it's like listening to someone tell you a story after you've gotten the point. Even if it was a good story, the longer they talk, the more the impact of the story dissipates. That said, respect how important this moment is, because it is the very last thing your audience or reader experiences. Though you have to wrap up and get out as efficiently as possible, you can't let your guard down and just phone this in.

The answer to the CDQ reveals the meaning of your story. Now, you need to decide how you want your audience to *feel*. This moment is sort of like giving all the kids a goody bag as they leave a child's birthday party. You don't just kick your guests into the street—you give 'em a little something for the road to smooth the transition back to reality. In a story, what you put in the goody bag is a specific feeling, and you make it count. Think of your very favorite story. I'll bet you don't just remember the final moment, I'll bet you still feel it too.

HOW IT WORKS

When you take in a story, you're fully engaged with the hero and absorbed by the Central Dramatic Question. As the hero moves closer to and further from their object of desire, and your emotions whip back and forth from sorrow to joy, tranquility to stress, rage to acceptance, your body tightens up and releases tension over and over until, finally, the CDQ is answered. This moment is emotionally charged and intellectually engaging. Even when the CDQ is answered in a quiet, understated way, as it is in this chapter's masterwork, Yasijuro Ozu's film *Late Spring*, it is intense because it is filled with meaning.

So, the most common rhythm you see is the story hits a high point of tension at the moment when the CDQ is answered—which is most often called a climax—and the story wraps up with a quieter, more reflective tone. This is for obvious reasons. The audience needs a little room to process the meaning of what's just happened. It's not a coincidence that the word *climax* is the same word we use for an orgasm. Most people don't move from the finale of a sexual encounter onto a pogo stick. We collapse and take a few deep breaths, maybe share a stunned look or giggle, snuggle in or lie on our backs, and gaze through infinity.

After the CDQ is answered, master storytellers get out of there like jewel thieves who just snatched a multimillion-dollar necklace with the cops on their way. You can turn this section into a mini story complete with its own dramatic question. For example, after a courtroom drama, when the defendant is found guilty, the final moments might be fueled by another dramatic question, "How will the hero meet death?"

Great stories are wrapped up quickly and in a way that leaves the audience with an emotion that is appropriate to the genre. The 2015 horror film *The Witch* ends with someone walking toward a fire in the woods at night. It's profoundly disturbing. *The Brothers Karamazov*, Fyodor Dostoevsky's classic 1879 family and crime drama, ends with a young man encouraging a group of boys to never forget each other and their fallen friend.

It's bittersweet and leaves one feeling sad but hopeful. The 2013 series finale of the TV show *Breaking Bad* ends with a man laughing and crying as he speeds his car through a gate, and another man lying down to die as Badfinger's mournful rock ballad "Baby Blue" wails. It's an emotionally complex ending that leaves you with both a trace of hope and a profound sense of loss.

HOW A MASTER DID IT

Late Spring (1949)
Yasujiro Ozu

The humanity of his actors, the simplicity of his compositions, the minimal camera movement, and the gentleness of his nature as a writer and director all combine to make Yasujiro Ozu's masterpieces particularly poignant. One of them is the 1949 classic drama *Late Spring*. On the surface, it is a simple story. It's about an aging professor, Shukichi (Chishu Ryu), who is fully engaged in his work. He's a widower who lives alone with his daughter, Noriko (Setsuko Hara). They are very close. She takes care of the house—does the cooking and cleaning and looks after him. He pays the bills. Though nowadays this may seem sexist, the film is set in 1949, during a time in Japan where the father's role and traditional family values were still firmly in place. Though it was not unusual for women to work, the expectation was still that they would get married and take care of the home and children, while men worked. But Noriko has no desire to get married; she's content living with and caring for her father. If she left him, he would be alone, unable to cook and clean for himself, and that would break her heart. They are both happy with the way their lives are set up.

Shukichi's sister and Noriko's aunt, Masa, is concerned. If Noriko, now in her mid-twenties, doesn't marry soon, no man will have her. When Shukichi dies, what will become of her? Shukichi reluctantly agrees to let Masa find Noriko a husband. Masa sets

Noriko up with a promising candidate, Hattori. They go on a date. He is handsome, seems kind, and they get along well. But later Noriko tells her father that he is already engaged. Though Hattori may be willing to break his engagement to be with Noriko, she has no interest. She will not leave her father. She is willing to give up any chance of her own happiness to take care of him.

Masa, undeterred, convinces Shukichi to remarry. There's a young widow named Mrs. Miwa who would be perfect for him. Once Noriko realizes that she would only be in the way, she will accept that she must find a husband and build a life of her own.

Late Spring is a love story. The two "lovers"—as in people who love each other deeply—just happen to be father and daughter. And the CDQ of all love stories is ultimately "Will the lovers stay together?" Though nowadays a father/daughter love story sounds perverse, there's nothing incestuous or creepy about Shukichi and Noriko's love. They simply enjoy each other's company and run a nice little home together in a way that works for both people.

When Noriko hears about Mrs. Miwa, she is hurt, and doesn't believe her father is interested. One afternoon, they go to the theater together to see a Japanese Noh play. During the show, Shukichi sees Mrs. Miwa and the two exchange smiles. Noriko leaves the theater distraught. She knows that her father no longer needs her to care for him.

Masa sets Noriko up with another man, whom we never see. We learn only the odd detail that he is kind of handsome—half his face looks like the American movie star Gary Cooper. Noriko, with an air of resignation and no true passion, agrees to marry this man. She goes on vacation with her father and, as the two are leaving, she pleads with him to let her stay. She doesn't want to get married and doesn't mind if he is married. She just wants to stay by his side. He explains to her that she will one day find true happiness with her new husband. Happiness is something you build, over time. He tells her that her mother too was unhappy in the beginning of their marriage but gradually he built a life with her. Noriko apologizes for being selfish and promises to find happiness in her new marriage, after she leaves her father.

Shukichi visits with her one last time before the wedding. He goes upstairs to see her dressed as a traditional Japanese bride. She is profoundly sad, but, before they part, she thanks him for being a kind, loving father. And he sees her off. Keep in mind, she is moving far away and will soon be consumed by her own life. They may never see each other again. This answers the Central Dramatic Question: They will not stay together.

Shukichi has a drink with Noriko's childhood friend Aya, who asks him if he really plans to remarry. She tells him that Noriko was very much against it. He says that he will not remarry. He lied because it was the only way to convince her to marry. He walks home alone at night. This man, who has been cared for throughout his life by his mother, his wife, and his daughter, comes home to an empty home for the first time. He weakly dusts off his jacket with his hands and hangs it up. He sits down and slowly peels an apple. His knife works its way around until the peel hangs weakly and drops to the floor. Unable to bear his grief, his head drops. We cut to the sea at night; the tide rolls out as the waves roll in. And the film ends.

After the CDQ is answered, Ozu ties up one loose end—does Shukichi really plan to marry? He does not. Then Ozu shows us exactly where the hero is and how he feels. He is alone and heartbroken. Ozu ends with a shot of the sea—the world moves on as it always has and always will. The credits roll. There is no wasted time or extraneous detail. The meaning of the story is clear and resonant. No matter how much we love each other, no matter how happy we are together and how well we get along, we must eventually separate.

HOW YOU DO IT

The following bullet points will help you think through and execute the principle.

▶ After you answer your story's Central Dramatic Question, take a step back and consider every question your readers might still have—about the hero's emotional state, other characters, the world you've created, anything they might wonder about. All of this information must be clearly conveyed.

▶ Focus on efficiency. The story is essentially over. Your goal is to communicate any additional information as quickly and clearly as possible. If it's key information about what actually happened, say or show it and get out.

▶ Think about the image you want to conjure. Anton Chekhov is widely considered to be the greatest short-story writer of all time. His final images always land hard. In "The Kiss," a dejected soldier walks alone by a river in winter, then bitterly rejects an offer to attend a party. He's quit on life. In "Gusev," a dead body sinks past a school of fish as it descends to the bottom of the ocean. In "The Steppe," a little boy is left alone with an old woman he doesn't know but now has to live with. Focus on crystallizing the feeling you wish to leave your audience with. What visual image can you evoke to amplify that feeling? Define it clearly, then amplify it.

▶ Consider what you want your final message to say about the nature of life. The film *Ordinary People* ends with a father sitting by his son. After what they've been through, it is a powerful, bittersweet image that captures the vital importance of parental love and the price a man pays to save his child. If you have an idea to express, how can you express it as quickly, meaningfully, and emotionally as possible?

▶ For additional inspiration, consider the final moments of your three favorite stories. Carefully examine how they make you feel and what you can "steal" from them.

MINI FINAL EXAM

Read the following, then answer the question below.

You're writing a coming-of-age/sports story whose CDQ is "Will a young superstar goalie lead the Canadian Olympic hockey team to a gold medal?" She is hard-driving and hypercompetitive, and struggles with depression, drug abuse, and codependency. Her only sense of self-worth comes from winning. During her training and the Olympics, she turns her life around—she goes to counseling to manage her anger and anxiety, quits drinking, confronts the neighbor who once abused her, and, after a series of bad relationships, falls in love with a good man. At the final game of the Olympics, the team plays their hearts out but loses in triple overtime to their archrival after the hero lets in a bad goal. With the CDQ clearly answered—she will not lead her team to Olympic gold—which of the following most effectively wraps up the story?

a) The ghost of her grandmother appears and tells her that the family has always known defeat, and, she learns that her fate, and the fate of all humankind, is predestined.
b) She apologizes to the team. The captain tells her she doesn't need to apologize. They never would have gotten so far without her. The team gives her a standing ovation, and she's able to accept defeat.
c) As the winners celebrate, her face contorts with horror. She wanted this so bad. She barely makes it off the ice before collapsing in misery.
d) Tormented by the loss, she returns to a life of drinking and drug abuse. Her bad attitude costs her a spot on the next Olympic team. She goes to night school, studies accounting, and takes a job at H&R Block. After a series of failed attempts to get clean, she finally surrenders herself to God and finds peace.
e) She wakes up and is thrilled to realize that this was all a dream. The game is later that night!

CONTINUING ED

In Martin Scorsese's 1990 true-crime drama *Goodfellas*, Henry Hill is an Irish Italian kid who grew up idolizing gangsters. At a young age he was brought into the crew of mob boss Paul Cicero. Along with his two closest friends, Jimmy "The Gent" Conway and Tommy DeVito, Henry lives a hardcore criminal life. Whatever these guys want, they take, and they thrash or kill anyone who stands in their way. Together, the crew pulls off one of the biggest heists in New York City history. But they turn on each other. The CDQ is "Will Henry survive the mob life?" The CDQ is answered when Henry Hill flips and testifies against his crew.

As Henry walks off the stand, he addresses the camera directly to let us know the story is over. The CDQ is answered. It's a mixed ending, positive in that Henry survives, negative in that he had to betray his friends to do it, and must give up the exciting life he loves. After he walks off the stand, Scorsese and co-screenwriter, Nicholas Pileggi, need only let us know where things stand—in other words, where exactly Henry ends up.

How long does it take for the film to go from Henry on the witness stand to the final credits? What feeling do the writers leave you with? How do they make this section compelling? And why is the last line—the last word—Henry utters so memorable?

MINI FINAL ANSWER

The correct answer is **b) She apologizes to the team. The captain tells her she doesn't need to apologize. They never would have gotten so far without her. The team gives her a standing ovation, and she's able to accept defeat**.

This gives us the information we need to have a satisfying conclusion in a short scene that, if well written (and acted), could be moving and meaningful. She will overcome this loss because she has grown as a person. The other choices are either not relevant to the previous action, too long, or meaningless.

"Some mystery should be left in the revelation of character in a play, just as a great deal of mystery is always left in the revelation of character in real life, even in one's own character himself."

—TENNESSEE WILLIAMS, Playwright

PART TWO

ESSENTIAL PRINCIPLES of CHARACTER

In this section, you'll learn nine principles to help you create dynamic characters that drive your stories forward with purpose, and accurately express your personality, intellect, passion, and imagination. Characters are not real live human beings. They do not exist beyond what they do in your story. So free yourself from feeling as if you must depict every last detail of an entire human life in order to realize a character. That will drain your battery and kill your confidence.

Instead, focus on executing the principles in this section—provoking dilemma, making characters active and decisive, writing characters to the top of their intelligence, etc.—that serve your story's needs. If you nail these nine simple principles, your characters will not only be entertaining, engaging, and thought-provoking, they will also be uniquely your own. And you will have all you need to tell your tale—authentic, compelling characters who are fully motivated to play out their fate.

11

Make your hero active and decisive.

"Make up your mind to act decidedly and take the consequences. No good in this world is ever done by hesitation."
—THOMAS HUXLEY, Biologist

QUICK TAKE

When your hero is active, it keeps your story moving, enables you to show instead of tell, and makes the story more entertaining. When your hero is decisive, they infuse your story with meaning by making themselves accountable for their actions. An active, decisive character is essential to a great story. But being "active" doesn't just mean the hero physically does things. It means they take progressively bolder actions that move them closer and closer to their ultimate fate. These actions include talking and thinking. When a protagonist takes a minute to make sense of things, asks a question, or finally says what's on his mind, these are actions. (We'll talk more about this in Chapter 22, "Craft actionable dialogue.") A cop grilling a suspect might take twenty different actions—sweet-talk, cajole, threaten—without ever leaving his seat.

> Because it is essential to your hero to acquire their object of desire, they cannot quit until the matter is permanently settled. And when it's all on the line, they enter a heightened state and become fully aware of what they do and why. They make a decision and then act on it, make another decision and then act on that one. And this brings them fully to life. Only an active and decisive character has the substance and *gravitas* necessary to carry the story.

HOW IT WORKS

Imagine two different characters, one active and decisive, one passive and indecisive. They are both victims of late-night home invasions. In bed, they hear glass shatter. The passive one sits up and trembles. The other tries to dial 911, but his phone's dead. He races around looking for a weapon but can't find one. We cut back to the passive one, still trembling. Cut back to the active one. He tries to open the window but it's frozen shut, so he puts his fist through it and places pieces of glass between his fingers to make his hand a lethal weapon. Back to the passive character—still trembling as the intruder walks toward the bedroom. Back to the active character—with a bloodied fist full of glass, he conceals himself behind a door and whispers the Lord's Prayer. One character takes one action, the other takes five. Each new action says something about the character.

This is not about believability. When faced with danger, people freeze, fight, or flee. It's entirely believable that someone would freeze. They're just not likely to reveal much or entertain while they're stuck in a state of paralysis.

Your audience or reader has come to you to help make sense of the world. When your characters are active and decisive, your story fills with meaning. Each decision and action reveals something. If a character responds to a slight with a punch, it means they're a hothead. It means if you insult a hothead, you get punched.

All twenty-seven principles are tightly connected. But this one goes particularly well with its sister principles, "Escalate risk" (Chapter 5) and "Clash expectation with reality" (Chapter 6). Your hero makes a decision and takes an action, then something unexpected happens. This unexpected incident or response from the world is meaningful, and forces them to take a bigger risk to acquire their object of desire. From the moment you drop the hammer, your hero springs to life, makes decisions, and takes actions that involve greater risk, and keeps going until their fate's decided. Think of story construction like triggering an avalanche that's fueled by an active and decisive main character.

HOW A MASTER DID IT

Red Dead Redemption (2010)
Dan Houser, Michael Unsworth, and Christian Cantamessa for Rockstar Games

In this Western video game, set in a fictionalized version of the American West in 1911, you play as the former outlaw John Marston. It takes roughly thirty-five hours to play the entire game, and over the course of the experience, as any fan of the game will attest, you build a strong connection to the character. This is because John is exceptionally well drawn, furiously active, and makes compelling decisions from start to finish.

John comes from the street. His mother was a prostitute and it's highly likely—he doesn't know for sure—that his father was her customer. She died in childbirth, and while John was still a little kid, his father was blinded in a bar fight and died from his injuries. John was put in an orphanage but escaped from it to live on the streets. He got himself into trouble, killed a man, and was about to be hanged when a man stepped in to save and essentially adopt him. That man was Dutch Van der Linde, a radical libertarian who believed that civilization was inherently evil. His dream was to build his own society, free from the corruption, oppression, and tyranny of governments and their big-business cronies. Dutch was highly literate and way ahead of his time in terms of treating everyone equally—American Indians, black people, and women all had a place in Dutch's budding society.

Dutch was the only true father John ever had and he followed him faithfully for years. The Van der Linde gang was, for a period, a true family. But making ends meet meant robbing banks and trains, and no shortage of murders. Sadly, Dutch's mind started to go as his hatred consumed him. The endless battles he waged against the powers-that-be took their toll. Marston was one of his most loyal soldiers—a fierce gunslinger and, when necessary, cold-blooded killer. But as time wore on, John grew weary of the endless cycles of violence. He fell in love with a fellow gang member, the former prostitute Abigail Roberts. Though she had slept with most of the guys in the gang, and did what she had to do to survive, John truly loved her and the two broke off from Dutch together and had a son, Jack. They bought a little farm and committed to going straight.

But John got busted by two federal agents, Edgar Ross and Archer Fordham, who kidnapped Abigail and Jack and basically threatened to kill them if John didn't do their bidding. They wanted him to go after one of his former associates, Bill Williamson, who had become a major badass, terrorizing communities with his new gang. Ross and Fordham knew that John was an elite killer and wanted him to eliminate Williamson by any means. When he completed his mission, he'd get his family back, and be able to live in peace on his farm.

The game starts when the feds put John on a train to Armadillo, where he quickly locates Williamson at the abandoned Fort Mercer. John calls out for Williamson to speak with him, and Williamson, a burly, bearded, nasty sumbitch, appears on a ledge above the gate and tells John to get lost. John tells him they can't win this war anymore and that he's got to give it up. Williamson guns John down and leaves him for dead. John is saved by a rancher who nurses him back to health. As soon as he pays his debt to her and recovers from his wounds, John sets out to build a small army of mercenaries to attack Williamson's gang at Fort Mercer.

The Central Dramatic Question is "Will John get his wife, kid, and ranch back?" The first Subordinate Dramatic Question is, "Will he take out Williamson?" But to do this, he'll need to win allies, get money, and score enough firepower to take out the heavily armed Williamson gang. This means doing odd jobs, hunting down outlaws for rewards, and pulling robberies. Here's the basic outline of the story:

- John puts together a ragtag band of misfits who score a large machine gun. They hide it in the back of a medicine man's carriage and pull a Trojan horse routine, sneaking into Fort Mercer and slaughtering Williamson's gang. But Williamson escapes into Mexico, where he's rumored to be aligned with their old friend, Javier Escuella.

- John rides into Mexico on his own and gets caught up in the Mexican Civil War. He's enlisted by a Colonel Allende, who offers to help him take out Williamson and Escuella if he'll fight by their side against the rebels.

- After John does his part helping the army win a battle, Allende screws him over—and is about to execute him, when he's saved by the charismatic rebel leader Abraham Reyes. John helps Reyes win some major battles and the two capture Escuella. You're offered the chance to kill him or just bring him to the feds.

- Then John and Reyes finally locate Allende and Williamson—and kill them both.

- The two men part ways and John heads back to the feds, Ross and Fordham, to get back Abigail and Jack, so he can return to his ranch and live in peace. But Ross goes back on his word. They've located Dutch Van der Linde and want John to track him down and take him out.

▶ John goes through hell as he treks into the mountains to find Dutch, who is holed up with a tribe of American Indians battling the US Army. John chases Dutch through an old mine and traps him high up on a snowy cliff. Badly injured and spent, Dutch drops his weapon and makes a beautiful speech to John about his inability to quit fighting—against his own nature—and falls gently backward off the cliff.

▶ John is reunited with his wife and son, and they're joined on the ranch by an old man he calls Uncle. They work hard to build a new home, buy and raise livestock, and make ends meet. But the story takes a dark turn. One day, as John's working on the ranch, Uncle warns him that there's a fast-approaching battalion of soldiers. He hustles Abigail and Jack onto a horse and the two make a narrow escape. Uncle makes his last stand and is shot down by the soldiers. John peeks out of his barn to see Agent Ross and a long line of soldiers ready for war. Maybe he knows too much. Maybe Ross would sleep better at night knowing the last of the Van der Linde gang is taken out. Whatever it is, they've come to kill John. He comes out, guns blazing, and after taking out as many soldiers as he can, is lit up by a hail of bullets. Ross lights a cigar and watches John, covered in blood, fall to his knees, take one big last painful breath, collapse, and die.

Though people may talk about the incredibly detailed, hyperrealistic world that *Red Dead Redemption* built with its awe-inspiring attention to detail, that's not what made the game a multibillion-dollar franchise. The success of this franchise was built on the character of John Marston. He is born into an immoral world, the result of an ignoble birth, and is forced to do whatever it takes to survive. Throughout the story, he kills outlaws, murderers, thieves, soldiers, rebels, lawmen, American

Indians, the good, the bad, and everyone in between. He's strong and courageous, but he's weary and scarred. He would much rather be a decent man and simply take care of his own, but this world betrays him at every turn. His mother was killed. His father was killed. He was cast out into the streets and society tried to kill him. And the only man who ever cared for him just happened to be both enlightened and borderline insane. So, dealt an impossibly bad hand, he did what he could to build an honorable life. And just when he had it in his grasp, the "law" betrayed him.

But what ultimately, above all, builds the exceptionally strong bond between player and character is not just John's rich history and emotional complexity, it's that he is so active—you do so many things as John, and he makes so many difficult decisions—you feel as if a real life was lived. If you're not familiar with video games, what you need to understand is that to complete a mission—to rob a train, take out a band of rebels, capture an outlaw—requires countless actions and many difficult decisions. As John, you work so hard, for so long, to finally gain a little place of your own in this big bad world. To see it come to nothing, to see it ripped from your grasp after you've finally paid your debt, genuinely hurts. When the history of video games is written, the death of John Marston will stand as a pivotal moment. For thousands, if not millions, of players, it was likely the first time a game made them cry. Rest in peace, John.

HOW YOU DO IT

The following bullet points will help you think through and execute the principle.

▶ Get clear on your hero's worldview and their values. You want your character's actions and decisions to have an intuitive logic and consistency. In *A Clockwork Orange*, Alex DeLarge, a teen gang leader in a dystopian future England, believes that in life, some people do the knifing and others get knifed. He prefers to do the knifing. This attitude fuels his actions and decisions. Define your hero's worldview in a simple statement—for example, Alex believes that it's better to knife than to get knifed.

▶ From the moment the hammer drops, your hero works to acquire their object of desire—even in quiet moments or conversations, they're working to satisfy their need. A man plotting a murder might go for a long walk to analyze his options. Like talking, thinking can be action. Start by making a massive list—go for quantity—of everything you can think of that your hero might do to achieve their goal.

▶ As you work through your story, give the important decisions to your protagonist. They must drive the action and make the key calls. Walter White makes the big decisions in *Breaking Bad*, Liz Lemon makes them in *30 Rock*, and, though often hopelessly ineffective, Oscar makes the final decision that seals his fate in *The Brief Wondrous Life of Oscar Wao*.

▶ To practice this, imagine a woman whose sole purpose in life is to win the Strawweight title of the Ultimate Fighting Championship. List three actions she can take to move toward her goal, and force her to make at least one big decision. For example, her husband tells her she must choose between her family—they have two young kids—and her dream.

▶ Have fun with this. Gamify it. With your hero's need firmly in mind, see if you can think up fifty actions your hero could take to achieve their goal. You can do it. In the story of the cop hunting his son's killer, he could interview witnesses—hostile witnesses, helpful witnesses, bizarre witnesses. He could study the crime scene, talk to experts, analyze security camera footage from homes and businesses. He could go through his son's phone, drawers, pockets. He could beg his captain to let him work the case, rally friends in the department, fight with the cops assigned to the case. He might need therapy, or to work out, or drink, to ease the pain caused by such monumental loss. Go nuts, list as many actions as you can—and don't stop until you get to fifty.

▶ Once you have a massive list of actions and can identify some big decisions your protagonist makes, ruthlessly weed out the uninteresting ones. Now, play with the order and see if you can structure your story from start to finish. Get as far as you can. Many pro writers will place individual actions the hero takes on separate index cards and just play with them to see how they fit together. And, as always, use the other principles alongside this one—for example build chains of action by connecting events with "therefore"—this happens, therefore that happens.

MINI FINAL EXAM

Read the following, then answer the question below.

A serial killer has a man tied up in his basement. The man tells the serial killer he'll pay him a hundred grand, no questions asked, if he'll let him go. He can show him an app right now and once the money goes through, it's done. The serial killer says nothing. The man says that the serial killer looks just like his father and jokes that they could be related. The serial killer grins and lights a cigarette. The man asks him where he's from and suggests that crazier things have happened. The man asks if he can just call his daughter to say goodbye. The serial killer reacts—this seems to strike a chord—but then he shakes it off. The man asks the serial killer if he believes in God. The serial killer turns and slowly walks up the basement stairs, unmoved. The man shouts that he will make the serial killer pay for this, as the sound of Haydn's oratorio *The Creation* drowns out his screams. Horns blare in celebration of the birth of life as the lunatic descends the staircase, axe in hand.

Which of the following are true? The man is:

a) Inactive, because he never moves.
b) Active, because he tries six different things to achieve his objective.
c) Both kind of active and kind of inactive.
d) Deserving of respect because he fights so hard for his cause.
e) Decisive, because all his actions are well thought out and boldly taken.

CONTINUING ED

In the 1960 children's classic *Green Eggs and Ham*, author Dr. Seuss uses just fifty words to tell a simple story. In it, a small furry creature named Sam-I-am tries to convince a larger, seemingly older creature to try green eggs and ham. Sam-I-am's strategy is to launch a relentless assault on his target's peace of mind until he achieves his objective. How many different tactics or actions does Sam-I-am take to execute his strategy? And how does the sheer number of things Sam-I-am tries up the emotional intensity, comedy, and scope of the story? Why do you think this story is one of the all-time bestselling children's books? What does it mean? And would its status as a "classic" be impacted if Sam-I-am did 50 percent fewer things to achieve his objective?

MINI FINAL ANSWER

The correct answers are b), d), and e). The man is very active. In this short tale he works constantly to achieve his objective, deserves respect for working so hard, and is decisive. He consciously decides to use new tactics after each one fails.

12

Provoke dilemma.

"No pressure, no diamonds."
—THOMAS CARLYLE, Philosopher

QUICK TAKE

Great writers put unbearable pressure on their characters, most notably the protagonist. They infuse their stories with impossible choices—choices between the lesser of two evils or two wonderful things of which the hero can only have one. We learn who your characters are by exploring how they respond to the most difficult decisions. If a character is heading to work and sees an old lady fall down in the street, this is not a dilemma. Of course, she should stop and help the woman. But if her tyrannical new boss told her that lateness is a firing offense, things get interesting. The character who slinks past, hoping someone else will help the lady, and gets to work on time is very different from the one who rushes to the prone woman, wipes the blood off her face and hands, then stays with her until an ambulance arrives.

Stories that force your characters to confront dilemmas are more engaging, reveal more about your characters, and are more entertaining because they make the story active. Dilemmas can't be ignored. When a character falls madly in love with two fantastic people at the same time, they must inevitably reveal their nature in how they respond to this delicate situation. If you're struggling to write, if you read your work and it meanders, if the dialogue feels pointless and full of clichés, it's almost certainly because the stakes are not high enough and the choices your characters face are too simple. Stories are charged by dilemmas. The more difficult the decisions your characters face, the more engaging the story.

HOW IT WORKS

You're reading a story about a young marketing executive just out of graduate school. She gets two job offers. One is from a company that works with the most exciting businesses and organizations around the world. It pays well and is located a block from her house. The other works with stodgy old insurance companies, pays half what she's worth, and requires an hour-long commute each way. Which will she choose? Which would you choose? Which would any sane human choose? It's not only obvious, it's predictable. You know the ending before she's actually made her choice. So, we learn nothing and it's boring. Awful.

Now let's say she gets the following two offers. One pays triple what she expected, lets her do what she's best at, and the company is growing like wildfire. Her success is virtually guaranteed. She'll be working for one of the biggest oil-and-gas companies in the world. The other one pays a third of the money, but works to protect the environment. She believes climate change is the most important issue we face and spent countless nights in grad school railing against the evils of fossil fuels. But she's mired in debt, has aging, sickly parents who are living on a small pension, and shares a stuffy apartment with an obnoxious roommate. She's dying to move into her own place. How she makes this choice tells us who she is.

She could meet with executives at the oil company and convince herself they are doing all they can to care for the environment. She could study the evidence against climate change and convince herself the threat is overrated. She could go to her parents, explain the situation, and ask for permission to take the lower-paying job. Though it means she can't help them pay their bills, it's best for the world at large. All these actions tell us who this character is and what she values most, and *show* how her mind works. Whatever she does, she's going to have pain. How does she decide which pain to accept? What's more important—her parents, who raised her and loved her and cared for her? Or the environment that she fears could become uninhabitable for future generations?

The master storyteller makes the choice as difficult as possible. Let's say she meets with her future boss at the oil company. If he's a cold, arrogant jerk, that makes the choice easier. She's already feeling negative about the company. If he's the nicest guy in the world and known for taking care of his team, that makes the choice more difficult. Think of these choices like watching a balloon fill with air. Some choices let the air out, some put more in. The more the balloon expands before it pops, the more entertaining the story.

The challenge here is that when you, as the writer, increase the pressure on your characters, *you* need to work harder, think deeper, and feel more as you process the implications of how characters respond. In real life, we dread dilemmas. Not many people wake up thinking, "Boy I sure hope today brings some brutal choices that force me to reveal who I truly am!" So, of course, you'd rather clean out the garage, go to the gym, or alphabetize your book, than afflict your characters with difficult choices. But that's the task at hand. You, the writer, are the hero of your own story. And the CDQ of your story is "Will you finish a meaningful, well-crafted story?" Do you feel the tightness of that connection between you and your main character? You both have to face dilemmas and face the truth of who you are.

HOW A MASTER DID IT

"The Best of Times, the Worst of Times" (2003)
Anthony Griffiths

"The Best of Times, the Worst of Times" is a story told by comedian Anthony Griffiths. It was recorded live at the US Comedy Arts Festival in Aspen on February 28, 2003. As of this writing, you can watch it on YouTube or listen to it on the Moth at themoth.org/stories/the-best-of-times-the-worst-of-times. It's only ten minutes long, so it's a quick listen and it will give you a richer experience than just reading the synopsis.

In 1990, Griffiths, a tall, handsome African American man, moves his wife and then-two-year-old daughter from Chicago, where he grew up poor on the South Side, to LA, to seek his fame and fortune as a stand-up comic. This was a time when network television was a much bigger deal than it is today. The king of late-night comedy was NBC's Johnny Carson, host of *The Tonight Show*. To be asked to appear on Johnny Carson was the pinnacle of any comedian's career. There were no Netflix comedy specials, no YouTube or websites or DVRs. Playing Carson was the key way to get in front of an audience of millions. If you nailed it, your status, earnings, and potential skyrocketed.

Just after arriving in LA, Griffiths gets two phone calls. The first is the answer to his prayers. It's the talent coordinator for *The Tonight Show*, inviting him to appear on the show. The second is from his toddler daughter's doctor, who tells him her cancer has returned. She had cancer before, but it was in remission, and Griffiths is confident that they beat it once and they will beat it again. But his life is turned upside down. He and his wife want to keep their daughter at home, which means during the day they have to undergo medical training to learn how to do CPR and administer her medications. They also have to take her to specialists, etc. At night, he has to play clubs and work closely with the talent coordinator from *The Tonight Show* to perfect his act. As he plays the top rooms in Los Angeles, he meets the biggest comedians in the world, including Jerry Seinfeld and Roseanne Barr. He plays *The Tonight Show* and, though he's terrified and can't recall a thing afterward, he's interrupted with six applause breaks. After the show, he walks to his car and sees Johnny Carson going to his car. They share a private moment and Johnny Carson tells him he was funny—and will be invited back. This means all his years of struggle, every gig he ever played, every time he bombed, all the hardships he's endured to make ends meet, are paying off. He's not only played *The Tonight Show*, he's won over the big man himself, Johnny Carson.

But there's no time to celebrate. When cancer returns, it comes back harder. His little girl has to be admitted to a pediatric cancer ward. And the treatment is severe—chemotherapy, radiation, the works. Her hair falls out. She can't keep her food down. Griffiths's heart is broken. He can't make sense of it. He fears it's his fault or his wife's fault. He can't fathom how it's possible for an innocent child to be made to suffer so much pain. This little girl had cancer before she reached her first birthday and she is not even two years old when it comes back. He feels ashamed of his powerlessness. He's a six-foot-four man who has overcome every challenge in life, but he can do nothing to protect his baby girl. And no one can help. He says that in the black community, people, especially men, do not go to therapy. That's something for rich white people. But he must dig deep and find a way to keep going. The medical bills are piling up. He is one missed payment away from being kicked out of his home or having his car repossessed.

As he works on his second set for *The Tonight Show*, his comedy grows darker. He's in agony, and his act is the only outlet he has to express the fear, anger, and sorrow in his heart. The talent coordinator tells him he has to tone it down. His act has become too dark and bitter. But Griffiths pushes back. He's filled with rage and wants the world to suffer as he suffers. He wants to make someone—*anyone*—pay for the pain his little girl must endure. And comedy is about truth. If he gets on stage and pretends to be happy and does a lighthearted routine, that would be a lie.

These are the hard choices that make stories interesting, that reveal character, and are filled with meaning. Griffiths could leverage the truth of his experience, convert his pain to comedy, and do blistering sets that pay respect to his pain. If he does this, he defines himself as an outlaw comic, a badass who blew up his own shot at big time fame and fortune to tell the truth as he sees it. Then again, taking this route could lead to playing empty rooms in no-name clubs for no money. But, he would get the benefit of staying true to his art. If he does *The Tonight Show* and delivers a professional, feel-good set, he makes money to pay the bills and gets big-time accolades and the respect that comes from doing what it takes to provide for your family. The downside is, his art is disposable and lacks meaning.

He chooses to tone down his act and play *The Tonight Show*. He nails it and is even asked back a third time—a gig he plays well after his little girl passes. On the upside, he achieves the dignity that comes from excelling on the biggest stage, not just once but three times in a single, brutal year. The trade-off is he no longer cares about his art. It's a painful story, but throughout we learn what kind of man Griffiths is—passionate, loving, intense, enraged, resilient, and profoundly vulnerable, as all parents are. The more dilemmas you provoke your characters to move through, the more likely your story is to be compelling.

HOW YOU DO IT

The following bullet points will help you think through and execute the principle.

▶ As you did in the last chapter, get clear on your hero's worldview. State it in a few simple words. For example, in the 1950s sitcom *The Honeymooners*, Ralph Kramden is a working-class guy who is certain he'll hit it big. He goes all in on everything he does because mediocrity and building success slowly are for chumps.

▶ Now you're going to create a dilemma. Think up something your hero desperately wants. Then think of another thing your hero desperately wants. Give them a very real chance of acquiring both—but they can only keep one. For example, a woman is offered her dream job and also given the chance to go on a once-in-a-lifetime trip. But they both start on the same day.

▶ Now let's create a different kind of dilemma, the high price. Think of another positive thing your hero wants—for example, to spend a night with the person they have been wildly attracted to since junior high. Give them the chance to make this dream come true. But make it costly. The person is married to a friend.

▶ Now let's create a third kind of dilemma, the lesser of two evils. Think of something awful that may happen. The hero might lose their job for making a big mistake at work. But they can pin the mistake on a close friend.

▶ Up the pressure on their decision. The hero's wife gets sick and he can't afford to lose his health insurance. But his friend is in debt, and losing his job would mean losing his house.

▶ As you make these decisions, as always, trust your gut. Make sure they align with *your* worldview.

MINI FINAL EXAM

Read the following, then answer the question below.

You're writing a drama about Chip Whalerson, a US infantryman fighting in World War II. His unit is overrun on the battlefield by fast-approaching German tanks. He turns to see a grenade explode behind him. His two best friends, Wally Wallcraft from Spokane and Gus Pickett from Oxford, Mississippi, get lit up. Their bodies fly ten feet in the air and disappear into a muddy trench. Chip rushes over to find both men severely injured and in shock. Chip stands between them, eyes darting from one of his friends to the other. His sergeant shrieks at him to hurry up—there's a plane a hundred yards up ahead. They have to get out of here now-right-now! Tears stream down Chip's face. There's no way he can carry both men. But he loves them both so much!

Which of the following choices increases the pressure on Chip and provokes an even more intense dilemma?

a) Wally's eyes roll back in his head—he's not going to make it.
b) Gus pleads with him to save Wally as Wally pleads with him to save Gus.
c) Gus threatens him—you best take me or God will strike you down.
d) Wally coughs up blood but tries to cover it with a joke.
e) Gus swears that he can see the Angel of Death descending upon him.

CONTINUING ED

In Mel Brooks's 1967 comedy film *The Producers*, Zero Mostel plays Max Bialystock, an aging theater producer who has fallen on hard times. He has no money, works in a dingy, depressing, cramped little office, and has sex with wealthy old widows in the hopes that they'll write him checks to put on plays. One day, a middle-aged accountant, Leo Bloom, arrives to audit Bialystock's books. Bloom is a nebbish—a frail sad sack—who casually observes that if Bialystock were a dishonest man, he could make more money from producing a flop than a hit. He could raise more money than he really needs to produce the play. Then, when the play flops, he can just keep all of the extra money because no one will expect any payouts on a flop. Bialystock trembles with greed. The idea is genius! He begs Leo to help him pull off the scam. But Bloom insists that he was only kidding. How hard does Max push Leo, and how emotional does this make Leo? At first glance, there's no dilemma for Leo. All he has to do is walk out. How does Max provoke a dilemma for Leo by framing Leo's life in a way that makes the scam feel like the lesser of two evils?

MINI FINAL ANSWER

The correct answer is **b) Gus pleads with him to save Wally as Wally pleads with him to save Gus.** This provokes an even greater dilemma for Chip because it shows that both of these men are good men, true heroes who each deserve to be saved. Leaving either one would be tragic. If they threaten each other or their health dissipates, this releases pressure on Chip as it either makes them less likable or less likely to survive, simplifying his choice.

13

Layer conflict.

"Be kind; everyone you meet
is fighting a hard battle."
—attributed to PHILO OF ALEXANDRIA,
Philosopher

QUICK TAKE

Imagine a human being represented as the rings in an archery target. The bull's-eye is the epicenter of your being, all you think and feel. The next layer out is your personal connections—friends and family, neighbors and coworkers. The circle outside personal connections is society at large, the institutions that run the world—religions, corporations, and governments. And beyond that is the physical world, our surroundings, natural and man-made environments. This circle includes everything you must interact with as you move through physical space: wind and rain, animals, passing cars, all sights and sounds, etc.

There are times when all these things are in harmony, when you feel strong, healthy, and comfortable in your own skin. When your loved ones are content, at peace, and by your side. Your tribe is gathered in rituals and events that are meaningful to you. The sun shines, the winds are calm; all is well in every conceivable way.

But there are other times when conflict erupts. It can be on any one of these levels of existence—you break a bone or have an anxiety attack. Your boss laces into you for poor performance. Your mother won't speak to you. Your religion calls you a sinner and threatens your soul with eternal damnation. Your car hits a patch of black ice and skids off the road. This dynamic, the way you move back and forth from tranquility to chaos, reveals your true nature. When sketching out your characters, consider all four layers available to you: conflict with self, personal connections, society at large, and the environment—both the natural and man-made worlds, and all things in them.

HOW IT WORKS

The number and types of conflicts your characters confront depends on the type of story you're telling, its length, and your temperament. There's no one-size-fits-all formula. If you're writing a teen slasher film, you may not need to give the chain saw–wielding maniac any more conflict than hatred of sex-crazed, drug-abusing teenagers who are terrible at hiding. When you write a Looney Tunes cartoon about Elmer J. Fudd hunting "wabbits," you don't need to get into how he feels about his mother. But if you're writing *Anna Karenina*, and you want to keep your novel compelling for 1,000 pages, you need to explore every last conflict in your heroine's and all major characters' lives—with their sexuality, spouses, lovers, families, religion, and rapidly changing societies. Or you will have some very bored late-nineteenth–century Russian readers.

Story at its heart is about exploring, raging against, and dignifying the human experience. No one has it easy. As the adage at the start of the chapter says, "Be kind; everyone you meet is fighting a hard battle." What this means is we all really do have to struggle through a lot—on all levels of existence—to care for our loved ones, to stay happy, healthy, safe, connected, sane. When your characters wrestle with conflicts on all levels, you reveal who they are, you show us what they're made of, validate our suffering, and help us figure out how to live.

Keep in mind (yet again) that these principles don't exist in a vacuum, and that these distinctions dissolve as you tell your story. For example, if a middle-aged woman finds a tiny wrinkle above her lip while she's brushing her teeth, it's not important to formally classify whether she's in conflict with herself or her environment. The wrinkle may have been caused by stress, genetics, the passage of time, or the sun. What's important is what it means to her, what it says about her character, and how it affects what she *does*. You want to pay particular attention to how these conflicts move the story forward, and, as we explored in Chapter 6, how they clash expectation with reality. For example, if she's in a joyful mood, preparing to go on a first date with someone special, and this tiny wrinkle sends her into a tailspin that makes her cancel because she feels unworthy, that's interesting. And if she's a lovely, brilliant woman with a great sense of humor, it's heartbreaking, absurd, and meaningful. This is why filling your story with conflict is so important. Look at how much mileage you can get from a tiny wrinkle.

Conflict with Self

We wrestle with ourselves—with our mind, body, and spirit. Our minds are full of conflict—anxieties, fears, anger, hurt, shame, confusion, lust, envy, bad memories, guilt, regrets, and broken dreams. We have thoughts and feelings we don't understand. We worry about our mortality. We struggle to figure out what's real and not just a figment of our imagination or paranoia. Our bodies, too, fill with conflicts. Our head, teeth, stomach, and feet ache or swell or burn. The slightest movement sends jolts of pain shooting up an arm or down a leg. Our spirit—our will to live—can suddenly go out. One day your eyes open but you can't find the strength or desire to get out of bed. Try as you might, you just can't bring yourself to care anymore.

Conflict with Personal Connections

We long to have stress-free relationships with our family, friends, coworkers, bosses, and employees. But they do and say things that we don't understand, that sadden, infuriate, or embarrass us. They hurt our feelings. They betray our trust. They disappoint us. They move away, get sick, fall on hard times, break our hearts in a thousand different ways. And we do the same to them.

Conflict with Society at Large

We must deal with companies, local government, state government, federal government, the governments of other nations, the news, entertainment, advertising, religious institutions, and charitable organizations. They pass laws, impose regulations, levy fines and penalties, make arrests, raise taxes, hire, and fire. They sell products. They ask for your time and money. They influence how you feel, what you do. They get you enraged, aroused, excited, terrified; they make you feel guilt-ridden, inappropriate, lacking, hungry. They want you to buy their product, use their service, watch their show, serve their needs. They bring threats, real, hyped, and imaginary. They come at you *hard*. They'll talk you into destroying your body, wrecking your peace of mind, fearing the future. They threaten your soul, your everlasting place in eternity. They put your ass in stir.

Conflicts with Our Surroundings

As we move through the world, through physical space, we must deal with icy roads, blazing sun, and blistering heat. There are flashing lights and loud noises. There are blighted landscapes, putrid smells, potholes, and turbulence. There are robots, machines, and artificial intelligence that exceed our ability to even remotely comprehend how they work. Things rust, decay. Stuff breaks and fails to work as intended. All of it affects your perception, feelings, and ability to get through the world without stress, pain, and the risk of loss.

• • •

One of the most important choices writers make is what medium to work in. Sadly, we'll never know how many writers might have found success, even great success, had they chosen to write a novel, for example, instead of a screenplay, a comic book instead of a TV series, etc. There are many factors that go into this decision, including your personality, where you prefer to live, and how much you enjoy—or dislike—collaborating with other people. A staff writer on a TV show obviously has to deal with many more people than someone who writes short stories.

But what is probably the most important factor in this decision is the level of conflict you find most interesting (which may or may not correspond with the one you personally experience the most conflict on). For example, if you live in your head, and often wrestle with aspects of yourself, then you are probably meant to write fiction, which allows you to explore your characters' thoughts and feelings. If you study the great novels (among them *Pride and Prejudice*, *Crime and Punishment*, *Beloved*), they go deep into the minds of their characters. Playwrights and television writers are often most interested in conflicts between people—friends, family, and coworkers. The great plays (*A Doll's House*, *The Glass Menagerie*, *August: Osage County*, just to name a tiny handful) and TV series (*All in the Family*, *The Sopranos*, *30 Rock*) are all focused on tight-knit groups of people. Movies, on the other hand, tend to focus on people vs. society and the world at large. Superhero films often deal with costumed heroes tearing through the heavens, battling armies and governments. Or they pit a human against the elements. Think about Sandra Bullock or Matt Damon trying to return from space in *Gravity* and *The Martian*, respectively. That said, of course film can explore quieter themes that focus on everyday struggles and the complexities of life.

As always, do not be absolutist about this. Arthur Miller's play *The Crucible* is about a man against society at large. Jack London's novels pit man against nature. And there are loads more exceptions to these "rules." They are general guidelines. You can tell whatever kind of story you like in whatever medium you prefer. It's just helpful to be aware of the unique strengths of each medium, and to match it to the story you want to tell.

HOW A MASTER DID IT

Ms. Marvel: No Normal (2013)
G. Willow Wilson

This critically acclaimed comic book won the 2015 Hugo Award for Best Graphic Story. It tracks heroine Kamala Khan's transition from a sixteen-year-old Muslim kid with an identity crisis to Ms. Marvel, a superhero. The story works so well because Kamala struggles with ever-expanding conflicts on all four levels. Below, we'll explore the first chapter, then look at how the writer leveraged conflict to build empathy and develop her character. (Of note, there have been other series featuring a different version of Ms. Marvel. Prior to Kamala Khan, the character was portrayed as an ample-bosomed, blond, blue-eyed air force officer whose costumes were often provocative and showed a great deal of skin.)

Scene One

In the first panel we are close on a bacon, lettuce, and tomato sandwich. Kamala hovers over the glass case of a Jersey City grocery store, playfully moaning, "Delicious, delicious infidel meat." She is with her childhood best friend, Tiki, a Turkish Muslim girl who insists on being called Nakia, as she connects more comfortably with her faith than Kamala does. Their friend Bruno works behind the counter. We'll learn shortly that this well-mannered, hardworking white kid could be the perfect guy for Kamala, if they were not from conflicting cultures.

In walks Zoe Zimmer with her meathead boyfriend, Josh. Zoe is blond-haired, blue-eyed, and wears clothes that expose ample flesh. She is passive-aggressive, self-involved, and condescending. Even while complimenting Nakia's headscarf, she rudely questions whether Nakia is being forced against her will to wear it. Nakia says her parents wish she would not wear it. Zoe is flirtatious with Bruno. Though Bruno and Nakia see through Zoe, Kamala is smitten by her all-American good looks and envies her popularity. Josh and Zoe invite them to a party by the waterfront, but Kamala can't go because her parents won't let her. Nakia declines as well, because she chooses to avoid parties with alcohol and other temptations.

In just the first three pages, Kamala's world is riddled with conflict. There's inner conflict (Kamala longs to look like blond, blue-eyed Zoe), personal conflict (with Nakia's embrace of their religion), and the ever-present conflicts of being Muslim in a Western culture. Even the air she breathes is saturated with the smell of forbidden food. As we watch Nakia handle the same conflict, being Muslim in a secular Western culture, this sharpens our understanding of Kamala's conflict with her religion. Nakia is more at peace with her faith and culture than Kamala.

Scene Two

That night, alone in her room, Kamala entertains herself by writing fan fiction about her favorite superheroes, the Avengers. Her mother, a Pakistani immigrant, scolds her for not doing homework and for being late to dinner. She shows no respect or appreciation for the fact that Kamala's fanfic has almost 1,000 upvotes on freakingcool.com, and she never imagines that Friday night should be more fun than a regular school night.

At the dinner table, Kamala's older brother, Aamir, a devout Muslim who wears a carefully clipped beard, traditional robe, and kufi cap, prays at the table before the meal. He argues with their father, Abu-Jaan. Aamir is unemployed, and criticizes his father for offending Allah by working at a bank and promoting usury. Abu-Jaan is skeptical of Aamir's devoutness, which he feels is an excuse to avoid work. Mom stands by her son (clearly her favorite child), who she believes will find the right job in time.

Bored, frustrated, and tired of the same bickering that erupts at every dinner, Kamala asks to go to the party with Josh and Zoe. Her father refuses and encourages her to be more like her hardworking friend, Bruno. Kamala insists that if she were a boy, her father would let her go. The two fight and her father, disgusted, lets her be excused.

Here, she has inner conflict with her own boredom and frustration, as well as personal conflict with her mother's lack of respect for her creativity and her parents' sexism in favoring Aamir. The conflict between her brother and father wrecks the vibe at dinner. Aamir's orthodoxy sends ripples of conflict through the family. His character, a devout, unemployed, young male Muslim in America, is fraught with potential conflicts.

Abu-Jaan's handling of the conflict with his son's faith reveals his character. He is a devout Muslim, but moderate in temperament and willing to balance the needs of his family with those of his culture. He is also psychologically sophisticated and able to be honest with his son without demeaning him. These are multidimensional characters struggling through the conflicts of modern life on all levels.

Scene Three

Kamala sits alone in her room feeling sorry for herself and questions why she must always bring funny food for lunch, observe weird holidays, and be excused from health class. She laments that "everybody else gets to be normal." She thoughtfully navigates her inner, personal, and societal conflicts with a mixture of naïve innocence (failing to see Zoe's true nature), respect for her parents and Islam, and her teenage need to rebel.

She sneaks out of her window to go to the party. As she approaches the waterfront, she's intimidated by the large size and harsh vibe of the party. Music—"Boom Boom Shaka Shaka"—rattles the air. Zoe spots her and immediately jumps on her for "hanging out with us heathens." A couple of drunk jocks trick her into taking a sip of alcohol, which she spits out, embarrassed. Bruno urges her to return home to avoid getting into trouble. She shouts at him for acting like her parents—then marches off.

As she walks alone through darkened streets, a thick, green mist floods the city. She struggles to walk through it and grows woozy, fearing that just tasting vodka has made her drunk. She berates herself. "No matter how hard I try I'll always be poor Kamala with the weird food rules and the crazy family." As the bizarre mist envelops her, she leans on a telephone pole. On it is a hand-drawn sign seeking a missing child. On the surface, you have a simple scene—a teenage girl walking home from a party. But she's consumed by conflict on every level. Her religion, culture, parents, peers, own mind, the miasmic air, all weigh heavily on her. The detail of the sign is both symbolic of her lost soul and emblematic of the harsh realities of modern life.

Unable to continue, unable to bear the weight of her conflicts, she collapses. From a distance, we see her passed out on the street, enveloped in mist, yet her hand remains sadly touching the pole. Her myriad conflicts build both sympathy, as we feel for her suffering, and empathy, as we all have to struggle with parents, siblings, and the need to fit in.

Scene Four

A harsh light falls on her. She is greeted by a vision (or is it real?) of Iron Man, Captain America, and Captain Marvel. They're joined by odd birds and furry creatures. Captain Marvel speaks Urdu, an Arabic-influenced language spoken in Pakistan. They inform her that they are an incarnation of faith, and a vision of what she needs to see. Captain America scolds her for disobeying her parents, religion, and culture. She is torn between her Pakistani heritage and her need to feel at home in Jersey City, the only place she's ever lived. Kamala tells Captain Marvel that she doesn't know who she is *supposed* to be but knows what she *wants* to be—a sexy superhero, one who wears a "politically incorrect" costume with high boots and giant wedge heels. Captain Marvel jokes about Kamala's boot fetish, then warns her that she will grant her wish but that "it won't turn out the way you think."

Scene Five

The green mist turns black and forms a cocoon around Kamala. With a furious fist she punches her way out to find that her skin is now white, her hair is long and blond, and she wears a sleek costume featuring thigh-high boots and a top that barely covers her behind. Her first response to her new look is to ask if it's too late to change her mind.

• • •

Note that all these conflicts alter Kamala's moods, affect her decisions, and cause her to take actions she wouldn't otherwise take. No conflict exists in a vacuum, and one often impacts another. In the first chapter, there are eighty-one panels—in each one Kamala is handling multiple conflicts. She experiences:

- **Conflict with Self**—She is uncomfortable with her brown skin, dark hair, and conservative clothing. She feels like an outcast, and longs to be blond, blue-eyed, and popular. She has too much time on her hands and spends much of it wishing she were someone else.

- **Conflict with Personal Connections**—Her mother is hostile and demanding. Her brother is extreme. Her father is kind and patient, but doesn't understand her feelings. She can't relate to Nakia's dawning faith. Bruno's the perfect boy—but not for a Muslim girl. Zoe is popular, but a selfish jerk. The jocks trick her into drinking alcohol. And when she is greeted by her beloved superheroes, they are critical of her choices.

- **Conflict with Society at Large**—Being a Muslim kid who is excused from health class, forced to eat different-smelling food, and attend a mosque is a constant source of stress. She can't go to the store, attend a party, or sit comfortably in school without her faith and culture being questioned.

▶ **Conflict with Her Environment**—Everywhere she looks, there are girls dressed in tight clothing, kids listening to edgy music, drinking, dating and having premarital sex, all things she can't do. She is constantly tempted by "unclean" things, like BLT sandwiches. And then there's the mist that envelops the city and consumes her. Her middle-class New Jersey town has an edge.

In this age of big data, let's think of this as a mathematical formula. Kamala appears in eighty-one panels, and each panel could put her in conflict on up to four levels. So the aggregate conflicts she could deal with is 324 (81 × 4). Actually, she can theoretically have a trillion conflicts on each level, but let's stay reasonable and keep it at one per level. It's not important to get the exact number, just to note that the greater the amount of conflict in your story, the more likely it is to succeed.

This is a key reason Ms. Marvel won major awards, racked up strong sales, and is still going strong as of this writing. But obviously this is not just about mindlessly larding your story with truckloads of conflict. The conflict must be authentic, interesting, personal to you, and explored with heart and depth. The reason Kamala Khan is a strongly written character, and not just a pathetic attempt by Marvel to add diversity, however clichéd, is that the writer, G. Willow Wilson, has a deep connection to the material. She is a white woman from New Jersey who converted to Islam and spent time in Egypt where she worked as a journalist. She knows the world she is writing about and also about being an outsider, and the story radiates authenticity.

In an interview with NPR's *All Things Considered*, Wilson says she spent a great deal of time discussing the nature of "hyphenated" identity with friends who were from African-, Arab-, and Pakistani-American immigrant families. This research helped her fill in the gaps in her own knowledge. Combining personal experience and investigative research enabled her to load Kamala with a wide variety of inner, personal, societal, and environmental conflicts. They work not just because of volume, but because of volume and authenticity. They're meaningful to her.

HOW YOU DO IT

The following bullet points will help you think through and execute the principle.

▶ Generally speaking, the longer your story, the more conflict you need to force your hero to deal with. *Breaking Bad*'s Walter White is besieged by conflict on every level in the pilot episode because he will have to carry an entire television series—one that went on to not only last five seasons but worked in consecutive order. So it's essentially a nearly forty-eight-hour story! Incredible. Therefore, to really launch Walter, creator Vince Gilligan needed to flood him with troubles.

▶ For the purpose of this exercise, let's err on the side of bombarding your character with conflict on every level, just to see how it feels—to see how it lends insight into the character and sparks ideas to drive the narrative.

▶ Start with a basic biography. A forty-year-old farmworker and father of four, a garbage collector on his first day of work, a teacher with twenty-five years of experience teaching kids in Washington, DC's most elite prep school. Or, of course, you may have a character you're already working with.

▶ Let's work from within and build out. Picture concentric circles. Your character has problems with herself. (This is dead center, at the bull's-eye.) Maybe she hates her body, struggles with an illness, thinks she's stupid, regrets her wild years, knows she needs to have more fun, has blood-curdling nightmares, is beset by allergies, or is positive she could have been more successful in every way. One way or another, it's hard to be inside her head.

▶ The next circle out is conflict with the people in her life: immediate family, extended family, friends, next-door neighbors, and coworkers. Make her conflicts difficult: a sick in-law, a friend desperate for money, an adult son who won't leave home. Once you identify the conflict, intensify it. Why is this person's problem particularly hard for your hero? For example, she was once very close with her mother and idolized her for her brilliant mind, but now Mom's losing her memory.

▶ The next circle out includes institutions in society at large—multinational corporations, the church, government, the media, the news. On the sitcom *All in the Family*, Archie Bunker could not stand liberal culture, "commies," and "pinkos." What conflicts does your character have with the world's big entities? For example, she might be a socialist who hates capitalism, an atheist who is enraged by the church, or a religious person who believes we must put God at the center of public schools.

▶ The next circle out is the environment. Here we'll include the weather, landscape (natural and man-made), seascapes, and all external things—technology, crumbling sidewalks, falling pianos—any nonhuman thing that might cause conflict. In the Coen Brothers film *Fargo*, there's a darkly charming scene when the hero, police chief Marge Gunderson, investigates a gruesome murder on a lonely stretch of highway in winter. She's so pregnant she practically waddles. She wears large boots, a thick jacket with a big hood, and huge mittens. As she walks across the icy snow she suddenly drops a few inches and nearly falls. The cold winds, frozen grounds, and whiteout conditions all make her job more difficult. It's a challenge just to walk. This gives her things to respond to that reveal her character. For example, she makes a funny face after she nearly falls that shows her pleasant demeanor. This is especially notable as she's in the midst of an awful crime scene. When you live in such harsh conditions, you learn how to take everything in stride.

▶ Give your character at least three conflicts on each level of existence—inner, personal, societal, and external/environmental. As you do this, consider how it makes you feel about the character and about life in general. If you get stuck, make it personal. List all the conflicts you have right now, with yourself, loved ones, society, and the world at large.

MINI FINAL EXAM

In this exam, we'll explore the relationship between conflict, character, and plot. Review the following sequence from the comic *Ms. Marvel: No Normal*, then answer the question below.

1. Kamala is late for dinner because she is working on her fanfic of the Avengers.
2. Her mother enters and scolds her for being late and wasting time on fanfic.
3. Kamala comes down to dinner grumpy and gets in a tiff with her father. She asks to be excused and he angrily accepts.
4. Kamala goes up to her room and fumes about being an outcast—then sneaks out to the waterfront party.
5. Kamala is tricked into drinking alcohol and storms away from the party.
6. Kamala is enveloped in fog and greeted by a vision of Captain Marvel.
7. Kamala is transformed into a young, sexy superhero.

The second point reads "Her mother enters and scolds her for being late and wasting time on fanfic." Imagine that instead, Kamala has a loving, supportive mother who encourages her creativity. For the following, pick all that apply. Removing the conflict with her mother would:

a) Deplete the momentum that drives Kamala to sneak out.
b) Diminish our sympathy for Kamala and her struggle.
c) Have no effect on the story.
d) Make the story more enjoyable because it would add levity.
e) Make the arrival of Captain Marvel feel unnecessary.

CONTINUING ED

In the pilot episodes of two of the most critically acclaimed TV shows of all time, *The Sopranos* (1999–2007) and *Breaking Bad* (2008–2013), the respective antiheroes, Tony Soprano and Walter White, are both so overloaded with conflict that they literally pass out. For each character, list all the conflicts you can think of—with their minds, health, families, coworkers, the law, and their surroundings, both natural and man-made. Consider how removing conflicts might kill story ideas and make the characters less interesting.

MINI FINAL ANSWER

The correct answers are:

a) Deplete the momentum that drives Kamala to sneak out.

b) Diminish our sympathy for Kamala.

e) Make the arrival of Captain Marvel feel unnecessary.

Again, the point here is to explore the relationship between conflict, character, and plot. Making the mother more supportive might do what writers call "pulling threads," as in when you pull a thread, you can unravel the entire garment. If the mom was supportive, Kamala would come down to the dinner table in a good mood and thus be far less likely to get into a tiff with her father, depleting the momentum that drives Kamala to sneak out, so choice **a)** is correct. What's more, if her mother is supportive instead of critical, it would diminish our sympathy for Kamala and her struggle, so choice **b)** is also correct. Lastly, Captain Marvel arrives in Kamala's life with a purpose: to help her find her true self. If Kamala's mother was fulfilling that role, Captain Marvel's arrival would feel unnecessary. Therefore, choice **e)** is also correct.

14

Peel the onion.

"There are only two mistakes one can make on the road to truth, not going all the way and not starting."
—BUDDHA, Philosopher

QUICK TAKE

A well-told story presents characters, then gradually peels away layers, like an onion, until the core truth of who they are is revealed. As the story progresses, you learn more about how the characters think, what's essential to them, and how far they'll go to protect what they have or to acquire what they need. Each new thing they do, each detail revealed, gives you new insight and forces you to reevaluate your take on them. It's interesting and entertaining to watch a compelling personality unfold, especially when it's done in a surprising but satisfying way.

This principle will help you think more holistically about designing your characters, and constructing narratives that penetrate to the center of their being, by moving through four layers: surface (how they look, their basic biography), mental (how they think), spiritual (what they value and believe), and core (who they are as defined by a final, definitive action). There's something comforting in being able to reach the core of a character in a way that you can't always do in real life, where everyone and seemingly everything is always changing.

HOW IT WORKS

The "onion" we're peeling here is based on a common-sense progression we move through when we get to know someone intimately over time.

When we first meet someone, we take in their appearance—height, weight, hair, eyes, skin, their posture, how they dress, how they carry themselves, and their mannerisms. Often, we learn a few things about their most basic biography: their name, where they're from, if they have a family or significant other, what they do for a living. We make assumptions based on these first impressions. This is the surface layer.

Over time, we learn how people think. We get a feel for how they approach problems, process information, and make decisions. Some people move slowly and take forever to make a move. Others put almost no thought into anything. Some people are fantastically creative and always seem to have a unique approach to solving problems, others are methodical. Then, of course, there's the range of intelligence, which in plain English goes from imbecile to super-genius. And, as noted above, some people are brilliant in one area and clueless in another. This is the mental layer.

The next layer deals with ethics, morality, values—how people decide what's right and wrong. Inevitably, as we discuss at length in Chapter 6, "Clash expectation with reality," life throws us curveballs and forces us to make decisions under intense pressure. Here, we learn how mature or immature someone is, how warm and compassionate or cold. Our spiritual nature is shaped by our personality, genetics, and defining experiences. Someone raised in a ruthless, cutthroat home might believe that anything goes if you can get away with it. Another person waits for the light to change to cross the street, even though it's 3:00 a.m. and there's not a car in sight, because that's the law. This is the spiritual layer.

The layer beneath this is the core. This can only be revealed through an action someone takes when the stakes are high—

when big money, hearts, or dignity are on the line. If you think about the people that you have the most intense feelings about—for better and worse—it is almost certainly because you believe that you know their true nature. And it was likely revealed by something they did when you were both in a heightened emotional state. This is why old war buddies love each other so much. They *know* that when surrounded by enemy fire, they can trust each other. If you have a coworker who made a false accusation against you when the company was about to start layoffs, or a spouse who cheated on you when you were out of work, these actions tell you, definitively, who this person is deep inside.

These layers all affect each other. Our appearance often reflects our emotional state. Someone who thinks everyone else is out to screw them behaves differently from someone who is naturally trusting. As you move through drafts, and your characters take shape, it's valuable to consider where they're at on each layer and to track what you reveal when. This will help you create richly detailed characters and give you levers to pull as you shape the story as a whole. For example, as events unfold you may need to make one character smarter, another less ethical, and a third more attractive.

HOW A MASTER DID IT

"Interpreter of Maladies" (1999)
Jhumpa Lahiri

"Interpreter of Maladies" is the title story in Jhumpa Lahiri's debut collection of short stories. Set in India in the mid-1990s, it is both a scathing satire and a moving drama that explores the nature of delusion and cultural alienation.

Mr. Kapasi is a middle-aged Indian man hired to drive a young Indian American family from their hotel to visit an ancient sun temple. The family of five, visiting India from New Jersey, includes Mr. and Mrs. Das and their three young children. During the long drive, Mr. Kapasi becomes enamored with Mrs. Das. He secretly plots to win her heart after she refers to his other job translating ailments for patients at a doctor's office as "romantic."

Below, we'll explore how the author gradually presents, then peels away, layers—physical, mental and spiritual—to reveal her characters. By constructing her narrative with precision, compassion, and a biting sense of humor, Lahiri exposes the indignity we suffer when we can't bear to face the reality of our lives. Note that the layers are not always peeled in a clearly delineated progression, neatly moving from physical to mental to spiritual to core. Stories are never as neat in practice as they are in theory. The layers bleed into each other and overlap.

While we get a full sense of each character, it is always the hero who moves most cleanly and fully through this progression. In this story, it is Mr. Kapasi. The story is told in the third person from his point of view.

The Physical Layer

The story begins on a sunny day with an ocean breeze, perfect for sightseeing. Driving a bulky white Ambassador, Mr. Kapasi must pull over almost immediately because the Dases' daughter says she needs to use the bathroom. (Of note, the Ambassador, created by Hindustan Motors, was once an iconic Indian vehicle, modeled after an English car. It was the only one Indian politicians traveled in. The company fell on hard times and the brand lost its prestige. By modern Western standards, an Ambassador seems both charming and a bit silly, a regal version of a VW Bug.)

Mr. Kapasi watches the parents fight over whose turn it is to take the kid to the bathroom. The dad "wins" because he did her bath the night before. Mrs. Das drags her bare legs across the seat as she exits the vehicle and leads her daughter away without holding her hand. When Mr. Kapasi greeted Mrs. Das he pressed his palms together, but she shook his hand, squeezing so hard he felt it in his shoulder.

The Das family looks Indian but dresses like foreigners. The children wear brightly colored clothes. The girl is in a purple dress with bows and has a doll with chopped-off blond hair. The boys wear caps with translucent visors and their teeth are "covered in a network of flashing silver wires."

Mr. Das is clean-shaven and looks just like his eldest son, Ronny. He wears shorts, a t-shirt, and cap with a visor. His head is buried in a tour book labeled "INDIA," and a large camera with a huge telephoto lens is strapped around his neck.

Mrs. Das wears a red-and-white checkered skirt, shoes with large square heels, and a close-fitting blouse with a calico appliqué strawberry in the middle. Her short hair is parted to the side. She is slightly plump and wears frosty pink nail polish that matches her lipstick and sunglasses. She carries a large, bowl-shaped straw bag. Lahiri describes her hands as small and "like paws." In short, they are all dressed like cartoonish American tourists.

The parents, in their twenties, have traditional Indian names—Raj and Mina—but their children are named Ronny, Bobby, and Tina. Mr. Das teaches science in a middle school. Mrs. Das is a stay-at-home mom. They live in New Jersey. Both were born in America. They have returned to visit their parents, who moved back to India years ago.

Mr. Kapasi is forty-six, with silver hair and a "butterscotch complexion." He is self-conscious about his appearance—he dabs lotus oil balm on his brow and wears tailored clothes made of synthetic material, because it keeps its shape on long drives. His trousers are gray. He wears a "jacket-style" shirt tapered at the waist with short sleeves and a large pointed collar. That he puts such effort into his appearance but wears clothing that his clients are unlikely to find stylish gives him a unique blend of awkwardness and dignity.

The car ride starts off with Mr. Das and the younger son, Bobby, up front, while Mrs. Das is in back with Tina and Ronny. As Mr. Kapasi shifts gears, he notices that Bobby has paler skin than his family. The children are poorly behaved. They snap gum, fidget with the locks, call each other names. The parents do nothing about it. Mrs. Das, putting clear nail polish on her nails, angrily tells her daughter to leave her alone after the girl asks to do her nails, too.

Monkeys line the trees. One jumps onto the hood of the car and another blocks the road, causing Mr. Kapasi to honk his horn. The monkeys have "shining black faces, silver bodies, horizontal eyebrows and scratch themselves with black leathery hands." They stare down at the car as it passes. We'll meet them again later.

Lahiri uses the first third of her story to detail the physical layer of her characters. We have the soft-spoken, self-conscious, middle-aged driver Mr. Kapasi, and the unruly Das family. The author finishes this layer with subtle humor: "The car rattled considerably as it raced along the dusty road, causing them all to pop up." It's going to be a bumpy ride.

The Mental Layer

Mr. Kapasi looks over the family and thinks that Mr. and Mrs. Das seem more like older siblings than parents. Mrs. Das complains about the car's lack of air conditioning. She accuses her husband of being too cheap to spend a few "stupid rupees" and he snaps back at her. It never occurs to her that she's insulting Mr. Kapasi. Mr. Das jumps out of the car to take a picture of an emaciated man sitting on a cart. He doesn't show the slightest interest in the man. He just wants to take a cool photo.

As Mrs. Das stares up at passing clouds, Mr. Das asks Mr. Kapasi if he gets tired of making the same drive week after week. Mr. Kapasi says that he doesn't. He looks forward to visiting the sun temple as a reward for doing his other job. His other job is working in a doctor's office. Since the doctor doesn't speak Gujarati and many people in the area do, the doctor needs an interpreter. Mr. Kapasi's father was Gujarati, so it was a language he learned. After Mr. Das notes that he never heard of such a job, Mr. Kapasi says with a shrug, "It's a job like any other." Mrs. Das responds, "But so romantic." This drops the hammer. Mr. Kapasi is struck by her words. She lifts her sunglasses, propping them on her head "like a tiara." Mr. Kapasi catches her gaze in the rearview mirror, and she offers him a piece of gum. As she munches puffed rice, she asks him to tell her about his job. Mr. Kapasi tells her of a patient who felt as if he had straw in his throat. After Mr. Kapasi helped detail the symptoms, the doctor was able to cure him. Mrs. Das is impressed, suggesting that his role is even more important than the doctor. Without his accurate translation, the cure could not be found.

Mr. Kapasi is struck by her interest in his work. He has thought of his job as a failure. He spends his days in a small, stale room with a doctor who is half his age and has no personality. The patients struggle with swollen joints, cramps, and bowel disorders. He once dreamed of being an interpreter for diplomats and dignitaries. Self-taught, as a young man he would stay up late analyzing the etymology of words, and once felt he could translate many languages, including French, Russian, Portuguese, and Italian.

But none of this was to be. After his parents arranged his marriage, the young couple had a son who got very sick. Mr. Kapasi worked full-time teaching grammar school. But, to help pay his son's medical bills, he took on extra work, doing translation for the doctor. Sadly, the boy died. Mr. Kapasi did all he could to provide for his wife, who often cried in her sleep. They had more children. He bought a bigger house, paid for nice clothes and tutors. But his wife resents him working for the doctor who could not save their son. She tells others he's an "assistant" and this makes him feel like more of a lackey than a translator.

With the others distracted by passing monkeys and tour guides, Mr. Kapasi feels his talk with Mrs. Das is private. She keeps her head back with her eyes closed so she can take in his stories. He senses that her marriage to Mr. Das is fraught with tension, and suspects they too are a bad match. They stop for lunch, and Mrs. Das makes room for Mr. Kapasi to sit next to her. When the kids run off, Mr. Das asks Mrs. Das to move closer to Mr. Kapasi for a photo. Like a smitten schoolboy, he fears she can smell his perspiration. After the photo is taken, she asks for his address, so she can send him the photo. He is stunned and excited.

As he neatly prints his name and address on a torn-out page of a film magazine with a picture of lovers embracing, he fantasizes about the two of them developing a relationship by mail. They'll share details about their failing marriages and become friends. He'll tell her about his work and she'll laugh at his stories. Her interest in him makes him feel like he felt when he picked up a new language. He feels as if life is fair, that hard work is rewarded. He thinks of the spot where he'll hide the photo from his wife.

There's a childlike innocence to his thoughts. He worries about his perspiration and has no clue how badly the odds are stacked against his plot to woo Mrs. Das. Compare his timid dreams to the way a player would stalk a married woman.

The Spiritual Layer

The car arrives at the ancient sun temple, bringing the story, literally, into the spiritual realm. This is no accident. Whether it's conscious or intuitive, the author knows that as stories progress, they move into more profound places. Here, it is a massive temple shaped like a chariot, constructed in the thirteenth century, and designed to honor the sun. Mr. Kapasi, who has been here countless times, has expert knowledge of the magnificent structure. He discusses its origin (to honor a king's victorious battle), the twelve hundred artisans who built it, and the rich symbolism of its sculptures and design.

Mr. Das reads aloud from his tour book, "The wheels are supposed to symbolize the wheel of life. They depict the cycle of creation, preservation, and achievement of realization." He adds, "Cool," then lists details, including that the spokes are "carved with women in luxurious poses largely erotic in nature." Mr. Das has no passion, no depth, no ability to experience things directly, without the filter of his guidebook and camera. He's more interested in getting a picture of the family for their Christmas card (though they're not Christian) than instilling a sense of history or a connection to their homeland in his children.

The primal sexuality of the female figures carved into the temple—topless with thrusting hips, legs wrapped around their lovers—affects Mr. Kapasi. Though he's seen them many times, today is different. He thinks of his own wife, whom he's never seen naked. She keeps her top on during sex. His eyes drift toward Mrs. Das and her bare legs. He has seen the bare legs of many foreign women. But they never noticed him or cared about his work. She did. As he watches her ignore her children and refuse to let her husband take her picture, he feels she is walking for his benefit alone. Moments later, he stares at a sculpture that symbolizes the setting sun. It's a weary-looking sun god, and it's his favorite. He is startled to find Mrs. Das beside him. He tells her about the sculpture. She responds, "Neat." He doesn't know what the word means, but thinks it's positive. He looks at her bag, giddy with the thought his address is among her belongings. He wants to wrap his arms around her. He imagines the letters they'll send. He'll teach her about India. She'll teach him about America. And this will satisfy his dream of interpreting between nations.

When they return to the car and start the long drive back to the hotel, Mr. Kapasi steals glances at Mrs. Das in the rearview mirror. He dreads returning home, where his wife will serve him tea in silence. He can't deal with another night of loneliness and disconnection. Desperate to spend more time with Mrs. Das, he convinces them to visit another site, monasteries built deep in the woods.

We now know how Mr. Kapasi feels, deep inside. He's lonely and insignificant. He is a thing, a service. He provides for his family, but his wife doesn't speak to him or give herself freely. Tourists care only about him getting them from point A to point B. Patients use him to translate their words, but they're talking to the doctor. He is invisible and desperate for respect.

The Core

Mr. Kapasi plans to reveal his feelings to Mrs. Das if given the chance. He'll compliment her smile, the strawberry on her shirt, and even take her hand. They arrive at the next site: desolate monasteries that face each other across a "defile," a steep path lined by trees on both sides. The heavily wooded area is now free of tourists as the sun sets. Dozens of monkeys line the road and watch from the trees. Mrs. Das doesn't want to exit the car—the monkeys creep her out and her feet hurt. Mr. Das berates her for wearing high heels and walks off with the kids. Just as Mr. Kapasi is about to get out of the car, Mrs. Das climbs in the front seat beside him and asks him to stay. His heart pounds. This is it.

The story that began on a busy strip of hotels and restaurants with five people bathed in sunlight is down to the two main characters, seated beside each other, in a darkened wood. Mr. Kapasi watches monkeys follow and surround Mr. Das and the kids. One of the boys, the younger one with paler skin, Bobby, takes a stick and plays with a monkey, passing it back and forth. "A brave little boy," says Mr. Kapasi. To his shock, Mrs. Das blurts out that it's not surprising because the boy's father is another man.

As she snacks on puffed rice, she tells Mr. Kapasi that she has known Raj since they were kids. Their parents are close friends. As teenagers, they used to have sex upstairs while their parents socialized. Because she spent so much of her life alone with Raj and had kids at a young age, she has no friends. She's never told a living soul the secret that's tormented her for eight years. Raj once invited a friend to stay with them. He was in from London, job hunting. While Raj was at work one day, the friend made love to her on the couch. It was a sudden, meaningless encounter. Though the man was far more skilled than Raj, teething toys dug into her back on the sofa. Her son, Ronny, cried in his playpen. The man didn't take a job in the States. He doesn't know that Bobby is his son and never will.

Mr. Kapasi is rattled and depressed to think that such a young woman has already given up on life, that she doesn't love her own children. After he asks why she told him her secret, she scolds him for calling her "Mrs. Das." He must have children her age. "Not quite," he says, upset that she thinks of him as a parental figure. She pleads with him to ease her pain, like he does with the patients at his job. He's insulted, and feels she has no right to compare her transgression to the suffering of his patients. Still, he feels compelled to help her and even considers offering to mediate a discussion with her husband. He starts with the most obvious assertion, that what she feels is not pain but guilt. She glares at him hatefully but holds her tongue. Her scornful look makes it clear he's not even worth insulting.

She storms off, dropping puffed rice as she goes, attracting monkeys. Bobby cries out. He's terrified and surrounded by monkeys. One lashes his legs with a stick. Mr. Kapasi gets out and shoos the monkeys, takes the terrified child, and returns him to his mother. Mrs. Das pulls a bandage from her bag and, as she does, Mr. Kapasi sees the little piece of paper with his phone number fly out and rise into the trees among the monkeys.

The story ends definitively. He will never connect with Mrs. Das on any level. The core of each character is revealed. He is a kindhearted person whose dreams are too big for his ability. She is a selfish, stunted young woman who won't take responsibility for her life. The idea that Mr. Kapasi could ever win over Mrs. Das was absurd, just like his dream that he would become a noted translator for diplomats without the proper education and connections. Both will remain unhappy, trapped in loveless marriages. Because these two characters progress so cleanly through related journeys, the themes of miscommunication and the dangers of seeing what we wish to see, instead of how the world really is, are fully explored.

HOW YOU DO IT

The following bullet points will help you think through and execute the principle.

- We're going to create and "peel" down a character from the external, or physical, layer to their core. Start with what the character looks like. Imagine meeting them for the very first time. How do they make you feel, what first impression do they give? Do they seem comfortable in their own skin or twitchy? Are they stylish and well put together or a mess? How's their hair and skin? What do they smell like? Do they radiate insecurity or confidence, aggression or tranquility, joyfulness or rage?

▶ How do they think and solve problems? Are they naïve or cunning? How smart are they? Is this a rocket scientist, a knucklehead, or something in between? Remember, people are smart in some areas of their lives and idiotic in others. I fancy myself well versed in the world of investing but give me a toolbox and I'd be lucky to pick out a wrench.

▶ Get clear on their ethical makeup. What are their beliefs about right and wrong? How aligned are their actions with what they claim to believe? Is this someone you can trust with a secret? Are they warm, empathic, and true to their word, or a snake who will betray you the first chance they get? Or might they be something in between—for example, kind to those who can help them, dismissive to those who can't.

▶ You get to the core of a character at the end of a story. For example, in *Jaws*, Chief Brody mistakenly leaves the beaches open and this leads to the death of a young boy, whose mother famously smacks the chief across the face in her funeral attire. This doesn't define Brody's core because he still has time to redeem himself through his final action: risking his own life to kill the shark. You may not know your ending until you've written it—that's fine. Just know that what your characters do at the end, when all the chips are down, defines who they are.

▶ Remember the old adage—show, don't tell. If your character is intelligent, show them solving a problem. If they're a good person, show them taking care of someone else, or doing the right thing when no one's watching. If they care deeply about their appearance, show them spending two hours meticulously attending to every last detail of their outfit.

MINI FINAL EXAM

Read the following, then answer the question below.

You're sketching out a character. He's a wrestler who dreams of becoming a champion in the WWE. He grew up on a vast estate in New England. His parents are big-time WASP socialites. Their lineage goes back generations. His father, an investment banker with a military background, insists on a rigid formality in all matters. His mother is a day drinker—always has been—and regrets marrying his father, who is a bully at heart. The wrestler has bright blue eyes and a big head of wavy blond curls.

Rumors have it his mother had an affair with an ex-football star, a 350-pound defensive tackle. But this was never proven. His father always rode him harder than his two siblings, a brother and a sister, and it could be that his dad feared he was not really his son. Whatever the reason, nothing he ever did was good enough. But this wrestler is kind, empathetic, and always sticks up for the little guy. Every time anyone was in trouble or getting taken advantage of, he stepped in to help, no matter the cost. He wants to become a WWE champion to use his platform to stop bullying. A defining experience came when he was eighteen. His father hit him in a drunken rage. It took all his strength not to tear the old man to shreds, but out of respect for his mother, and feeling no hate, just pity for his father, he stayed calm and simply left.

Which layer is missing?

a) His core.
b) His appearance, or his surface layer.
c) How he thinks, or his mental layer.
d) How ethical he is, or his spiritual layer.

CONTINUING ED

In a 1956 episode of *The Honeymooners*, "The $99,000 Answer," Ralph Kramden, a bus driver from Brooklyn, New York, goes on a game show where you answer trivia questions for a chance to win up to $99,000. Note how his physical stature, tone, uniform, the way he thinks—particularly his strategy for winning money, how hard he works, and ultimately how he performs on the show—all contribute to the full revelation of his personality. Carefully walk through all four layers—physical, mental, spiritual, and core—to see how the writers created such a memorable character.

MINI FINAL ANSWER

The correct answer is **c) How he thinks, or his mental layer.** We have a clear physical description and we know he's a good guy both spiritually, in general, and in his core, because he was able to keep his composure in a climactic showdown with his father. But we don't learn how he solves problems, builds strategies, and uses his mind to get out of trouble.

15

Write characters to the top of their intelligence.

"Always play to the top of your intelligence. If you're going to make a stupid joke make it brilliantly stupid."
—DEL CLOSE, Actor/Director

QUICK TAKE

When you write characters to the top of their intelligence, you show them acting at the upper limits of their potential. They might not be smart. But when you put them in a situation, they do the best they can—because what they're doing is critically important. When you drop the hammer and shatter reality as they knew it, you provoke the Central Dramatic Question, which is always "Will the hero acquire their object of desire?" The more the hero cares about acquiring their object of desire, the more the reader cares about the hero. The best way to show that your character cares *deeply* about what happens is for them to do the hard work of thinking. When characters operate at the top of their intelligence they reveal more of their true nature and become more active and compelling.

Think about how you feel when a coworker messes up an important project, not because they don't understand it or are not up to the task, but because they just don't care. You lose respect for them. Similarly, think about a lazily written chapter. Let's say it's a medical drama. A patient is rushed to the ER with odd symptoms. And the brilliant doctor instantly figures out what's wrong, and cures the ailment. This is uninteresting because the doctor is not forced to operate at the top of her intelligence. It's a form of *telling* us the character is intelligent instead of *showing* how their mind works.

As writers, we are always interested in how the storyteller creates a character that we, as readers or audience members, inhabit. If the storyteller doesn't care enough to write characters operating at the top of their intelligence, they don't care enough to give us an inspired, meaningful experience. Not cool. Thinking harder, smarter, longer, deeper about your choices is your best competitive advantage. How else will you rise to the top of the pack?

HOW IT WORKS

The reason we love watching competitions of all kinds play out is they are living stories that unfurl in real time before our eyes. Let's imagine two versions of the same event. Two of the greatest chess players in history are competing in the final match of the World Chess Championship. They are both going to retire after this match. They have played each other one hundred times and each player has won fifty matches. This is the most important match of their careers, the one that will define their legacies.

In the first version, the match begins and we can see instantly that one player is having an off day. No one knows why. Maybe she got a bad night's sleep, maybe her breakfast didn't agree with her. Who knows? She's just not at the top of her game. After a few moves, she makes an idiotic mistake and loses. You can reasonably say the winner is better. While you might learn something important about the loser—that she is nervous, weak, or ill-fated—it's not as revealing and interesting as the following version of the match.

Both players come out swinging with inventive openings, each one's style fully expressing their personality. They go after each other with furious intensity, and computer models have to update their predictions after each move. They set ingenious traps for each other, but each brilliantly solves puzzle after puzzle and escapes. The game rages on with every fan around the world on the edge of their seat. Both women control their nerves and execute at the very top of their game. This continues for hours until finally one player makes a move so brilliant, so unpredictable, so astonishing, that even her opponent must tip her king and bow with respect.

This version of the match is more meaningful and entertaining. We can now explore the tactics each player executed, the best moves they made, the opportunities missed, how they handled stress, their body language, the mind games they played, how bad each one wanted it, how devious their strategies were, and more. We can't just dismiss the game as one player having an off day.

Again, this is not to say you can't write a character with a low IQ. But they too must operate at the top of their intelligence. There's a famous line from the comedy film *Dumb and Dumber*. Lloyd Christmas falls madly in love with a woman who left a briefcase in his limo. He treks across the country to find her and, after spending some time with her, confesses his feelings. He begs her to be straight with him, to give him the odds that a "girl" like him can get a "guy" like her. She says, "Not good." His heart sinks. "Not good, like one in a hundred?" She says, "More like one in a million." He takes this in, stunned. Then he smiles and cries out, "So you're telling me there's a chance!" The bit works so well because Lloyd is genuinely doing his best to interpret her meaning.

To put a darker spin on the same idea, look at slasher films. These are actually dark comedies that let out our aggression against people who consistently fail to operate anywhere near the top of their intelligence: teenagers. The fun comes from watching drug-abusing, sex-crazed, narcissistic knuckleheads make terrible decisions. They stand frozen, screaming for an entire minute, when they can just run. And when they run, they run into the most confined spaces where they're sure to be caught by the chain saw–wielding maniac. If the teenagers made consistently brilliant decisions to escape, and still got slashed to pieces, the films would be tragic and unbearably painful. Inevitably, these films always end with a showdown between the lone survivor and the maniac. For the ending to work, we need to care about the last gal standing. This only happens if we feel she's operating at the top of her intelligence.

In the classic 1976 slasher film *Halloween*, Jamie Lee Curtis plays a high school senior, Laurie Strode. Early in the film, Laurie notices that she's being followed by the mask-wearing homicidal lunatic Michael Myers. Her friends Annie and Lynda ignorantly dismiss her concerns. Only Laurie, the most conscious and intelligent of the three, survives. Though these films are not often taken seriously, there is an important idea at play: The world is a dangerous place. And you need to bring your A-game, day in and day out, or risk paying the ultimate price.

HOW A MASTER DID IT

"Stan" (2000)
Marshall "Eminem" Mathers

The song "Stan" was a single from Eminem's third album, *The Marshall Mathers LP*, and deals with his struggle to adjust to becoming a superstar. His previous album, *The Real Slim Shady LP*, was a smash hit, reaching number two on the Billboard 200 charts. *Shady* went quadruple platinum and catapulted

Eminem, a white, blond-haired rapper, into the upper echelons of rap superstardom. "Stan" is constructed as a series of letters, and tells the story of an obsessed, mentally ill fan named Stan who is desperate to connect with his idol, Eminem.

The challenge is, Stan has no money, no connections, no power, nothing he can offer Eminem to become a meaningful part of his life. He desperately loves Eminem; he believes that Eminem is the only one in the world who understands him, and that he is the one who knows Eminem best. Stan can think of nothing else. He clearly suffers from a mental illness, unable to accurately assess the world around him, and is struggling in life. As his feelings of ineffectiveness and worthlessness intensify, his rage at Eminem grows, leading to a tragic conclusion.

Below, we'll explore the actions Stan takes to reach his idol. He is relentlessly active and uses his words as weapons. We'll explore this in detail in Chapter 22, "Craft actionable dialogue," but for now, it's important to know that Stan attacks Eminem from many different angles in order to sear himself into his consciousness. If you ask your friend to borrow money and you tell him he's handsome, that you respect how successful he is, and that you desperately need a break, you've taken three distinct actions to acquire your object of desire. You buttered him up, made clear he can afford it, and asked him to sympathize with your needs. When you consider how impossible it is for Stan to achieve his objective—the odds of this guy connecting with Eminem are infinitesimally small—you see that he actually does a fantastic job. He makes a real connection. But he'll never know that, as it occurs after his own anguish and self-hatred consume him.

"Stan" is one of Eminem's most critically acclaimed songs; it was performed at the Grammys and has been streamed over a hundred million times. In fact, the word *stan* is included in the *Oxford American Dictionary* as a term for an obsessed fan. The main reason Stan has become such a powerful archetype is that Eminem, a master storyteller, beautifully executes the principle of writing characters to the top of their intelligence. He creates a three-dimensional, compelling, contradictory, darkly comedic, and authentically tragic character. The amount of depth and detail Eminem packs into Stan's three-verse attack on Eminem is extraordinary. Let's go through each one to see how Eminem leveraged the principle of writing characters to the top of their intelligence to create a definitive archetype of the outcast, of all of us who dream of making it to the big time, but know we'll never get there.

Verse 1 (as Stan)

Dear Slim, I wrote you, but you still ain't callin'
I left my cell, my pager and my home phone at the bottom
I sent two letters back in autumn
You must not've got 'em
There probably was a problem at the post office or somethin'
Sometimes I scribble addresses too sloppy when I jot 'em
But anyways, fuck it, what's been up, man?
How's your daughter?
My girlfriend's pregnant too, I'm 'bout to be a father
If I have a daughter, guess what I'ma call her?
I'ma name her Bonnie
I read about your Uncle Ronnie too, I'm sorry
I had a friend kill himself over some bitch who didn't want him
I know you probably hear this every day
But I'm your biggest fan
I even got the underground shit that you did with Skam
I got a room full of your posters and your pictures, man
I like the shit you did with Rawkus too, that shit was phat
Anyways, I hope you get this, man, hit me back
Just to chat, truly yours, your biggest fan, this is Stan

Right out of the gate, Stan declares exactly what he wants—to connect directly with Eminem. And he calls him by his alter ego's name, Slim, as in Slim Shady. He lets him know that he did all he could to reach him: wrote two letters, left all his contact information, and waited patiently for months, but still nothing. He's trying to make Eminem feel guilty for not calling, but doesn't hit the guilt trip too hard.

He then shows maturity by taking the blame. It must have been his own fault for writing too small and sloppy. He knows he is one of a million fans, yet he can't bear the thought that his letters might be lying in a pile of thousands of fan letters, unread, or worse, that Eminem did read his letters but didn't care enough to respond. So, he lies to himself and suggests the post office must have lost the letters.

He talks to Eminem in the poetic language of the street as if they're close friends. He's working to humanize himself, to make Eminem see that they have so much in common. He tells Eminem that his own girlfriend is pregnant. When he says he's going to name his daughter "Bonnie," this is a reference to Eminem's song "97 Bonnie and Clyde," in which Bonnie is Eminem's daughter Hallie. That song is a dark fantasy about Eminem taking his daughter to the beach while he has his ex-wife, her mother, dead in the trunk. Telling Eminem that he plans to name his daughter Bonnie is a confession, a secret warning of the dark deed lurking in the back of his mind. It's a plea for help. It's the start of a threat. It's foreshadowing.

When Stan pays condolences to Eminem's Uncle Ronnie, who killed himself "over some bitch who didn't want him," the reference is accurate. Eminem did lose his Uncle Ronnie, whom he loved, to suicide. Stan is showing empathy and trying to prove that he doesn't just take, he gives. He sees himself as Eminem's true friend. And when he says that he's Eminem's "biggest fan," he backs it up. His room is covered with posters and photographs. He knows the old school stuff only the most hardcore fans know. He wraps up by staying calm because he knows if he comes on too strong, he'll scare Eminem off. So, he pretends all he wants to do is chat. Then, like a professional salesman, he asks for the close, "hit me back."

Verse 2 (as Stan)

Dear Slim, you still ain't called or wrote
I hope you have a chance
I ain't mad, I just think it's fucked up you don't answer fans
If you didn't want to talk to me outside the concert
You didn't have to
But you could've signed an autograph for Matthew
That's my little brother, man, he's only six years old
We waited in the blisterin' cold for you
For four hours, and you just said no
That's pretty shitty, man, you're like his fucking idol
He wants to be just like you, man, he likes you more than I do
I ain't that mad though, I just don't like being lied to
Remember when we met in Denver?
You said if I'd write you, you would write back
See, I'm just like you in a way; I never knew my father neither
He used to always cheat on my mom and beat her
I can relate to what you're saying in your songs
So when I have a shitty day, I drift away and put 'em on
'Cause I don't really got shit else
So that shit helps when I'm depressed
I even got a tattoo of your name across the chest
Sometimes I even cut myself to see how much it bleeds
It's like adrenaline, the pain is such a sudden rush for me
See everything you say is real
And I respect you 'cause you tell it
My girlfriend's jealous 'cause I talk about you 24/7
But she don't know you like I know you, Slim, no one does
She don't know what it was like for people like us growin' up
You gotta call me, man
I'll be the biggest fan you'll ever lose, sincerely yours, Stan
P.S. We should be together too

Stan falsely claims that he's not angry. He's smart enough to try to keep it together, but his hurt and shame are too intense. He scolds Eminem for ignoring his fans. He tries to make him feel guilty for ignoring his six-year-old brother, Matthew, who waited in the "blistering" cold for an autograph. This is both intelligent and ridiculous—what the hell is a six-year-old doing up late at night, in the freezing cold? And how can Eminem, whose work deals with sex, violence, and other adult themes, be his favorite? The kid is six. Stan then accuses Eminem of lying to him, because one time after a show he said he'd write back. Stan knows that he's just one of millions of fans, but he can't bear that thought. He is too narcissistic to see the world through Eminem's eyes.

He changes tactics to strengthen their bond by sharing more secrets. His father used to cheat on his mother and beat her. He then ran off on him, just like Eminem's father did. He ups the ante, confessing that he cuts himself, that he got a "tattoo of your name across the chest." He can no longer hide the depth of his devotion. He thinks about Eminem every waking hour.

Finally, he ups the ante yet again with his most shocking revelation yet. He's sexually attracted to Eminem and dreams of being his lover. This is both moving and darkly comedic as Eminem is straight and would find this level of attraction off-putting. But Stan's desperation is skyrocketing and he's disconnecting from reality. When he threatens to become "the biggest fan you'll ever lose," he's throwing the most explosive bomb he can. Surely Eminem doesn't want to lose his biggest fan. It also has a double meaning. He's trying to say that he's thinking seriously of suicide.

Verse 3 (as Stan)

Dear Mr. I'm-Too-Good-to-Call-or-Write-My-Fans
This'll be the last package I ever send your ass
It's been six months and still no word—I don't deserve it?
I know you got my last two letters

I wrote the addresses on 'em perfect
So this is my cassette I'm sending you, I hope you hear it
I'm in the car right now, I'm doing 90 on the freeway
Hey, Slim, I drank a fifth of vodka, you dare me to drive?
You know the song by Phil Collins
"In the Air in the Night" about that guy who could've saved that other guy from drownin'
But didn't, then Phil saw it all, then at a show he found him?
That's kinda how this is
You could've rescued me from drowning
Now it's too late, I'm on a thousand downers now, I'm drowsy
And all I wanted was a lousy letter or a call
I hope you know I ripped all of your pictures off the wall
I loved you, Slim, we could've been together—think about it!
You ruined it now, I hope you can't sleep
And you dream about it
And when you dream
I hope you can't sleep and you scream about it
I hope your conscience eats at you
And you can't breathe without me
See, Slim—shut up, bitch! I'm tryin' to talk
Hey, Slim, that's my girlfriend screamin' in the trunk
But I didn't slit her throat, I just tied her up, see, I ain't like you
'Cause if she suffocates she'll suffer more
And then she'll die too
Well, gotta go, I'm almost at the bridge now
Oh shit, I forgot, how am I supposed to send this shit out?

In his final letter, Stan's hatred goes parabolic. He rages at Eminem, now referred to as "Mr. I'm-Too-Good-to-Call-or-Write-My-Fans." In this desperate attempt to assert his own masculinity and effectiveness, to make his mark on Eminem's conscience, he records this letter on a cassette while speeding down the highway drunk and on downers with his pregnant girlfriend tied up in the trunk. He compares his own situation to the one in a Phil Collins song, "In the Air Tonight." But he gets the title wrong, referring to it as "In the Air in the Night." Stan mistakenly believes the myth that the song is about Phil Collins shining a light on a man at his concert, a man that Collins allegedly witnessed letting another man drown. Stan views this song as identical to Eminem allowing him to drown, and pitifully notes that all he wanted was a "lousy letter or a call." This is again both true and not true. It's technically accurate that all he asked for is a letter or a call, but what he really wants is validation, a best friend, true love, a soul mate. And when Stan talks of drowning, he's not just speaking metaphorically.

He viciously curses Eminem's soul, his ability to sleep and breathe. He declares himself superior, contradicting all his previous declarations. Now he claims "I ain't like you" because he is ultra-hardcore. He is not just writing about being a killer, he's about to become one. And not just a killer, but the most vicious kind, one who inflicts maximum suffering on his victim, his girlfriend, who screams from his trunk in terror. He didn't slit her throat, wanting her to experience the agony of suffocation. His wish for Eminem to lose the ability to breathe has been grotesquely transferred to his woman. And this is all Eminem's fault. Stan's descent into hell ends with his plunging his car off a bridge into the water where both he and his girlfriend drown.

In just three short, poetic letters Stan declares what he needs; he guilts, empathizes, connects, validates, expresses, exposes, confesses, pleads, vows, rages, curses, threatens, murders his girlfriend and their unborn child, then kills himself. Though he makes many mistakes, though he goes full evil, he executes the most intelligent plan that he possibly can. And here's the thing: He achieves his objective. In the last verse, Eminem writes back to him, urging him to get counseling. He sends his brother Matthew an autographed hat. And he genuinely does connect with Stan—with affection, care, honesty, and respect. What makes Stan so tragic is if he were more emotionally stable, he'd have the skill and passion to be successful. It's not hard to imagine him putting his passion, intensity, and persuasion to work in a more productive way.

Eminem set out to express some of the intense challenges of moving from poverty to superstardom and to talk directly to his most passionate fans, many of whom were young, angry, disaffected men. He wanted to both validate their feelings for him and to show his appreciation for their support. He also wanted to warn them not to emulate his lyrics, to relax and not get too carried away with their support. That he does this through the lens of a disturbed fan is clever and interesting. But what takes this to the next level is the fierce intelligence of the fan. It's Stan's intelligence that makes him a substantive, fascinating, and genuinely tragic figure.

This may sound cruel to say, but it's true. Stupid people are dismissible. If someone talks to you about politics, your job, marriage, a mutual acquaintance, or even insults you, and what they say is just plain illogical or poorly thought out, you pay it no mind. But if it's insightful and instructive and challenges you to think differently about the subject at hand, it stays with you. It rattles around in your head and forces you to deal with them. In story, the more intelligent you make your characters, the more interesting and dynamic they are, the better the dialogue, the more compelling your scenes, and the richer your themes.

HOW YOU DO IT

The following bullet points will help you think through and execute the principle.

- This principle applies to all characters. Every character sees themselves as the hero of their own story and has their own object of desire. Whenever someone takes an action—physical or through dialogue—get clear on what they need.

▶ Remember that there are different kinds of intelligence. A person may be strong in one area and weak in another. The cliché is the rocket scientist who can't talk to girls. Some people are brilliant in action—the quarterback who makes calculations at high speed while running around a football field. Others can read emotions. Know when your character is at the top of their game, and where they struggle.

▶ Once you know what your character needs, how they think, and what can trip them up, think as hard as you can, *in character*, about the choices laid out before you. Your objective as your character is to get what you need as quickly as possible with the least amount of effort, and to make decisions at the top of your intelligence.

▶ Characters can, of course, do stupid things. But the reason they do them must be clear and meaningful. For example, an entrepreneur makes a presentation to a group of high-powered venture capitalists. He might get resentful when they ask pointed questions, or let his nerves get the best of him. This reveals essential information about his character and gives insight into the nature of doing business.

▶ If a scene's not working, go back to what the characters need and study how they're going about it. Smart choices breed smart choices. Give yourself options. List out all that you might do if you were in their shoes.

▶ Take pride in doing this work. Your characters, in aggregate, reflect *your* intelligence. In Shakespeare, every character—from a gatekeeper with one line to King Lear—is interesting because they're all doing the very best they can, always.

MINI FINAL EXAM

Read the following, then answer the question below.

A teenage girl, Maddy, plans to sleep at her boyfriend's house. His parents are going away for a night and she wants to be with him. But she knows her parents will never allow it. So, to butter up her way-too-strict mom, she does all of her chores, keeps her room clean, and talks about the excellent grades she has been getting and how excited she is to start college next year. She then schemes with one of her girlfriends, Noelle, to say that they're having a sleepover at Noelle's house. The big worry is that Maddy's mom will call Noelle's mom that night to confirm the girls are safe and sound in the house. They consider asking Noelle's mom to cover for them, but realize she would most likely rat. They consider stealing Maddy's mom's phone, but realize she would borrow Maddy's dad's. They consider murdering Maddy's mom, but decide the risk of jail is too high. Finally, the big night comes and Maddy must decide what to do. She lies to her mom, says she's sleeping over at Noelle's, goes to her boyfriend's house, and just hopes her mom will forget to call.

Which one of the following should be cut from the story because the character is not operating at the top of her intelligence?

a) Maddy involves her friend Noelle.
b) Maddy and Noelle consider asking Noelle's mom to help.
c) Maddy considers stealing her mom's cell phone.
d) Maddy does the sleepover with her boyfriend despite the possibility of getting busted.
e) Maddy and Noelle consider killing Maddy's mom.

CONTINUING ED

In Henrik Ibsen's 1879 play *A Doll's House*, Nora is a housewife, mother of three young children, and married to Torvald, who works in a bank. They live in a tight-knit community where people place a high value on morality and guard their reputations. Prior to the action of the play, Torvald fell ill and needed to spend time in a warmer climate to heal his illness, but the family lacked funds. Desperate to help her husband, she forged Torvald's signature at the bank to secure a loan and lied to him, claiming that her father gave them the money. Torvald's rival at the bank, Krogstad, discovers Nora's secret and threatens to blackmail them. Torvald viciously berates Nora for risking his reputation.

Eventually, they escape disaster when Krogstad agrees to keep their secret. Upon hearing the news, Torvald cries out, "Nora! Nora! I'm saved! I'm saved!" Nora sees that she is no more than a prop to him and decides to leave the family to find herself. Torvald is speechless—the idea of a woman leaving her husband and children in 1879 was unthinkable. In the final scene, he pleads with her to reconsider. But he fails. The final moment when she slams the door is widely considered one of the most powerful sound effects in theater history. Carefully read the scene in which Torvald begs Nora to stay. Look at everything he does and says to keep her. Given who he is, what more could he do? Though he's been self-absorbed throughout the play, how does he earn our sympathy and make her decision more impactful?

MINI FINAL ANSWER

The correct answer is **e) Maddy and Noelle consider killing Maddy's mom**. There is not the slightest indication in the story that Maddy is anything but a good kid. The idea that she would actually kill her mom, risking her soul and life in prison for a single night with her boyfriend, is absurd. It's also weak storytelling as it's not set up by any of the previous action.

16

Mask everyone.

"We all wear masks, and the time comes when we cannot remove them without removing some of our own skin."
—ANDRÉ BERTHIAUME, Author

QUICK TAKE

Imagine you're on a train. It's early morning, quiet. People are dressed neatly for work. Typical commute. Then someone gets on wearing a mask. No matter what kind of mask it is—Halloween, hockey, Lone Ranger, surgical—it sets off an alert. You need to know what's up with this person. Are they unstable? Dangerous? Diseased? Or are they just having fun? In the first section on plot, we talked about dramatic questions. When you mask a character's true personality, you infuse them with their own personal dramatic question: Who are they?

Now of course we're not just talking about physical masks. How people behave, dress, what they're obsessed with, can all mask hidden desires, intentions, or even the most innocent crush. It's entertaining and engaging to discover that a character is not who they seem to be and to watch their mask gradually come off throughout a story. Therefore, you want to control the relationship between how a character looks and who they are. You're saying to your readers/viewers—"See this clean-cut, soft-spoken guy with the warm smile? He just got out of prison." "See this teacher showing her history class government buildings in DC? She's plotting a terrorist attack."

Things get interesting when the mask slips.

HOW IT WORKS

Again, these principles are not puzzle pieces to snap together to create the same picture everyone else does. You can't just make a scar-faced, wild-eyed hulk a nursery school teacher and shout, "Voila!" That might work, it might not. The key factors to consider when masking characters are:

- How it's discovered, stays on, or comes off.
- Why it's worn.
- What the mask reveals about the characters.
- How it works within the context of the story's genre.
- What it means—how it elucidates or amplifies theme.

How it's discovered, stays on, or comes off

You first have to sell your reader/viewers on the authenticity of the mask. In Jane Austen's *Pride and Prejudice*, Mr. Darcy at first seems cold-hearted, arrogant, and cruel when he makes cutting remarks about the heroine, Elizabeth, at a dance, and then torpedoes her sister's budding romance with his friend Bingley. Elizabeth also gets an earful from the questionable Mr. Wickham, who assails Darcy's character. Though Mr. Darcy is attractive, and there's clearly chemistry between the two, we have every reason to think he is a negative character.

The novel would fail if readers figured out too quickly that Mr. Darcy is actually a warm-hearted, deeply moral person, if a bit prideful. Therefore, the moment you let the reader/viewer know of the mask's existence must be handled very carefully in order to lead them to the realization that the character is not who they seem. And the mask must be carefully and gradually removed—or ultimately kept on—as the story progresses and new information about the character is revealed. When the mask slides out of place, it propels the narrative. Mr. Darcy writes Elizabeth a passionate letter, detailing the reasons for his previous actions, and we quickly realize there is more to this man than it seemed.

Tracking a character's struggle to protect their hidden self is engaging and entertaining. In Judith Guest's 1976 novel *Ordinary People*, Beth Jarrett appears to be a loving, dedicated wife, mother, daughter, friend, and neighbor. But deep down, she has an injury, or strange limitation, which prevents her from loving her younger and only surviving son, Conrad. Her older and favorite, Bucky, was killed in a boating accident that Conrad survived. The narrative is structured around the question of whether or not Beth, her husband Calvin, and their son Conrad, can live with the truth of who she is behind her mask. When it's ultimately removed, it's a devastating moment that ends the story. You can structure an entire plot based on the question of whether a mask will be kept on or torn off.

Whether a story ends on a positive or negative note often depends on whether or not the main characters can accept the truth of who they are. Mr. Darcy is able to hear the entire truth of how Elizabeth feels about him and fully confront her feelings. Beth Jarrett can't accept the truth that she lacks the capacity to love her younger son. She can't deal with the complexity of her feelings. Once her husband calls her on her inability to deal with the messy reality of life, she leaves.

Some people are so terrified of being exposed, so unable to deal with their pain, they will give up everything—a loving spouse, beautiful home, their own son—rather than face the truth of who they are.

Why it's worn

Characters wear masks for noble reasons. An undercover cop assumes an identity to catch a serial killer. Characters wear masks to protect vulnerabilities—though terrified, a mother assumes a can-do persona to help her children through a difficult time. Characters wear masks for evil reasons. A corporate executive joins a company to steal its secrets. Some characters wear masks in some situations, but not others. For example, a rock star, politician, or CEO may need to assume a persona in public in order to do what must be done. Bob Dylan, whose real name is Robert Zimmerman, once said, "I'm Bob Dylan when I need to be Bob Dylan." Some characters don't know why they're wearing a mask because they don't even realize they are wearing one. In the 1987 supernatural thriller *Angel Heart*, Mickey Rourke plays a detective who carries a secret so dark he had to completely reconstruct his identity to escape it. Regardless of what the character knows or doesn't know, you, as the storyteller, must know why the character wears their mask and how aware they are that it's on.

What the mask reveals about the characters

What people hide, why they hide it, and how they go about keeping their secrets hidden reveals who they are. What we hide is more meaningful than what we show the world. The person who posts endless photos on social media of himself working out, climbing mountains, riding motorcycles, and doing martial arts may be hiding the fact that he feels weak and vulnerable. It may even be an attempt to cover a traumatic experience.

In story, masks always come with high stakes. People wear them for deep-seated psychological reasons, and it's painful and frightening to have those reasons exposed. It can also be extremely liberating. But either way, it's not easy. If one goes to the trouble to construct a mask, to hide something from the world—a past action, incident, or trait—the thing hidden is obviously important. No one constructs a mask to hide the fact that they think nachos are yummy. And the mask gives insight into all the characters, not just the one who wears it.

We discover who people are by how they respond to the mask. In families, corporations, and in politics this dynamic plays out all the time. For example, when a CEO straight out of central casting—tall, gorgeous, with a sparkling résumé—turns out to be corrupt, incompetent, or in over their skis, some executives will callously use it to their advantage, while others risk their own careers to rip off the mask. Arthur Miller's 1947 play *All My Sons* deals with a son's realization that his father is not the great man he thought. The old man knowingly sold busted airplane parts to the military, causing the deaths of American pilots during WWII. When the mask comes off, we find out who both men are by how they handle it.

How it works within the context of the story's genre

I started this section with the crack that you can't just make a scar-faced, wild-eyed hulk a nursery school teacher and shout, "Voilà!" This is because you have to be fully aware of the type of story you're telling. A choice that works perfectly in one genre fails in another. In a screwball comedy, the tattooed hulk that turns out to be a nursery school teacher could be funny. In a dramedy it could be charming. In a straight-up drama, it could feel strained and fake.

The mask must work within the context of the story's genre. In the 1949 film noir *White Heat*, James Cagney plays Cody Jarrett, a seriously damaged middle-aged gang leader who suffers from brain seizures and leans heavily on his mother for guidance. She's a hateful, cunning old woman, but she truly loves her boy and tells him repeatedly that he'll make it to the "top o' the world." The story centers on an FBI agent, Hank Fallon, who masks himself as a fellow convict and befriends Cody in prison. The FBI knows Cody is planning a big job as soon as he gets out, and Hank's job is to stop it. As their friendship develops, we see a softer, gentler side of Cody, who never had a true friend—except his mother. Back then, epileptic seizures were considered a mental illness, and Cody was never able to make friends because he was an outcast.

There's a famous moment when Cody learns that Hank has betrayed him. He laughs bitterly, maniacally repeating "a coppa!" because he can't believe he was foolish enough to trust anyone, to believe that he could ever have a true friend. It's a painful and emotionally complex moment because even though Cody's a killer, it hurts to see him so intimately betrayed. This works well because it's a film noir and this is what noir does: It blurs lines. It makes us question our ability to tell who's truly good and who is evil.

What it means—how it elucidates or amplifies theme

Why characters wear masks, how they respond to being called out for wearing them, how others respond to them, and whether or not the mask is kept on is full of meaning. In *Angel Heart*, when the hero, or antihero, Detective Harry Angel, has his mask ripped off—by the Devil himself—he steps up to a mirror with tears streaming down his exhausted face. He stares into his own eyes and pitifully repeats, "I know who I am," as we flash back to all the cold-blooded murders he's committed. That he can't accept the truth of who he is when this mask comes off means that human beings can't bear to face the truth of our own sins.

It's always surprising when a mask comes off. Whether the surprise comes from how the mask comes off or how the character responds, the moment is charged. Whenever a mask comes off, there's a clash between expectation and reality. Anyone who puts one on assumes they can keep it on. Or control how and when it comes off. And even if they fully expect it to come off, they can't know how it will feel and how the world will respond. Therefore, the moment is full of meaning. What people do in these heightened states, when fully exposed, defines who they are. This is a powerful way to sharpen and highlight your story's theme.

HOW A MASTER DID IT

Harry Potter and the Prisoner of Azkaban (1999)
J. K. Rowling

In this novel, the third in the Harry Potter series, the Hogwarts School of Witchcraft and Wizardry is abuzz with terrifying news. The mass murderer Sirius Black has done what no one has ever done before—escaped from Azkaban prison. A traitor to his former friends, including Harry's parents, Black is a dedicated servant of Lord Voldemort and rumor has it he is coming to Hogwarts specifically to kill Harry. The school is encircled by Dementors, creatures that serve as Azkaban prison guards. They are humanoid with gray, rotting skin and they hover in the air. Though blind, they can sense the presence of human beings, and can drain a person of their happiness by "kissing" them—sucking out their soul.

Into this tense atmosphere comes the students' new professor of Defense Against the Dark Arts, Remus John Lupin. It's his job to teach the kids how to protect themselves from malicious magic and the evil creatures spawned by it. Since our interest here is in Lupin's character, and not the plot as a whole, we'll just give a brief synopsis of the main storyline that includes him.

Lupin, an old friend and schoolmate of Harry's father, James, cares deeply about Harry. He teaches him a powerful spell called a Patronus charm, which is specifically designed to protect against attacks by the Dementors who now surround Hogwarts. They are hell-bent on nailing the escaped prisoner, Sirius Black, but they are wretched, dangerous creatures and will come after anyone who gets in their way. To cast a Patronus charm, the wizard or witch summons the power of their happiest memory. If successful, a silver guardian spirit animal with a direct connection to the spell caster appears to ward off the assailing Dementors.

In a shocking twist, we learn that Sirius Black did twelve years in Azkaban for a crime he didn't commit. He was framed by a former friend, Peter Pettigrew, and forced against his will to wear the mask of a deranged serial killer. He's escaped to clear his name and protect his godson, Harry Potter. In the story's climactic finale, Harry is called upon to save Sirius from a large pack of Dementors by casting the Patronus charm.

As fans of the Harry Potter books and movies know, the universe of characters in the series is filled with wizards, witches, muggles, and animals that are not what they appear to be. From Dolores Umbridge, who wears the mask of a well-mannered, even sweet, middle-aged woman, but is the incarnation of evil, to Ron Weasley's pet rat, Scabbers, who turns out to be the traitor, Peter Pettigrew, to student Neville Longbottom, who appears to be a hapless nerd but is in fact a courageous warrior, the list of characters whose true selves are masked by their outward appearance is long. Though there are many factors that contribute to the success of these books, a major one is J. K. Rowling's ability to draw complex characters who are not what they seem. It's hard to navigate what Paul McCartney called "this everchanging world in which we're living." These books validate this fact and teach kids to be careful who you trust.

Of all the characters Rowling created, she's said in interviews that Lupin is among her very favorites. He is a tragic character. He wears an "extremely shabby set of wizard's robes that had been darned in several places." He's tall, pale, prematurely gray-haired, and looks sickly and older than he is. Throughout the novel, we get hint after hint that Lupin has a secret. He often misses classes and returns looking frail and spent. During one class, when he's teaching the students a spell that requires envisioning your deepest fear, his own is revealed. It's a "silvery white orb hanging in the air." When he misses class, the ill-tempered Professor Severus Snape fills in for him and forces the students to jump ahead in their textbook to study werewolves. At another point, Harry sees Snape give Lupin an herb. Though Harry's worried about taking anything from Snape, Lupin doesn't question this at all.

As the novel's climactic action erupts, Hermione accuses Lupin of being a werewolf. He's impressed. She's right. Hermione, always operating at the top of her intelligence, figured out that his worst fear is the moon and that he always misses class after a full moon. The herb that Harry saw Snape give Lupin was to lessen the devastating effects of transforming into a werewolf. And Snape, of course, jumped ahead to teach the kids about werewolves because there was a very real chance that Lupin could fail to lock himself away during a transformation and harm them. In fact, when the novel concludes, he almost does. Caught up in the stress of confronting Black and discovering that Ron Weasley's rat is actually his former friend Peter Pettigrew, Lupin loses track of time and misses the arrival of a full moon, causing him to transform into a werewolf and nearly slaughter Harry and Hermione.

Now let's review the five key factors of masking characters and see how Rowling handles them. Again, they are:

- How it's discovered, stays on, or comes off.
- Why it's worn.
- What the mask reveals about the characters.
- How it works within the context of the story's genre.
- What it means—how it elucidates or amplifies the story's theme.

How it's discovered, stays on, or comes off

The discovery that Lupin is a werewolf is integral to the plot, as the reader is fed clue after clue that this is his secret. And once the mask finally comes off, he is as terrifying as any werewolf. Rowling hides his dark secret by making him not only kind, but one of the students' favorite and most competent teachers. After his secret is revealed, he resigns his position to avoid putting the school through the drama and chaos that will surely erupt when parents realize Hogwarts has a werewolf on staff.

Why it's worn

The wizard world is as prone to fits of hysteria as the human, or muggle, world, and people who suffer from "lycanthropy" (becoming a werewolf) are treated as outcasts to be feared and shunned. This is especially true for men teaching children, however noble and well-intentioned they may be.

What the mask reveals about the characters

Lupin expends a tremendous amount of energy to conceal his affliction. This is on top of the physical pain and suffering the transformation puts him through. The beast that hides behind his mask is diametrically opposed to the kind man he is. That he must spend so much of his energy concealing the truth of who he is, and that a part of him is truly a monster, is archetypal. We all know kind-hearted people who are capable of exploding with rage if certain nerves are struck. That Lupin is willing to work so hard to contribute what he can, that he has never given in to his condition and the animosity it provokes, speaks to his integrity, courage, and perseverance.

The fact that Hermione figures out Lupin's secret and tells him so shows, yet again, her intelligence and honor. Snape helps provide him with herbs to ease the agony of his transitions, but is also instrumental in letting the world know about his condition, which further reveals his own complex nature. That Albus Dumbledore (the headmaster of Hogwarts) allowed Lupin to attend the school as a child and return to teach, despite his condition, speaks to Dumbledore's faith in people. We also learn that while Lupin was a student, his friends, James Potter (Harry's father), Sirius Black, and Peter Pettigrew, learned how to transform into animals in order to spend time with young Lupin during his painful transformations. Werewolves, in the world of Potter, don't attack animals. This speaks to just how close these men were in school. And makes the fact that Pettigrew would betray them all the more despicable.

How it works within the context of the story's genre

The Harry Potter series is both fantasy and drama. The genre is rife with stories of humans transforming into animals, magical creatures, and monsters. That Lupin's mask hides the fact that he's a werewolf fits in the dead center of Rowling's hybrid genre, fantasy-drama. It is fantastic (in a supernatural sense), emotionally complex, and moving.

What it means— how it elucidates or amplifies theme

Lupin's affliction is symbolic of those who live with misunderstood illnesses or disabilites. That Dumbledore allows someone who is suffering from a condition that could harm students makes a powerful statement about the nature of goodness. To be a good person and a noble leader means having to make difficult decisions. Dumbledore must factor the odds of Lupin actually harming students against the benefits of his teaching at the school—and the benefits to Lupin himself. Interestingly, Dumbledore decides it is best *not* to inform the students' parents.

Rowling's theme is that ethical societies don't cast out the afflicted, even if they can be dangerous. Rowling is saying that there is strength in goodness, as good people take risks for each other and form tighter bonds. Voldemort, a no-good, evil sonofabitch if ever there was one, casts out all those he considers weak, fragile, and impure. This means he never reaps the benefits of all that people like Lupin have to offer. Rowling was inspired to write Harry Potter while working with the human rights organization Amnesty International. There can be no doubt where her interests lie—on the side of the powerless, those in the most desperate need. Through the story of Lupin, and his attempt to keep his mask on, Rowling makes a bold statement about the value of compassion and what it really takes to be good.

HOW YOU DO IT

The following bullet points will help you think through and execute the principle.

- As always, make it personal, just to get the right mindset. Remember, it takes a great deal of energy to wear a mask and keep it on. And it can be terrifying when it comes off. When does your outward appearance conflict with the truth of who you are?

- Decide what your character is hiding and why. It could be a feeling, a past action, or an alter ego. Make sure there is a tight connection between the person's external appearance and what they're hiding. For example, a mixed martial artist who fights to prove he wasn't broken by childhood abuse, or a Sunday school teacher who longs to experience sin.

- Sell the mask. Take your time. As your readers/viewers settle into your story, they scour details to help ground them. If a character wears a cross, drives a Porsche, eats steamed vegetables, is named Red, all of these things lead people to draw all sorts of conclusions. To navigate life, we have to rely on shortcuts. We assume the guy in the mailman outfit is a mailman. Use this to trick readers/viewers into buying the mask.

- Enjoy the slip. In life it's disarming to realize someone is not who you thought. In story it can be too, but it's fun. The cliché here is when, in film, a seemingly good character slowly squints as eerie music plays at the end of a scene—this means they're bad! Have fun striking the first discordant note.

- Consider your genre. In certain genres—comedy, horror, soap opera—you can go big with these choices. In other genres, especially drama, you need to be more subtle and walk the line. You want to drop clues that are big enough to be noticed, but not so big that they reveal what's beneath the mask. In *Harry Potter and the Prisoner of Azkaban*, Rowling inserts the bit about Lupin's worst fear being a silvery orb into a chaotic scene in which all the students are confronting their fears. She then touches it again when the character Lavender, exiting class, says, "I wonder why Professor Lupin's frightened of crystal balls." And this is quickly covered by Ron's joke about Hermione's worst fear being a homework assignment where she only gets a nine out of ten.

▶ Track every movement of the mask—how it moves closer to coming off or staying on. Make sure that you're not repeating moments, moving too slow, or too fast. Parcel it out throughout the story.

▶ Reflect on the meaning of this mask. Why was it put on? And why does it have to come off or stay on? What does this mean to you?

▶ Your goal is that its ultimate removal, or the moment it's put firmly back in place to stay, is both surprising and believable. You're clashing expectation and reality here. Make it count.

MINI FINAL EXAM

Read the following, then answer the question below.

In a small New York City apartment, a mom in her mid-forties plays Motown music and dances playfully as she cooks an elaborate meal. As her teenage daughters set the table, they exchange uncomfortable looks. This is weird—Mom hates cooking. Mom playfully bumps them as she dances. The younger daughter giggles, but the older one's irritated. Mom struts back into the kitchen and cuts a huge, crusty loaf of Italian bread with a little too much aggression, then eyes her eldest daughter's nasty glance and turns off the music. "Can't we just have a little fun? Just a little?" The dad comes in from his home office excited to talk about the deal he just closed, but immediately senses the tension and asks, "What's wrong?" Mom grabs his hand, puts her arm around his waist, dances him about, and kisses him on the lips. He mouths, "Knock it off," to his snarling eldest.

They enjoy a passably happy meal with some okay, if strained, conversation. But as the girls clear the table and Mom makes dessert, she whistles. Dad eyes them, validating their concern. Mom is acting weird. The younger daughter holds her stomach, suddenly nervous. A false, almost malicious smile crosses Mom's face as she puts out dessert, and a grim silence overtakes the room. They all sit but no one touches their food. Dad calmly asks, "What's wrong?" Mom grins at him, small and weak and scared. She then insists that she's going to be fine. Nobody moves. And she adds simply, "I have cancer."

Masking mom's fear with false cheer gives the scene which of the following benefits?

a) Increases tension.
b) Reveals character.
c) Heightens emotion.
d) Makes the ending more impactful.
e) All of the above.

CONTINUING ED

In the 2005 romantic drama *Brokeback Mountain*, Jack Twist and Ennis Del Mar are hired to work on a ranch herding sheep in Montana for a summer. They battle rough terrain, fierce storms, and the rigors of the job. The film begins in the 1960s and moves through the 1970s as we track the relationship between Twist and Del Mar. The two engage in a sexual encounter after a night of drinking and eventually have an affair that lasts years. However, both men eventually marry women, have children, and build lives apart from each other, though they remain in love.

How does their identity as old-school, all-American cowboys affect their relationship and individual identities? Why do they feel it's necessary to behave differently in public than they do in private? How does their relationship and the nature of their sexuality affect their respective marriages? How strong is the conflict between their outward appearance and private sexuality? How well do they understand their own behavior, personas, and identities? How conscious are they of the masks they wear?

MINI FINAL ANSWER

The correct answer is **e) All of the above**. By masking the mom's fear with false cheer, the scene is more tense, we get a deeper sense of who each character is by watching how they respond to her unusual behavior, their emotions are heightened, we feel more for their suffering, and the ultimate revelation that ends the scene is more impactful than it would be if Mom just came out with the bad news up front.

17

Earn transformations.

"Technically, chemistry is the study of matter, but I prefer to see it as the study of change."
—WALTER WHITE, Protagonist, *Breaking Bad*

QUICK TAKE

We find meaning in stories by studying how and why things change. If nothing changes, nothing substantive happened. This story doesn't work: "Once there was a noble king, who lived a noble life, then died as nobly as he lived." Even in Samuel Beckett's existential masterpiece *Waiting for Godot*, where two tramps spend the entire play waiting for a mysterious figure, "Godot," who never comes, there is a profound change in their sense of desperation. They transform from men with an ounce of hope to men with virtually none. Even those who seem to do nothing are at the mercy of an ever-changing world.

To master story, both you, the writer, and your characters must earn every transformation. By "earn," we mean you portray the transformation in a way that's convincing. Transformations must be earned for stories as a whole, and for the smallest changes that take place throughout the journey—in chapters, scenes, and even little interactions and bits of dialogue. Two women eye each other in a bar, then move from strangers to love interests. To make this transformation convincing, characters must do the work. So, if one woman smiles, gets nothing back, sends over a drink and gets a slight nod, then does something funny or interesting to win a smile, and we believe that these two specific women would respond to these interactions as they do, the transformation is earned.

When Michael Corleone transforms from a decorated marine to the Godfather in the first film, and from alive to spiritually dead in the second film, your heart sinks, because the change is so convincing. There's an inexorable quality to his ultimate transformation. We believe that this man, forced to endure what he endures—the loss of his father, older brother, first wife, and his unborn child, the betrayal of another brother, corruption at the highest levels of government—would lose his soul.

HOW IT WORKS

Before we get into how it works, let's get clear on why it's so important to earn transformations. A key reason we love the writers we love most is they face down chaos and tell us that life is not just a meaningless blur—that Macbeth was wrong when he said life is "a tale told by an idiot full of sound and fury, signifying nothing." Good stories are filled with meaning, they're not just a list of random events. When Noah crawls into bed with Allie at the end of Nicholas Sparks's *The Notebook*, it means that true love never dies. In *Crime and Punishment*, when Raskolnikov is consumed by madness after burying an axe in a hateful old woman's head, it means that murder is wrong, that even when we take the lives of the most despicable people, we give up our humanity. When the father at the end of the Harry Chapin song "Cat's in the Cradle" realizes that his own son has no time for him, it means we must prioritize each other, not the bullshit of life. If these changes are not earned, they feel like a hustle. They feel like lies.

We come to storytellers to find the truth. They help us better understand and deal with the inevitable changes that even the richest, most powerful, and most beautiful among us must endure. And the writers we love best inspire us because they validate our experience. They dignify the struggle. It hurts to change. Whether it's your body, job, home, relationship status, skill set—*anything*—it is not easy to manage the emotions, setbacks, and adjustments that are required to truly change.

We've talked before about the "math" of story. Every time something significant changes, we must believe it all adds up, that Character A experiencing events B, C, and D would become E. Here are three things to consider:

- Distance traveled
- Change comes hard
- Psychological insight

Distance traveled

If the story tracks a hardcore atheist's transformation into a priest, that covers more distance than one traveled by a man who has always loved Jesus. There's no right or wrong here. Every character has their own unique journey, every story its own needs. Some stories feature a change that covers a great distance—a homeless youth rises up from the street to become a billionaire. Others cover a small distance—a troubled soul asks for help. Either way, the change must be earned by making each step along the journey convincing. If the homeless youth excels at math, earns a scholarship to a top school, finds a mentor, invents a product, raises venture capital, generates sales, and takes the company public—and we believe every step—then that works. In stories that track change that occurs over a shorter distance, you need to lower the microscope in order to explore each step along the way. For example, if the character feels utterly hopeless and devoid of all feeling, just making it out of bed, into the shower, into clothes, and onto the train to work can require superhuman strength. If a step along the way to asking for help includes fully realizing that life cannot continue this way, this can be extremely compelling and convincing.

You also want to factor in your genre. Grand, sweeping, action-adventure stories tend to travel greater distances than family dramas. In Chapter 13 we discussed Kamala Khan's transformation from troubled teenager into Ms. Marvel. In Eugene O'Neill's play *Long Day's Journey into Night*, a family moves from a very dark place to an even darker one over the course of a single day, as they rage at each other and attempt to soothe their wounds with drugs and alcohol. The key point here is to be aware of the distance your hero's transformation travels, so that you can know what you'll need to make it authentic.

Change comes hard

As we discussed in Chapter 5, "Escalate risk," humans are hardwired to conserve energy and avoid loss. Things have to get pretty bad to get us to change. A smoker doesn't quit until he's had a heart attack. A worker doesn't switch jobs until his boss makes life intolerable. A married couple doesn't go to counseling until they've had a brutal fight in front of the kids. Even when it's for the better, we fear change. It's uncomfortable, it's unknown, it could make our loved ones see us differently. If you've ever tried to change how you eat or when you wake up, you know how hard it can be. Just when you make some progress, you backslide. Change rarely moves in a simple, straight line from A to B.

In the example above, about the wife coming to realize she wants a divorce, she's not going to simply decide that her husband is an intolerable bastard and call a divorce lawyer. If her husband is that awful, the marriage is probably not worth writing about. Maybe he is self-involved—but can also be kind, and is a wonderful father. The night she decides to tell him, she sees him playing with their sons and is struck by guilt at the thought of separating him from his boys. We move toward what we need, then back off. We dance around it, then recommit. As Jerry tells Elaine on *Seinfeld*, "Breaking up is like knocking over a Coke machine, you can't do it in one push. You gotta rock it back and forth a few times and then it goes over." This is also good for your narrative, as it keeps readers guessing how things will turn out.

Psychological insight

To get into the depths of Freudian psychology is beyond the scope of this book. But to realistically explore how and why characters change—or fail to change—requires some insight into how the mind works. The following is just the simplest overview to salt your tip jar. Freud believed that we have a conscious, subconscious, and unconscious mind—things we're aware of, only partially aware of, and not aware of at all. We have constructive and destructive secret desires fueled by our instincts. These desires must be managed and controlled to help us avoid negative consequences that can lead to punishment and humiliation. To protect ourselves, we repress our scariest and most uncomfortable thoughts, deny reality that terrifies us, and regress to childlike states. We sublimate urges by trading unacceptable desires for acceptable ones—an aggressive man becomes a surgeon so he can cut up bodies without going to jail. We project our insecurity and fear onto other people and accuse them of being what we fear we are. A preacher who doubts Jesus is the savior threatens everyone else with eternal damnation. A man who fears he's weak works out relentlessly to prove his masculinity. Again, this is oversimplified, but understanding basic psychology—the subconscious, repression, regression, sublimation, and projection—is very useful.

So how do you know if you nailed it, if the change that you've written has been truly "earned"? Two helpful words to consider are transcendence and resonance. When your story captures an authentic transformation, the character seems to transcend the story, and the meaning resonates. The character feels archetypal, what they've become at the end of your story represents a primal aspect of the human experience. When Adam and Eve are kicked out of the Garden of Eden and turn to see angels with flaming swords blocking the gate back in, they feel like the personification of the human disconnection from God. In Chapter 22, "Craft actionable dialogue," we'll break down the scene from *Death of a Salesman* where Willy Loman is stripped of his dignity as he loses his job. In his excruciating transformation from a man who feels valuable to one who feels worthless, he becomes a symbol of every person who has ever felt discarded.

• • •

Remember, these principles are not recipes you follow to bake a masterpiece. If you could just press a few buttons and yank a few pulleys to write a masterpiece, what fun would that be? What insight would you gain? So, how do you know when you've written a convincing transformation? You rely on your own judgment, intellect, taste, and style. If it feels authentic to you, that's good enough.

HOW A MASTER DID IT

Fun Home: A Family Tragicomic (2006)
Alison Bechdel

The author of the long-running comic strip *The Essential Dykes to Watch Out For*, Alison Bechdel, wrote *Fun Home* as an attempt to better understand herself by examining her troubled relationship with her father. The 232-page graphic memoir features psychologically complex characters, elegant prose packed with allusions to classic literature, and sharp, insightful dialogue. Deeply personal and uniquely revealing, it feels like equal parts comic strip, novel, and fine art exhibit. Like everything in this book, the title and subtitle are layered with meaning. The title refers to the funeral home her father ran, which she and her two brothers were allowed to play in as kids. But it also refers to the fact that this family, with a very unhappy marriage at its center, was often anything but fun. That it's a "tragicomic" alludes to both the genre—it's moving and often darkly comedic—and its form, a comic. At the heart of the story is a profound transformation that occurs within the narrator, who is also the main character.

Bechdel undergoes three transformations that coalesce into a whole, like rivers flowing into a sea. Her body changes from a child's to a young woman's. Her understanding of her own sexuality, or "erotic truth," changes from ignorance to understanding. And her feelings toward her father change from judgment to empathy, even love. In a November 5, 2017, interview in the *Guardian*, Bechdel said,

> I remember being so excited when I read about Virginia Woolf getting her mother out of her head by writing *To the Lighthouse*. I felt the same after *Fun Home*. I had been haunted by my father and I no longer was.

When you read this graphic memoir, which features nearly one thousand panels and took Bechdel seven years to finish, you sense this claim rings true.

The story, which is a pure character study (as opposed to a plot-driven page-turner), revolves around Bechdel's exploration of her father's life and the development of her own identity. The action takes place in a large, old home in the small town of Beech Creek in central Pennsylvania. Her father, Bruce, was almost pathologically dedicated to restoring and decorating their home. Though married, and a father of three, he was either bisexual or homosexual, and engaged in many affairs with attractive young men. His personal tastes veered heavily toward what is traditionally considered feminine—ornamental furniture and floral prints. But he aggressively stifled Bechdel's own preferences for traditionally male attributes. He was killed at age forty-four, when he was hit by a truck on a country road. Throughout the book, Alison gradually discovers her own sexual identity—she's a lesbian—as she tries to make sense of her father's life and mysterious death. He may have committed suicide by deliberately jumping in front of the truck, after learning that his wife wanted a divorce.

Now, let's go through the changes that fuel this coming-of-age story—to her body, sense of self, and view of her father.

Though the change to her body may seem obvious—every girl who moves through a story from roughly age nine to nineteen changes from a girl to a young woman—Bechdel captures the discomfort, confusion, awkwardness, pain, fear, and wonder of it so well, it plays a key role in the story. There's an understated humanity to the way Bechdel explores these intimate subjects—getting your first period, having your first orgasm, growing breasts—that makes them memorable and notable markers on her transition to adulthood. In one panel, she sits alone in the bathroom looking at her stained underwear. In another, she bumps her budding breasts on the edge of a pool and the pain jolts her. And in still another, she twists on her chair and doesn't know what's happening when she climaxes. She is so mortified by the thought of getting her period that she develops coded language to discuss it in her diary. And she buries the box of sanitary napkins her mother gave her way back in her closet.

These moments are infused with pathos because she has no one to talk to—no close friend or older sister. The changes hurt, physically and emotionally. When she finally works up the courage to talk to her mom about her period, her mother shares some bad news. Her father got arrested for buying an underage boy a beer. He may lose his second job teaching high school English. And if that happens, they'll have to move. The moment is far from the one that kids dream of, in which a dedicated parent lovingly explains the transitions of life. Alison's needs come second to those of her damaged parents. And she'll have to navigate the changes to her body on her own.

Her attempt to figure out her own sexuality is even harder, as she is not just navigating solo, but actively repressed. As early as she can remember, Bechdel wanted to wear her hair short, dress like a boy, and avoid anything feminine. But her father forced her to wear dresses and put barrettes in her hair—he would even threaten to smack her if she took them out. She liked to play games that boys play—pretending to be a cop, making a gun out of her fingers. Her cousins called her "Butch." She hated the flowers her father was always arranging. And one time, while visiting a construction site, she was overcome by the urge to convince the workers she was a boy whose name was Albert.

Another time her dad takes her on a business trip to Philadelphia and they stop at a restaurant for lunch. A thick-bodied woman with a flannel shirt, jeans, and close-cropped hair comes in. Little Alison is stunned. She writes, "I didn't know there were women who wore men's clothes and had men's haircuts. But like a traveler in a foreign country who runs into someone from home—someone they've never spoken to, but know by sight—I recognized her with a sense of joy." Her father cruelly asks, "Is *that* what you want to look like?" She's bullied into saying no, but adds, "The vision of the truck-driving bulldyke sustained me through the years."

Change comes hard. Here's this adorable little girl on a business trip to the big city with her dad. It's the ideal time to connect, to share, and be vulnerable. And here she has this revelatory, joyful moment. She's found her tribe. And what does her own father do? He *shames* her. This will condemn her to years of isolation and confusion. Keep in mind, this the 1970s. There's no internet to help you find like-minded souls, no TV shows featuring lesbian characters, no "woke" teachers to help figure things out. Alison's sexual identity is so repressed, she doesn't fully realize that she's gay until she reads about lesbianism in a book as a freshman in college. She eventually joins the gay student union, meets a girl, falls in love, and has her first sexual encounter. Though ultimately positive, her self-discovery is a long, painful process that takes over a decade to play out.

Like the transformation of her body, this one, too, is convincingly portrayed and feels earned, because Bechdel infuses each panel with pathos and psychological complexity. For example, in the panel where she answers "no" to her father's accusatory question, she's staring over the booth at the female truck driver with her back turned to her father. There are no tears, no histrionics, no expectations. She is too little then to understand what any of it means. A closeted homosexual, who as a child wanted to be a girl, her father is, on some level, jealous of the truck driver's openness about her identity. At the same time, he wants his daughter to be the girl he could never be. As a storyteller, Bechdel wrings so much emotion out of each panel, one feels that each step of her journey is fully realized. She "earns" her self-discovery by merely continuing to stay true to herself, even as a small child.

This brings us to the story of Alison and her father. Throughout the first part of the book, he comes off as a talented, driven man obsessed with beautifying his home. But he's negative, tyrannical, narcissistic, and often absurd. He flies into a tizzy if anyone comments on his appearance, and spanks the kids for little to no reason. No one else has any say in how their home looks, the kids don't even get to weigh in on their own bedrooms. Though he'll play cards and do things with the kids, he's not affectionate. He hardly ever touches his wife. Bechdel can recall very few instances of physical affection between anyone in the family, and the one time she herself tried to kiss her father, she awkwardly grabbed his hand and pecked, then rushed out of the room, embarrassed.

But their relationship changes when she gets to high school and enrolls in her father's class. They are both avid readers and enjoy discussing the classics. He feels she is the only student worth teaching, and she feels he's her best teacher. He begins to see her as almost a friend or mentee, someone he can share his love of literature with. And she relishes his attention. But when she goes off to college and studies literature, his obsessive nature and hyper-opinionated take on every book becomes overwhelming.

A pivotal moment comes when Bechdel sends her parents a letter, informing them that she is gay. She is devastated by her mother's response, which is to coldly encourage her to reconsider. Her father sends her back a letter casually mentioning his own decision not to "take a stand," which is odd, as the two never formally discussed his sexuality. He just assumes she knew. This causes her to consider his upbringing, and how it was even more difficult for a young man from a small town in the 1950s and 1960s to come out of the closet. When he went to college there were no organizations or outlets of any kind for kids to safely express their homosexuality. And she wonders what she would have done if she had come of age in an earlier and even more restrictive time.

Home from college for an extended visit, Bechdel attempts to broach the subject with her father as they polish silverware, but she can see the terror on his face from the very subtle way his eyes widen, and lets it go. Later in the week, her father drives her to see a movie. She steels herself to try again. The scene is laid out across two pages and is broken into twenty-four little, equal-sized boxes. The station wagon's roof is drawn in all black. There's nothing outside the window behind Dad but the empty night sky. It feels as if the car is moving and still at the same time. She asks him if he sent her a book by the lesbian writer Colette because he knows she's gay. He denies it. Then admits it. Then says there was an "identification." He tells her about his first encounter with a farmhand, which he describes as "nice." He mentions another experience in college. And confesses that as a boy, he wanted to be a girl, and used to dress up in women's clothes. In a flash of recognition and excitement, she exclaims, "I wanted to be a boy! I dressed in boys' clothes." But he doesn't respond, just stares coldly forward. She feebly asks, "Remember?" And then slips into comparing their lives to characters in mythology and literature. This is as close as they'll ever get.

After she returns to college, they exchange a few more letters, and, on her last visit home, he takes her to a gay bar for a drink, and they're mortified when they can't get in. They play the duet "Heart and Soul" on the piano. A family friend, watching them play, calls them "unnaturally close," then corrects himself, "unusually close." She thinks to herself that they were close, but not close enough. In the end, she finds a sense of closure. But it's not a simple, black-and-white thing. Her father never validates her experience, apologizes for his behavior, or offers helpful guidance. If anything, she feels more like *his* parent. The psychological complexity of their relationship, the convincing way it's portrayed, radiates authenticity. There's no great catharsis, no false moments of divine revelation, no radical change in their relationship. But there's the sense that, in her eyes, he became just human and fallible enough to ease her resentment and free her from his oppressive influence.

The authenticity of her hard-fought transformation from a repressed and troubled child to a free and confident young woman is a major reason the work has won so many accolades, and was turned into a Tony Award–winning musical. It tells us that if we fight the good fight long enough—if we stay on the path and reflect honestly upon the truth of who we are—we can make peace with our parents and, more importantly, ourselves.

HOW YOU DO IT

The following bullet points will help you think through and execute the principle.

▶ Identify the transformation that occurs in your character. Jot it down in its simplest form. A kid becomes a prince, a woman grows lonely, a good man becomes a killer.

▶ Break out a notebook and sketch a little timeline, with beginning and end points. At the first point, write a brief description of the character. Keep it simple. "Happily married, pharmacist, age 35." At the last point, do the same thing. "Age 37, miserable, enters prison to serve life sentence."

▶ Get clear in your mind that *change comes hard*. This is essential. As we discussed in the fifth principle, "Escalate risk," human beings are hardwired to conserve energy and avoid loss. We only change when we must, and even then it comes slow. I know a woman who knew on her wedding day that she was making a mistake. It took her twenty years to correct it. That meant two decades of lonely nights, countless fights, years of therapy, bouts of tormenting guilt, and falling in love with another man until she finally got divorced. Whether the change is positive or negative, it comes hard.

▶ Consider your story's genre and the distance traveled. Again, some stories travel a great distance and the hero undergoes immense change, others explore smaller transitions in minute detail. What kind of change are you tracking?

▶ Start with the essentials. What *must* happen for your character to make this transformation? If a character becomes a murderer, they must kill someone. If a couple splits up, they must agree to break up. Or one must realize the other's gone.

▶ Work around these necessary moments. If a couple breaks up, something must happen to cause the break—one cheats, they have a terrible fight, one finds God—and add these to the timeline. What caused the fight? Who cheated and why? Maybe you want to show the day one moves out. When you add something to the timeline, it often necessitates adding something else. This helps develop your plot.

▶ Add depth, texture, and detail to the key moments. Make them count. If your story's about a couple that's going to break up, and you put "fight" on the timeline, it must be a really nasty bit of business to drive the final nail into the marriage's coffin.

▶ You'll know you have it when you can do the math. Because character A does B, C, D, and E, they become F. As you develop your story and fill the timeline, be ruthlessly logical. Lay out your case like a prosecutor before a jury. Imagine a defense attorney attempting to poke holes in your argument. Keep working until the case for the transformation is airtight.

MINI FINAL EXAM

Read the following, then answer the question below.

A worker comes to his office excited. This is the day he's going to ask for a raise. They just gave one to his buddy and, since he's been there longer, they'll have to give him one too. He's so sure the boss will say yes that he's booked a table at the most expensive restaurant in town so he can break the news to his wife in style. He's struck by a jolt of nerves when he asks the owner if they can talk. She invites him into her office. They sit. A cloud passes across the sun and the room darkens. He lays out his case, then asks for the raise. The owner says she appreciates his candor and respects his points. But business is down, and she has to say no. He mentions the raise that his friend got. It's not fair. He's been there longer. She tells him flat out that his friend works harder and has a superior skill set. They don't give promotions based on longevity. With barely concealed anger, he says he will have to look for another job. She stays silent. They both know there are no better jobs in town. Rain pelts the windows. He thanks her for her time and slinks out.

True or false? The scene doesn't work because nothing changes.

CONTINUING ED

In the 1981 romantic comedy horror film *An American Werewolf in London*, David Kessler and his friend Jack Goodman are trekking across the moors at night on a trip through the United Kingdom, just after graduating from college. They are savagely attacked by a gruesome animal that looks like a cross between a wild boar and a wolf. It's a lycanthrope—a mythical creature that, once it bites you, causes you to transform into one whenever the moon is full. Jack is killed but David survives. One night, alone in his girlfriend's apartment, when the moon is full,

David sits alone reading a book. He suddenly rises to his feet and shouts at the top of his lungs that he is burning up. He completely transforms from a handsome, pleasant young man into a monstrous lycanthrope. You can find this scene online. (As of this writing, it is posted to YouTube as "An American Werewolf in London [1981]—Transformation Scene.") Carefully go through all two minutes and thirty-one seconds of the scene and list every single element of David's transformation. Study how his attitude gradually changes throughout. Notice how fully aware of this change he is.

This scene is an excellent metaphor for how to fully earn all transformations. Because it's so visceral, emotional, and painful, it is a beautiful (if ghastly) example of what it feels like to change. The storytellers painstakingly capture every last detail so that by the time the transformation is complete, it's convincing.

MINI FINAL ANSWER

False. Although the worker's employment status doesn't change, his feelings about himself and his job do. He changes from feeling excited to depressed, valuable to unappreciated.

18

Motivate fierce antagonists.

"Say you pick, as your villain a gutless pigeon, a gabby, twitching nobody. Your protagonist needs little heroic savvy to wipe him out. He almost has to stoop to do it. But if the heavy is a corrupt genius, towering with boodle and clout, then your hero must chop a lot of wood to bring him down."
—WELLS ROOT, Screenwriter

QUICK TAKE

The antagonist has one purpose: to prevent your hero from acquiring their object of desire. The hallmark of the weak writer is they make it too easy for the protagonist to get what they need. Consider a story about a little boy who wants to make it onto the best Little League baseball team in his area. There's only one spot left. So he goes down to the baseball diamond and walks up to the coach, who says, "Congratulations, kid! We were hoping you'd stop by. Welcome to the club." That's not a story. That's just some shit that happens. We learn nothing about the kid, the coach, the team, or life in general.

You, as the writer, have to work harder and make the character sing for their supper. If the kid gets to the field and sees ten other kids there who all want the same spot, and one of them is a bully from his class who he despises but who also happens to be a tremendous ballplayer, we're in business. The harder the hero has to work, the more compelling, entertaining, and necessary your story. Therefore, you must create fiercely motivated antagonists and write them with the same passion, intensity, depth, and commitment as your main character. These two forces go to all-out war and, as a result, reveal the truth of who they are.

HOW IT WORKS

The antagonist is as determined to prevent the protagonist from acquiring their object of desire as the protagonist is to get it. This is a big deal because protagonists are extremely determined. Consider the heroes and their respective objects of desire we've discussed so far—Hamlet to avenge his father's murder, Tish to get Fonny out of jail, Alison Bechdel to learn the true nature of her father—their honor, freedom, and peace of mind are at stake.

If a part of you feels intimidated, or even terrified, by the task of creating two conflicting forces who will stop at nothing to achieve their diametrically opposed objectives, who are active and decisive, who operate at the top of their intelligence, who are willing to escalate risk until there's nothing left to lose, and you realize how much energy and thought and feeling you're going to have to summon to pull this off, that's good. It means you get it.

Now let's look at different types of antagonists. An antagonist can be a person with good or evil intentions, any other living creature, a supernatural being, an element or force of nature, or an aspect of the hero's own personality. Sometimes there is no formal, single antagonist in a story. The forces that stand in opposition to the hero might vary, and function in aggregate as an antagonist. We'll explore each one of these possibilities below.

When the antagonist is a person or conscious being, they view themselves as the hero of their own story, and the hero as the antagonist. The hammer drops for them once they realize that the hero wants to acquire their object of desire. The antagonist may want to acquire the same thing for legitimate reasons. Apollo Creed doesn't have an evil bone in his body. He doesn't lie, cheat, or steal. He just wants to knock Rocky out because that's what boxers do. All villains are antagonists but not all antagonists are villains. In the next chapter, "Confront evil," we'll explore the dark side. For now, the important point is, regardless of their rationale, antagonists are dedicated to preventing the hero from acquiring their object of desire.

In the novel and film adaptation of *The Notebook* for example, Anne Hamilton wants to keep her daughter Allie from marrying Noah because she genuinely believes that marrying a working-class man will limit Allie's opportunities in life and kill her chance at happiness. She believes that preventing the lovers from achieving their object of desire (each other) is the right thing to do. And when she realizes that her motives are questionable, she adjusts her behavior. She is far from a villain.

It may be hard to tell who the hero and antagonist really are. In the TV show *Breaking Bad*, Walter White just wants to leave some money for his family before his cancer kills him, by manufacturing and distributing crystal meth. He believes that meth users are going to do drugs anyway, so he's not really doing anything wrong. In his mind, his brother-in-law, DEA agent Hank Schroeder, is the antagonist.

An antagonist doesn't have to be human—they can be an animal, a supernatural creature, or from an alien race. All of the same qualities that apply to people apply to non-humans. They too might be noble-intentioned beings with good reasons to stand in the way of protagonists. In Stanley Kubrick's classic 1968 science fiction epic *2001: A Space Odyssey*, the monoliths are markers placed by an unseen alien race to track human progress. They realize that human beings are not spiritually evolved enough to constructively participate in the universe. When Dr. Heywood Floyd travels to Clavius Base, an outpost on the moon, the monolith lets out a deafening noise that's as much for humankind's own good as anything else. It's telling them to turn back, that they don't belong this far out.

In Mary Shelley's *Frankenstein*, which we explored in Chapter 8, "Begin the end with a critical decision," the "monster" just wants to live in peace, to be loved, and to contribute what he can. He is understandably infuriated by his creator Dr. Victor Frankenstein's rejection of him and refusal to create a female fellow being who might love and understand him and assuage his intense loneliness.

An antagonist can be a mountain—with its impossible altitudes, high winds, and steep cliffs—as it is in John Krakauer's true story of climbers who were killed descending from the summit of Mt. Everest in the book *Into Thin Air*. On the smash hit TV series *Deadliest Catch*, fishermen battle powerful storms, driving snow, and freezing temperatures as they navigate the Bering Sea off the coast of Alaska in their never-ending quest to fill their thousand-pound pots with crab.

In John Valliant's book *The Tiger: A True Story of Vengeance and Survival*, the residents of a remote village in Russia's far east do battle with a man-eating tiger. But the more we learn about the history of tigers in the region, and the abuse they've suffered at the hands of humans, as well as their seeming consciousness and sense of justice, it is hard to tell who the real hero and antagonist are.

It's even possible for an aspect of the protagonist's personality to be the antagonist. In the 2000 slapstick comedy *Me, Myself & Irene*, Jim Carrey plays the hero, Charlie Balleygates, a Rhode Island motorcycle cop who falls madly in love with a young woman who is being pursued by her mobbed-up ex-boyfriend. But Charlie has a split personality and his dark alter ego, who calls himself Hank, has feelings for the same girl. Hank is played as if he is a completely different character from Charlie. They just happen to inhabit the same body.

The types of people, beings, and forces that can serve as your antagonists are virtually unlimited. They may be good or evil, active or passive, conscious or unaware of how they stand in the way of your hero. But what they *must* do is present powerful obstacles for your hero to overcome in order to secure their object of desire. And it is through this struggle to overcome all obstacles that your hero's true nature is revealed. By watching this struggle and analyzing its implications, we discover truths about the nature of life, gain insights into our own humanity, and find better, healthier, more authentic ways to live.

HOW A MASTER DID IT

The Piano Lesson (1936)
August Wilson

Set in a working class black neighborhood in Pittsburgh in 1936, August Wilson's play *The Piano Lesson* is fueled by its fiercely poetic dialogue, heartbreaking backstories, comedy, the supernatural, and the blues. The play explores the fear, hope, connections, and longing of people who are just a few generations past slavery. Haunted by its legacy of violence, degradation, and murder, they struggle to confront the past without being consumed by it. The action is set in a home owned by Doaker, a retired railroad worker, who lives with his niece, Berniece, and her twelve-year-old daughter, Maretha. The all-black cast features a diverse assortment of temperaments and storylines that revolve around borrowing money, sharing whiskey, sex, and romance. But the main storyline that we will focus on here is an intense sibling rivalry.

The action starts when Berniece's brother, Boy Willie, arrives at 5:00 a.m. after a long ride from Mississippi in a rickety old truck. He and his buddy, Lymon, have filled the truck with watermelons and plan to sell them in a white neighborhood when the sun comes up. Boy Willie's a farmer who wants to buy the land his ancestors worked as slaves. The land became available when its fat white owner, Sutter, fell down a well. Sutter's ancestors owned Berniece and Boy Willie's ancestors. The new owner told Boy Willie he would sell it to him, and promised to wait until Boy Willie got back from up north with enough money to meet his price. Boy Willie has a third of the money. He's going to make another third by selling the watermelons. And the last third by selling an old piano he and Berniece own together.

The watermelons are easy to sell and go like hotcakes in the white community. Boy Willie hawks them by falsely claiming the seeds were mixed with sugar, making them extra sweet. This is vintage August Wilson. He takes a loaded symbol, the watermelon, which whites have used to stereotype and insult black people for ages, and has his hero hustle them with that same symbol. White people love watermelon every bit as much as black people. Now that Boy Willie has the money from the watermelons, all that's left to do is sell the piano. The problem is, Berniece won't let him.

Let's quickly review the basics. From Boy Willie's point of view, he is the hero. His object of desire is the piano, which he needs to acquire some land. His uncle, Doaker, tells him a white man nearby pays good money for musical instruments, and once offered Berniece real money for the piano—easily enough for Boy Willie to buy the land. The situation is urgent. Boy Willie fears that if he doesn't get back down south immediately, the land will be sold out from under him. From this angle, the Central Dramatic Question is, "Will Boy Willie sell the piano?" And the antagonist is Berniece. She will not sell the piano under any circumstance.

From Berniece's point of view, she is the hero of the story. Her object of desire is to keep the piano. And her Central Dramatic Question is simply "Will Berniece keep the piano?" For Berniece, Boy Willie is the antagonist. In order to acquire, or keep, her object of desire, she must repel Boy Willie. Though he loves and respects her and would not stoop to violence or threats against his own sister, he comes after her with everything he's got.

From a neutral observer's standpoint, the CDQ is "Who will get the piano?" Both characters are so well drawn and fiercely motivated, and both have such a legitimate claim to the piano, that either one could be seen as the story's true hero or its antagonist. Now let's look at the two combatants.

Boy Willie is desperate to buy the land because he believes it is the only way to be equal to whites. He feels that through racism, intimidation, and corrupt application of the law, whites force blacks to either grovel at their feet or resort to lives of crime. The fact that his ancestors worked the land as slaves makes this land infinitely more valuable to him than any other land; it would not only provide him an income, but he'd be buying the dignity of his family. He has a monologue about watching his father staring at his hands and realizing that, although his hands are big, strong, and capable of doing anything, he has no valid way to put them to use. The look of futility on his father's face shaped Boy Willie's entire worldview and inspired his intense desire to control his own fate. He believes that his ancestors would be proud to see him own land. And since the land can provide a living, year after year, it's much more valuable than a piano. He is a big, intense man, with a loud mouth and unshakable spirit. Once he gets it in his mind to do something, no one can change it. (On a personal note, I saw the actor Charles "Roc" Dutton play the role, and the moment he describes the look of futility on his father's face was among the most moving things in theater.)

Boy Willie's cause is valid and inspired. And he is operating at the top of his intelligence. He knows farming (and has no other marketable skill), the land is affordable, and he can build a meaningful life on it. He can reclaim the place where his ancestors suffered unimaginable pain. So Berniece must be an inhuman monster to stand in Boy Willie's way, right?

Wrong.

Though smart, iron-willed, and attractive, Berniece carries herself with an air of defeat. She's been gravely wounded by life, and it permeates her being. She works as a cleaning lady for a rich white family. They are so venal and petty, they dock her bus fare if she's a few minutes late. They couldn't care less that she's a single mother. But these small indignities are nothing compared to the loss she suffered. Years ago, her husband Crawley, whom she loved dearly, was murdered. She not only still grieves his loss, she still blames Boy Willie, and harbors bitter resentment for Crawley's death. Boy Willie was moving wood for some white men. He kept (stole) some for himself to sell, by dropping it off in the woods. Boy Willie and Crawley went to get it late at night and got caught. Boy Willie claims Crawley tried to get tough and was beaten to death. He insists that Crawley knew what he was getting into and caused his own death. All Berniece knows is that Crawley left with Boy Willie and never came back. This is another key theme in Wilson's work, how oppression causes the oppressed to turn on each other. In Berniece's mind, Boy Willie killed her husband, not the men who actually did the killing.

The piano is not just any piano. It was once traded for their great-great-grandmother and her son, their great-grandfather. It has a rich history. Their grandfather was a woodworker who carved images of their family history into the piano. Their grandmother polished it every day, literally mixing her own blood and sweat into the wood. Though Berniece could play as a child, she never touches the piano now. It is the only thing she owns. She plans to get her daughter piano lessons one day, so Maretha can become a music teacher.

Whomever you regard as the hero and antagonist, both are not only fiercely motivated, but also three dimensional, flawed, and fully human. While Boy Willie is too cavalier in his willingness to sell the piano, Berniece's inability to even play it is symbolic of her inability to deal with the family's past. Both are active and decisive, constantly on each other to overcome the obstacle the other presents. And as a result, both ultimately grow from the experience.

Throughout the play, the house is haunted by the ghost of Sutter, the fat white guy who fell down the well. Berniece suspects the ghost has come to seek vengeance on Boy Willie for pushing him down the well in a scheme to steal the land. As Boy Willie moves to take the piano out of the house, the ghost rages, drawing Boy Willie into a fight upstairs. As they thrash about, Berniece is drawn to the piano. She plays and sings. Wilson describes it as an "old urge to song that is both commandment and a plea. With each repetition it gains strength. It is intended as an exorcism and a dressing for battle. A rustle of wind blowing across two continents." As her brother fights a ghost, she cries out to her ancestors, "I want you to help me." The ghost vanishes as Boy Willie rages for it to come back. Finally, he relents and leaves to catch a train back south. He warns her that if she doesn't play the piano, he and Sutter's ghost might return. Wilson writes, "A calm comes over the house." Berniece, spent and grateful, has the last line, her simple "Thank you."

The reason that this play works so well is that Wilson created not one but two main characters, and both serve as fiercely motivated antagonists for each other. The object of desire they seek is essential to them in the most personal and primal way. The piano connects Berniece to her ancestors and offers her a chance to express herself. She is teetering on the verge of spiritual death. Though she must live to provide for her daughter, she is almost zombielike in how she moves through the world after losing the love of her life to a senseless murder. For Boy Willie, the piano is a path to dignity, freedom, and success. That their own sibling stands in their way takes the stakes to the next level.

This is not to say that Wilson set out to write fierce sibling antagonists. In fact, in an interview with David Savran in the book *In Their Own Words, Contemporary American Playwrights*, Wilson says that this play was inspired by the question, "Can one acquire a sense of self-worth by denying the past?" and that he took the title from a painting called *The Piano Lesson*. When he first started writing, he had four men moving a piano onto the stage. He saw the creative process as one of discovery, and always trusted that he'd figure out the characters and story as he wrote. Those four men eventually morphed into the brother and sister battling over the piano. We don't know if he ever consciously considered the principle "Motivate fierce antagonists," we only know that he executed it in practice. And that's valuable information.

HOW YOU DO IT

The following bullet points will help you think through and execute the principle.

▶ When you create your antagonist, view them as the hero. The hammer drops on them as soon as they learn the hero wants to acquire their object of desire. The antagonist either has the same object of desire—again, Apollo Creed has every right to want to defeat Rocky—or the antagonist believes it would be a terrible thing if the hero acquired their object of desire. They feel it will hurt the hero, the world, or themselves. Whatever it is, from the antagonist's point of view, the worst thing that can happen is for the hero to acquire their object of desire.

▶ Go through every principle in this section and make sure you've created your antagonist with the same level of detail—and genuine love—as you have your hero. The antagonist too must be active and decisive, confront dilemma, be deeply conflicted, operate at the top of their intelligence, wear a mask, and transform as a result of the story. This will make them powerful enough to force your hero to work harder and reveal more of their true nature. If your story were a business, this would be the antagonist's job at the firm.

▶ Know *why* your antagonist is opposed to the hero acquiring their object of desire. Be specific. This will make it much easier to tell your story. But that said, the truth is sometimes you don't know what motivates your antagonist, only that they will stop at nothing to thwart your hero. Four hundred years after

Shakespeare wrote *Othello*, scholars still debate why Iago was so determined to destroy him. If you don't know what motivates your antagonist, you'll need to justify excluding this information. In *Othello*, it's essential to the story's theme, which is specifically that we'll never understand the true nature of evil.

▶ Make it personal. Leverage your experience. Have you ever had a friend or relative who wanted something that you were certain was terrible for them? For example, your son is dating a boy you feel is duplicitous. Did you ever fall in love with someone and have to watch in agony as they chose your close friend over you? Whether or not your feelings were justified or rational, all you knew was that you did not want your friend to get what they wanted. Once you're able to access this intense feeling, crank up the intensity and give it to your antagonist.

▶ Lastly, remember that even if your antagonist is evil, bad guys don't consider themselves evil. Hitler felt he was restoring Germany's honor, ridding the nation of filth, and building a more powerful race.

▶ Have fun. Remember, in a story no one really gets hurt. This is your chance to cause mayhem, to let out your inner trouble-maker, to break some hearts. Explore what you could be if you weren't constrained by morality and ethics. You might just learn something essential about yourself.

MINI FINAL EXAM

Read the following, then answer the question below.

A young mother, an event planner on her way to visit relatives in the country, schleps heavy bags and a stroller onto a Greyhound bus. Her three-year-old boy, Joey, relentlessly fidgets in her arms as she struggles to get situated. As the bus pulls out, she patiently explains to him that Mommy has to make a "very, very, *very* important phone call" for work. He moans "nooooo." She tells him not to whine, and fills a sippy cup with juice, but he swats it away. She pulls out some books and a tiny toy dump truck, but he ignores them. She puts headphones onto his ears and plugs them into her phone, then plays a little cartoon, but he's not interested in it. She checks the time as she walks him up and down the aisle, playfully kissing his cheek. With one hand, she finds the number she needs to call, then hesitates. "Okay, Jo-Jo, we're going to play a game." This gets his attention. He knows he might be able to play this for some cookies. She *hates* to make these nefarious deals, but sometimes a busy mom's gotta do what she's gotta do. "If you can stay quiet while Mommy talks, you can have a box of animal crackers." His eyes go wide. This he understands. He smiles mischievously and rests his cheek on her shoulder. She puts her headphones in and makes the call.

If the story was rewritten so that the little boy is a perfectly behaved little gentleman, this would most likely:

a) Reveal more about the mother's true character, because we would know she has great genes.
b) Make the story more compelling, as the mom would have more to do.
c) Make the boy's character more interesting, because well-behaved kids are rare these days.
d) Make the story less compelling and the mom less interesting, as there would be no dramatic question, nor anything for her to do.
e) Have no effect on the story, since it was hard enough to get the kid and all their stuff onto the bus.

CONTINUING ED

In Margaret Atwood's 1993 novel *The Robber Bride*, the antagonist is a woman named Zenia. Based on the number of lies she tells, the degree of damage she causes, and her level of commitment to destroying the romantic relationships of women who once considered her a friend, how "fierce" would you say she is? Why do you think the author Lorrie Moore wrote in the *New York Times* book review, "Zenia is what drives this book: she is impossibly, fantastically bad. She is pure theater, pure plot. She is Richard III with breast implants. She is Iago in a miniskirt."

MINI FINAL ANSWER

The correct answer is **d) Make the story less compelling and the mom less interesting, as there would be no dramatic question nor anything for her to do**. Because the kid is so difficult, he pushes her to work hard. Through her actions, we learn that she is resourceful, determined, empathetic, emotionally intelligent, moral, and willing to compromise.

19

Confront evil.

"God made man free to choose good or evil. And that is an astounding gift."
—ANTHONY BURGESS, Novelist

QUICK TAKE

Before we get into this heavy subject, it's important to note that you do *not* need to confront evil in every story. As mentioned in the last chapter, not all antagonists are malicious. So, if you favor lighthearted stories or you're particularly sensitive, you might want to skip this principle. But if you're interested in the dark side, if you're unafraid to stare down the very worst humankind has to offer, you need to approach this subject with respect. It is not easy. We're not talking about the cliché of evil—dastardly men with twirly mustaches who wear black capes. We're talking about reality—war, murder, rape, violence, terror, abuse, betrayal, and the suffering they cause.

When Toni Morrison confronts slavery in *Beloved* and Junot Diaz confronts dictatorship in *The Brief Wondrous Life of Oscar Wao*, you can feel the respect they brought to the task at hand. It's in their attention to detail, the depth of emotion, the clarity of their themes, and the poignancy of the questions they ask. *Beloved* is about the healing power of community, and raises questions about the nature of guilt. *Oscar Wao* is about the legacy of tyranny, and raises questions about masculinity and the risks inherent in love. When you confront evil in your work, rest assured that real people who have suffered real harm will find it. You owe it to them—and to yourself as an artist and yourself if you've been a victim—to approach the subject with love, courage, empathy, dignity, and respect.

HOW IT WORKS

Evil is the conscious infliction of suffering on people who do not deserve to suffer. The aggressor knows what they're doing. They *choose* to harm people. Though one can say that a mentally ill person who shoots up a school or a lover who erupts in a drunken rage upon learning of a betrayal have both committed evil deeds, this is not really what we're getting at here. We're talking about consciously inflicting extreme pain on innocent beings. And enjoying or drawing strength from it. And though tearing apart or abusing bodies is horrific, the damage goes far beyond the physical.

In his book *People of the Lie: The Hope for Healing Human Evil*, M. Scott Peck, a Harvard-educated psychiatrist and the author of the bestseller *The Road Less Traveled*, wrote,

> When I say that evil has to do with killing, I do not mean to restrict myself to corporeal murder. Evil is that which kills spirit. There are various essential attributes of life—particularly human life—such as sentience, mobility, awareness, growth, autonomy, will. It is possible to kill or attempt to kill one of these attributes without actually destroying the body. Thus we may "break" a horse or even a child without harming a hair on its head.

In story, death can of course be devastating. I don't need to remind anyone who has seen the films *Brokeback Mountain* or Pixar's *Up*, or watched Shakespeare's *Romeo and Juliet*, or read the kids' book *Charlotte's Web*. But we can't fathom what it means to be dead. It may be nonexistence. It may be a place in heaven or some higher realm. So, in story, it's often even more painful to experience a character giving up on life, being spiritually and psychologically defeated, than it is to have them die. And when this suffering is intentionally caused by an evil being, it unleashes a storm of emotion within us—rage, sorrow, confusion, hurt. Beyond these feelings are the two Aristotle identified as the hallmarks of tragedy: pity and fear. When we see a character suffer great harm, we pity them and fear it can happen to us.

On top of all this is the fact that we are all capable of committing evil deeds—each and every one of us could turn to the dark side. What the Devil sells is freedom and power. As Dostoevsky explored in *Crime and Punishment*, we're fascinated by the thought of being free from ethics, morality, guilt, and shame. We fantasize about acting on our desires, regardless of the pain we'd inflict on others or the perversity of our actions. And getting away with it. In *Crime and Punishment*, Raskolnikov is inspired to commit murder because he imagines that it if he can get away with it and handle the pressure, it will make him a superior man.

This brings us to your responsibility as a storyteller. If you are going to confront evil in your story, you must have something to say about it. Dostoevsky wanted to show that he understood—even sympathized with—Raskolnikov's desire to feel strong and free, but that Raskolnikov is wrong. He is upended by his own guilt. There is an inbred drive toward goodness in human beings that is repelled by evil.

Stephen King, whose work is arguably the greatest exploration of evil ever conducted by a single writer, said, "You must not come lightly to the blank page." This is especially true here, on the dark side.

HOW A MASTER DID IT

"The Lottery" (1948)
Shirley Jackson

It's a beautiful warm day in early summer; the flowers are in bloom. Children fill their pockets with stones as they head toward the town square for the drawing. Men arrive and exchange a few words about planting and tractors. They're followed by the women, who call for their children to come join them. Families stand together.

There is some talk of other towns abandoning the lottery, but this is dismissed by the elders as foolish, and something sure to result in the decline of their culture. They bemoan the degradation that's already occurred. The village used to conduct the lottery with a box full of wood chips, each with a citizen's name engraved on it, but now they do it with paper. There used to be songs and a chant, but that tradition has faded as well.

The lottery is held following strict rules. A round-faced, jovial man, Mr. Summers, calls out the names of men. These are the heads of households in this town of three hundred. He greets them kindly as they come up and one after another draw from the box. Everyone watches closely, nervously, excitedly. The men keep the slips of paper tightly in their fists and some hold them behind their backs. As the last man takes his slip of paper, a hush falls on the crowd. Each man looks at his paper and word quickly spreads that Mr. Hutchinson got it! His wife, Tessie, shouts, "You didn't give him enough time to pick any paper he wanted! I saw you. It wasn't fair!"

Mrs. Delacroix tells her, "Be a good sport, Tessie," and Mrs. Graves says, "All of us took the same chance." Mr. Hutchinson tells his wife to shut up. Mr. Summers asks if there are any other Hutchinson households. Mrs. Hutchinson shouts out, "There's Don and Eva. Make *them* take their chance!" But since Eva is married to Don, she is no longer a Hutchinson. The only ones included will be Mr. Hutchinson, Tessie, and their three children, Bill Jr., Nancy, and little Dave.

A town elder, Mr. Graves, helps gather five slips of paper, including the slip with the mark on it that Mr. Hutchinson drew. The five slips of paper are placed back in the black box. And one by one, each member of the family is called up to pick out a slip of paper. Mr. Graves helps little Dave fish one out, then Bill Jr. and Nancy each take one, then Tessie and her husband each take one as well. Then the kids open their slips of paper and are joyful to find that they're blank. Next, they ask Tessie to go, but she doesn't move. So her husband opens his. It's blank. Everyone knows what this means. It's Tessie Hutchinson! To confirm this, Mr. Hutchinson forces the slip of paper from her hand. He holds it up for all to see. There's the black spot drawn with a heavy pencil.

"All right," Mr. Summers says. "Let's finish quickly."

The crowd gathers up their stones. Neighbors rush to get in on the action. One woman picks up a stone so large, she has to use both hands. Little kids pull stones out of their pockets. Even Little Dave Hutchinson is given a few pebbles.

Tessie holds out her hands, desperate, terrified as a space is cleared for her to stand in and the mob forms around her. Someone throws a stone that hits her in the head. She cries, "It isn't fair, it isn't right." And the mob is "upon her."

• • •

Shirley Jackson was pushing her child in a stroller up a hill in Bennington, Vermont, when she was struck with the idea for "The Lottery." She ran home, wrote it fast, and dashed it off to her agent, who didn't get it at all, but agreed to send it over to *The New Yorker*. The editors, except one who felt it was "contrived," liked it and published it quickly. The response was immediate and overwhelming.

According to Jackson biographer Ruth Franklin, letters poured in, most from frustrated and confused readers who demanded to know what it meant. More than a few were enraged. Some found it so traumatic they said they could not read the magazine again. One woman said she read it in the tub and was tempted to drown herself. Several hundred people felt the need to write Jackson directly. They called her "perverted" and "gratuitously disagreeable." Jackson said that of the three hundred or so letters she received, only about thirteen were kind, and she joked that those were from friends. When an editor at the *San Francisco Chronicle* wrote that he was "stumped," Jackson replied, "I suppose I hoped, by setting a particularly brutal ancient rite in the present and in my own village, to shock the story's readers with a graphic dramatization of the pointless violence and general inhumanity in their own lives."

It's hard to fathom that after roughly one hundred million people were slaughtered in WWI and WWII, anyone could question a story about senseless violence. Franklin writes, "In 1948, with the fresh horrors of the Second World War barely receding into memory and the Red Scare just beginning, it is no wonder that the story's first readers reacted so vehemently to this ugly glimpse of their own faces in the mirror, even if they did not realize exactly what they were looking at."

There's a Yugoslavian proverb that says, "Tell the truth. And run." Whenever you decide to confront anything of substance, but particularly anything that confronts the nature of evil, know that you're playing with fire. This is especially true in our current climate, where so many are so outraged so often. As a rookie writer who dreams of hitting the big time, it's shocking to think that writing something profound about the nature of evil can provoke wrath. But the truth is that when you tackle this difficult subject, it's almost certain to infuriate people—the political party, religious figures, or any other group who feels accused or offended by your work. Jackson didn't just harmlessly point out that evil exists in the world. She set it in an all-American town that feels like an evil version of the cozy community in Thornton Wilder's *Our Town*. She took seemingly humble, decent, church-going folk, neighbors and families, and presented them all as killers. Little children enthusiastically help kill their own mother. She took iconic American imagery and ripped its mask off to show the murderous rage that lurks beneath all societies, no matter how seemingly pristine. And people were enraged.

Realizing this beforehand can help you prepare emotionally for that possibility, and make sure to work at the top of your game. In an interview with *The Paris Review*, the playwright Arthur Miller said, "When a play questions, even threatens, our social arrangement, that is when it really shakes us profoundly and dangerously, and that is when you've got to be great, good isn't enough."

In a figurative sense, when you tell a story that goes into full confrontation with the dark side, you're constructing a bomb.

HOW YOU DO IT

The following bullet points will help you think through and execute the principle.

▸ We're talking about evil, the conscious, willful destruction of human beings—not just their bodies, but their spirit, their ability to remain fully human. We're talking about acts of horror, torture, degradation, and humiliation, permanently scarring and disabling people. To do this right takes thick skin and the ability to stop and stare at the very worst we have to offer. Therefore, the first thing you need to do is approach the topic with respect.

▸ The psychologist Jordan Peterson talks often and eloquently about the need for human beings to honestly confront our own capacity for inflicting suffering on others. It is a necessary part of becoming a mature and decent person. As Anthony Burgess, the author of *A Clockwork Orange*, says, if a person can't choose to be good, they cease to be a person. It is our conscious decision to do what's right, to move toward goodness, that makes us fully human. It is the struggle against the darkness that gives us insight into ourselves and what life means. You know why you choose to be good. But what might cause *you* to hurt, even kill, someone who doesn't deserve it?

▶ In a 1972 interview with the film critic Gene Siskel, director Stanley Kubrick posited that there are four causes of violence, which is essentially evil: 1. Original sin (the theological view); 2. Unjust economic exploitation (the Marxian view); 3. Emotional frustrations and pressures (the psychological view); 4. Genetic factors based on the Y chromosome theory (the biological view). Which causes interest you? Which feel true?

▶ Get clear on where the evil in your story is located. Is it in a supernatural force, society at large, a group, or one character in particular? Who's gone dark and why?

▶ Once you locate the evil in your story, consider why it's necessary for you to confront this evil at this time in your life. What do you have to say about it that's essential?

▶ If you read "The Lottery" closely, you see that the woman who is stoned to death, Tessie Hutchinson, is not sympathetic. She says that the drawing was not fair. It was. She tries to get other, younger family members to take her place. And she doesn't express the slightest protective impulses toward her children. No matter how intense, a story is not reality. We get to act out our darkest impulses with relative impunity. List some things about yourself, or society at large, that you would enjoy seeing wiped out.

▶ Look for the connection between your hero and your villain. They're often reflections of each other. And both are part of you.

▶ You'll know you have it when it's not silly, when your skin crawls, and you feel afraid or like you might cry. The air itself around you gets heavy. It pushes you to the limits of your ability to cope.

MINI FINAL EXAM

Read the following, then answer the question below.

Erik Alden owns his own corporate law practice. He lives in a beautiful home with his lovely wife and two gorgeous little kids. He's made a lot of money throughout his career. Life is good. But he hits a rough patch and his fortunes rapidly descend. A big firm moves aggressively onto his turf and one of his partners jumps ship, taking major clients with him. One night at dinner with his brother, a wealthy venture capitalist, and their wives, his brother talks about scoring a four-hundred-million-dollar deal. Erik's wife jokes that he should have become a venture capitalist too. He laughs it off, but dwells on it for days . . . weeks . . . months. He plays the moment she made the remark over and over again in his mind, until he's certain she said it with condescension and malice. He convinces himself that she's going to divorce him, take what little dignity he has left, and wreck the family, So, one night, he downs a bottle of Scotch and guns her down in her sleep.

You decide to make the story darker and to explore the nature of evil. Which of the following works best?

a) Make it clear that his wife respects him, and have him destroy her peace of mind long before he kills her. Have him start by killing one of their kids first—and framing the other.
b) Change the victim to the brother, then pack the narrative with allusions to the biblical story of Cain and Abel.
c) Establish that his wife and brother are having an affair and then have him violently kill both of them.
d) Reorient the narrative to focus on his own demise so that he feels progressively more broken until he commits suicide.
e) Have him go full serial killer, taking out anyone who ever remotely doubted him, starting with his nursery school teacher.

CONTINUING ED

The 1980 film *Breaker Morant* is a courtroom drama set in 1902. It's the true story of three Australian lieutenants put on trial for war crimes that allegedly occurred while they were fighting for the English in what was known as the Second Anglo-Boer War. They are accused of murdering captured prisoners and a German missionary, and face death sentences.

How does the film confront evil? If all of the characters have blood on their hands, what is it that makes some characters—most notably the British commander, Lord Kitchener—feel eviler than others? What, if anything, makes Harry "Breaker" Morant worthy of redemption despite his sins? Note how you rank the degree of evil in each character as the story unfolds. Why do you dislike some more than others?

MINI FINAL ANSWER

All of these game plans for the rewrite are dark, but our focus is on the conscious nature of evil and how the evilest deeds inflict suffering on those who don't deserve to suffer. Therefore, the correct choice is **a) Make it clear that his wife respects him, and have him destroy her peace of mind long before he kills her. Have him start by killing one of their kids first—and framing the other.** This choice makes it clear that his wife meant no harm in her offhand joke, which makes the murder much darker. The husband not only plans it over a long period of time, he tries to destroy her psychologically first, on top of killing their innocent child.

"A good novel should be deeply unsettling—
its satisfactions should come from its
authenticity and formal coherence.
We must feel something crucial is at stake."

—DANA SPIOTTA, Author

PART THREE

ESSENTIAL PRINCIPLES of SETTING, DIALOGUE, and THEME

In this section you're going to round out your essential story-telling skill set by learning how to create fully realized worlds, write effective dialogue, and explore ideas that are critically important to you. For setting, we're going to use a broad definition that goes beyond the location of where the story takes place to include its form and tone. This will help you decide not only what to write but in what medium and genre.

In the first section, you learned how to structure events. In the second, you learned how to create compelling characters. This section will give you everything else you need to write a well-crafted, authentic story that's uniquely your own.

20

Link inextricably to your setting.

"Our histories cling to us.
We are shaped by where we come from."
—CHIMAMANDA NGOZI ADICHIE, Author

QUICK TAKE

This principle is about how setting impacts every other element of your story—the characters, what they do, how they live, how they communicate, and how their fates are sealed. "Linking inextricably to your setting" means that you evoke such a strong sense of place and time that the characters could not come from anywhere else at any other time. They are as tied to your setting as plants to earth. Some characters will be local, others fish out of water, some will embrace the world they live in, others will rebel against it. But no one is free from its influence.

When you think of virtually any master storyteller, the settings of their major works are intimately tied to their identity: Stephen King's haunted Maine, Jane Austen's rural England, Martin Scorsese's gritty New York City. They put immense effort into designing consistent, believable, evocative worlds that shape their characters. If you study Scorsese's characters—Johnny Boy

(*Mean Streets*), Henry Hill (*Goodfellas*), Jake LaMotta (*Raging Bull*)—you see that how they think, dress, walk, talk, eat, drink, fight, have sex, make money—all of it was forged in the working-class Italian American cityscapes of mid-twentieth-century New York's "Little Italy." They couldn't come from anyplace else without being fundamentally altered.

HOW IT WORKS

People are products of their environment. As we start our journey through life, we are vulnerable and dependent on others for survival and guidance—our parents and grandparents. We learn to speak by listening to how others speak. We get punished and rewarded based on what our parents and teachers believe is right and wrong. They get these ideas from their religion, the movies they watch, the books and newspapers they read, the type of work they do, the events and people that impacted and inspired them. These ideas flow down from them, and from all around us. They seep into our DNA and color how we experience the world. The people who came of age in the midst of the Great Depression are different from people who came of age during the development of the internet.

Even when we're old enough to think for ourselves, most people—not all, but most—prefer to move through life by taking the path of least resistance, which means conformity. We're imitative creatures. We wear what everyone else wears and believe what everyone else believes. This helps us avoid stress, reduce conflict, and play nicely with others. In the 1960s and 1970s, hair was cool. People wore long, thick, bushy, wild hairstyles. Men wore pork chop sideburns. Hairy chests and big mustaches were considered sexy. Today, men shave their heads, backs, shoulders, and chests, and both sexes spend fortunes on waxing and lasering off hair. This is just as true for ideas. Atheism, conservatism, populism, socialism—all move in and out of style as celebrities and politicians, popular books and events, move some ideas to the forefront and push others into hiding.

One of the fundamental elements of weak writing is a lack of specificity. You can take the generic characters and plop them into any world and it wouldn't change a thing. The following is a reference guide you can use to build richly detailed, atmospheric, authentic worlds that are instrumental in shaping dynamic, original characters. As you go through this list, trust your gut, *feel* how these things would impact *you* if you were exposed to different worlds.

- **Landscape**—Is it flat, hilly, mountainous, wooded, a desert, or a jungle? Is it urban, suburban, or rural? Is there water—ocean, lakes, or rivers? Are they full or dry? Think about the swamplands of Louisiana compared to urban New Orleans. What's the architecture like in your world—and how do the buildings reflect the temperament and worldview of the people?

- **Weather**—Is it sunny, cloudy, rainy, snowy, icy, bright, dark, prone to violent events—earthquakes, volcanoes, etc.? Does it have seasons or is it consistent? Think about the differences between London fog and Hawaiian sunsets.

- **Culture**—How do people dress? What do they eat and do for fun? And how is this impacted by religion, government, big business, and the powers that be? Think of the difference between how people behaved in America during the 1980s, after President Ronald Reagan exclaimed, "It's morning in America," compared to the early 1970s, during the Vietnam War and the Watergate scandal, and not long after the assassinations of President John F. Kennedy, his brother Senator Bobby Kennedy, and Martin Luther King Jr.

- **Economy**—Is this a boom time, depression, or something in between? Do people have money or not and how does this affect their behavior? Where do most people work? At which companies and in which industries? Are there lots of opportunities or only a few? Do people do what their parents and grandparents did, or this is a new economy? Is this a hypercapitalistic society with free markets or is the economy managed by the government? Or is this a society where money and what people do for a living is just not that important?

▶ **Government**—How fairly is this world run? Are the leaders responsible, caring, and elected by people who were able to vote without intimidation? Or is this land corrupt and tyrannical? Think about the differences between South Africa under apartheid, and since apartheid was ended in the early 1990s. There are always trade-offs as societies change for better and worse. What are they?

▶ **History**—What happened in the distant past and how does this shape the way people view their community? What are the defining experiences that shape the town's character—was there a battle fought here, a traumatic event, an amazing discovery? Think about the rich Civil War history of Gettysburg, Pennsylvania, or consider Roswell, New Mexico, where aliens allegedly landed. What's been going on in your world recently? Anything essential?

▶ **Religion and ethnicity**—What is the religious makeup of your society? What do the houses of worship look like, and how well-attended are services? Is the place diverse, filled with people worshipping in a wide variety of ways, or is everyone on the same page? Are there conflicts between peoples? For example, if your setting is the West Bank, it might be between Israelis and Palestinians, or if it's a small midwestern city, between blacks and whites. Conflicts between tribes can erupt more easily when there are only two groups than in more diverse communities.

▶ **Military and police**—Do people feel safe and secure? Are the military and police accountable to fairly elected government officials or does might make right? Do the police and armed forces exercise power with a commitment to justice and honor, or rule with an iron fist without regard for human rights? Think about the difference between American society today and Nazi Germany. Or a small town with a corrupt sheriff compared to one who reveres his community and is kind and decent.

There are no rules for how much of all this your story needs. You want enough detail to evoke a specific time and place, but not so much that you waste time and drain your battery crystallizing things that don't directly shape your characters and add insight into how they live. You want to approach this from two angles—one is the 30,000-foot view, the history, landscape, culture that's been formed over recent and even distant history. And then, within this larger framework, you want to create richly detailed locations—parks, lobbies, restaurants, hotel rooms, living rooms, etc., that are fully realized. You want to max out all five senses to bring them to life—how they look, feel, smell, sound and, if there's food cooking or dust or smoke, how they taste.

Above all, have fun with this. It's your world. When you imbue it with personality, depth, and specificity, your readers/viewers sense it and you earn their affection and respect.

HOW A MASTER DID IT

The Brief Wondrous Life of Oscar Wao (2007)
Junot Diaz

In a discussion at the 2013 Chicago Humanities Festival, Junot Diaz said,

> As an artist, I'll use local phenomena to access larger things. I always use this same example. Melville . . . ain't just talkin' about whalers. Right? You can't read

> *Moby-Dick* and say "Wow, he really didn't like whalers" or "whalers are like this." It's just a metaphor, you know? And for me it's useful because I am interested in the Dominican community. I am committed to the Dominican community. . . . But I also know that my work wouldn't have power if I didn't realize that this stuff, even for our own community is a shorthand. And it allows other people to engage it.

This is really just Diaz's take on the adage that you get to the universal through the specific. Never fear being too specific—it will not alienate your readers/viewers, it will draw them in.

There are two main settings in *The Brief Wondrous Life of Oscar Wao*—the Dominican Republic ("the DR") and Paterson, New Jersey, where many Dominican immigrants moved in search of a better life in America. This novel is saturated with all things Dominican. Almost all the characters are Dominican, and the novel is filled with references to people being real Dominican, un-Dominican, Dominicano, Dominicana, Old World Dominican, half Haitian half Dominican, and—an Oscar-generated word—Dominicanis. When people hear that Oscar wants to write books, he's the "Dominican James Joyce," and when he says he wants to write fantasy, he wants to become the "Dominican Tolkien."

There are many heavy themes explored in this book—the nature of masculinity, the way history intrudes on the present, the generational effects of dictatorship, and the insidious ways that racism infects a culture not just from without but within. But what really sits at the heart of this profoundly human novel is the tragic idea that love, even true love, brings only suffering. And not just a little suffering. To love someone will destroy you.

What essentially happens in the plot is that the five main characters—Oscar, his college roommate and the story's main narrator Yunior, Oscar's older sister Lola (who briefly takes over the narration), his mother Beli, and his grandfather Abelard—all suffer to varying degrees as a result of their longing to find love or protect the ones they love. Here we'll focus on just the two main characters, Oscar and Yunior, and the way their Dominican heritage and the story's two main settings, the Dominican Republic and Paterson shape their characters and develop the novel's main theme.

Oscar is a "ghetto nerd"; he's heavyset, homely, with dark skin and kinky hair, and he is obsessed with all things fantasy and science fiction. He falls madly in love with women over the smallest things—a glance, kind word, anything that acknowledges his existence. But when he finally loses his virginity at the end of the novel—with an aging prostitute, whom he's fallen hopelessly in love with on a trip to the DR—it leads to his being beaten to death in a cane field.

Yunior is a handsome, muscular young man who is genuinely in love with Oscar's older sister, Lola. But he is obsessed with sex and bedding as many women as he can. Though on the surface it fuels his sense of manhood, he doesn't understand or enjoy his own sexuality, and his persistent infidelities ultimately drive Lola to leave him forever. She moves away and has a child with another man while Yunior marries another woman he seems less attached to.

Both characters reflect powerful aspects of the author's personality. Diaz was a nerdy kid—overweight, wore bad glasses, and couldn't get a girl to save his life. In college he reinvented himself—started working out, dancing salsa, and became a major-league ladies' man. But this only led to him repeatedly hurting women he loved. Both Yunior and Oscar are profoundly impacted by their Dominican heritage and culture. Oscar is repeatedly derided for not being a "real" Dominican because he loves to read, write, and acts like a total geek. But mostly he's not Dominican because Dominican men are voracious and successful lovers. Yunior has the exact opposite problem. He is successful with women, at least in terms of getting them to sleep with him, but it only brings him—and them—pain.

Love for these two men is a curse. In fact, Yunior fears that all Dominican people are vulnerable to the *fukú americanus,* the curse that afflicts their island homeland; he is especially rattled by his close proximity to Oscar's family, who he's certain got the curse bad.

The novel begins with a detailed, and harrowing, history of the *fukú americanus*. The first line reads, "They say it came first from Africa, carried in the screams of the enslaved; that it was the death bane of the Tainos, uttered just as one world perished and another began; that it was a demon drawn into Creation through the nightmare door that was cracked open in the Antilles." Though Diaz fuels his prose with Spanish words and references to sci-fi/fantasy stories, he rarely explains them. He does this intentionally, to instill in the reader a sense of how it feels to be a foreigner, an immigrant, unable to fully grasp the language and customs of your new homeland.

Just as no story set in Nazi Germany could avoid Hitler, the DR is haunted to this day by the legacy of the dictator Rafael Trujillo, whose reign of terror many Dominicans feel was connected to the *fukú americanus*. In an extended footnote, Diaz writes,

> For those of you who missed your mandatory two seconds of Dominican history: Trujillo, one of the twentieth century's most infamous dictators, rules the Dominican Republic between 1930 and 1961 with an implacable ruthless brutality. A portly, sadistic, pig-eyed mulato who bleached his skin, wore platform shoes, and had a fondness for Napoleon-era haberdashery, Trujillo . . . came to control nearly every aspect of the DR's political, cultural, social, and economic life through a potent (and familiar) mixture of violence, intimidation, massacre, rape, co-optation, and terror . . .

The *fukú americanus* and Trujillo's legacy of terror are infused throughout the novel. One senses that Oscar's violent death was directly caused by an ugly chain of events that began when Trujillo imprisoned Oscar's maternal grandfather for refusing to give up his daughter to satisfy the dictator's near supernatural lust.

There is a clash at the center of this novel between America and towns like Paterson, where Oscar and many Dominican American immigrants live, and their homeland. You can feel this tension in that footnote, "for those of you who missed your mandatory two seconds of Dominican history," which goes onto mentions that Trujillo was backed by the United States.

The 1980s America and suburban New Jersey that Diaz describes is almost more notable for its absence of culture than culture. There are passing references to President Reagan and some current events, but one feels no sense of connection, community, or higher purpose. The places featured—Oscar's working-class neighborhood, his high school, strip malls, Rutgers University, even the boardwalk by the sea in Asbury Park—lack any semblance of magic, excitement, or romance. The people are hard-edged and tolerate no weakness. After Oscar graduates from college, he drives around at night to stave off depression. Diaz, writing as Yunior, says, "Every time he pulled out of the house he thought it would be his last. Drove everywhere. Got lost in Camden. Found the neighborhood where I grew up. Drove through New Brunswick just when the clubs were getting out, looking at everybody, his stomach killing him. Even made it down to Wildwood. Looked for the coffee shop where he had saved Lola, but it had closed." The towns lack any definition, specificity, soul. Diaz's New Jersey setting alternates between deadness and hostility.

After Oscar graduates from college, he gets a job teaching at his old high school. "Had Don Bosco, since we last visited, been miraculously transformed by the spirit of Christian brotherhood? . . . Negro, please . . . Every day he watched the 'cool' kids torture the crap out of the fat, the ugly, the smart, the poor, the dark, the black, the unpopular . . . and in every one of these clashes he saw himself."

It's not hard to see why the Dominican American immigrant community longs to return to their warm island homeland. Whatever problems it may face, whatever hardships and horrors—and there are many—it feels like what it truly is, the homeland. And it exerts a pull. Diaz writes,

> Every Summer Santo Domingo slaps the Diaspora engine into reverse, yanks back as many of its expelled children as it can: airports choke with the overdressed; necks and baggage carousels groan under the accumulated weight of that year's cardenas and paquetes, and pilots fear for their planes—overburdened beyond belief—and for themselves; restaurants, bars, clubs, theaters, malecones, beaches, resorts, hotels, moteles . . . swarm with quisqueyanos from the world over. Like someone had sounded a general reverse evacuation order. Back home everybody! Back home!

One summer, while Oscar's on vacation from teaching, he joins his mother, sister, and family in the DR. While there, he briefly comes alive. Diaz writes three chapters—"The Condensed Notebook of a Return to Nativeland," "Evidence of a Brother's Past," and "Oscar Goes Native"—that are among the most beautiful descriptions of setting that you will ever read. They intricately tie Oscar to the Dominican Republic and propel the narrative toward its tragic conclusion. At the end of this intense beckoning, Oscar meets the woman who will lead him to both the realization of his biggest dream—to lose his virginity—and his death.

These three chapters transform Oscar from spiritually vacant to a living, breathing human being. In "The Condensed Notebook of a Return to Nativeland" Diaz begins in a dark place . . .

> The beat-you down heat was the same, and so was the fecund tropical smell that he had never forgotten, that to him was more evocative than any madeleine, and likewise the air pollution and the thousands of motos and cars and dilapidated trucks on the roads and the clusters of peddlers at every traffic light . . . and people walking languidly with nothing to shade them from the sun and the buses that charged past

> like they were making a delivery of spare limbs to some far-off war . . .

Then Oscar's spirit begins to awaken. "It really was astonishing how much he'd forgotten about the DR: the little lizards that were everywhere, and the roosters in the morning, followed shortly by the cries of the plataneros and the bacalao guy . . ." Diaz evokes all five senses—you can feel the heat, see the bus with arms dangling out the windows, hear the roosters, smell and taste the bacalao (fish stew).

In "Oscar Goes Native" Diaz delivers a four-page riff that literally pulls Oscar back home . . .

> . . . after he'd gotten somewhat used to the surreal whirligig that was life in La Capitol—the guaguas, the cops, the mind-boggling poverty, the Dunkin' Donuts, the beggars, the Haitians selling roasted peanuts at the intersections, the mind-boggling poverty, the asshole tourists hogging up all the beaches . . . after he'd swum in the Caribbean, after tio Rudolfo had gotten him blasted on mamajuana de marisco, after he'd seen his first Haitians kicked off a guagua because niggers claimed they "smelled" . . . After he caught a cold because his abuela set the air conditioner in his room so high, he decided suddenly and without warning to stay on the island for the rest of the Summer with his mother and his tio.

The two settings—gray, dead New Jersey, and the DR that's teeming with life—are inextricably linked to the characters, themes, language, and narrative thrust. Diaz knows every detail about how these worlds work and affect the people within them. Every last element—the weather, landscape, architecture, economy, government, history, religion, degree of security, and culture—is fully realized. Whether it's putting a setting into historical context or simply creating vibrant locations and rooms where moments take place, Diaz, in *The Brief Wondrous Life of Oscar Wao*, offers a master class in setting.

Here's a good thought to wrap up on, a test to see how well Diaz executes this principle. Imagine you were hired to rewrite the novel and all you had to do was make one tiny tweak. You needed to make all the characters Norwegian.

Right.

HOW YOU DO IT

The following bullet points will help you think through and execute the principle.

▸ A setting can be as vast as a planet or small as a prison cell or motel room. Determine how big your setting needs to be. Even the smallest room can be an entire world within itself. But your world must be *specific*. You get to the universal through the specific. The more specific you make your world, the more universal it feels.

▸ Sketch out, with one quick thought, a line on each of the following:

- ▷ Weather
- ▷ Land or seascape
- ▷ Architecture
- ▷ Economy
- ▷ Government
- ▷ History (ancient and recent)
- ▷ Religion
- ▷ Military, police
- ▷ Culture

▶ Now imagine—*really* imagine—being in and of this world. How does it affect you? Does it make you harder or softer, more optimistic or pessimistic, more refined or crass? Picture a quintessential home, street, church, or restaurant. As you sit there and take it in, what do you see, hear, smell, taste, and touch? How do they affect you?

▶ This is not about quantity. It's about quality. Anton Chekhov once famously said, "Don't tell me the moon is shining; show me the glint of light on broken glass." As you create your world, look for those details that spark images in your reader's mind.

▶ Think about all five senses: sight, sound, smell, touch, taste. Consider how differently you feel and act in a dark room with a foul smell, the sound of dripping water, and footsteps creaking overhead vs. a cabana drenched in sunshine by majestic white sands and glistening blue-green waters. *Feel* the worlds you write.

▶ You'll know you have it when it's impossible to imagine changing the setting without changing something fundamental about the characters. Test drive this principle with any story you love. Imagine putting Offred, Gandalf, Vito Corleone, Cookie Monster, or Josephine March anywhere else at any other time. Odds are you'll laugh at the thought. Imagine Gandalf in Texas. That's not going to work.

MINI FINAL EXAM

Read the following, then answer the question below.

You're writing a TV series. It's a science-fiction adventure that merges the raunchy edge of adult-themed comedy with the quirky adventures of the original *Star Trek*. The setting is the starship USS *Endurance*, which was once the envy of the cosmos but was retired by the Intergalactic Transport Federation. It was bought cheap by a group of investors, led by the legendary fighter pilot Deke Blackstarr. After suffering grievous injuries to the left side of his face and losing his lower left leg on the planet Almathea in the Jupiter Six wars, Blackstarr fell into a life of drug abuse and crime. He did four years in a Mars work camp, pretended to find His Majesty Light-Jesus, and earned a fortune preaching questionable self-actualization strategies involving group sex. He painted the *Endurance* black and hot pink, christened it "The Galactic Penetrator," and then put in drug dens, fitness studios, basketball courts, and night clubs, and crafted a hundred-page manifesto for building a society based on "primal satisfaction." His mission is to seek out new life and new civilizations, and party his ass off with them. He's a good-enough guy, but not above a little piracy, and occasional murder, to make ends meet. This is especially true if he encounters a race of beings that he considers repressive. The man *hates* repression.

Imagine Blackstarr is building a crew. Which of the following characters would *not* feel inextricably linked to a noir-tinged space comedy set on a ship called "The Galactic Penetrator"?

a) **Dook Myun-Moon**—A Phyunesian (huge-eyed, orange-haired alien) and former attorney who was thrown out of the Interplanetary Office of Contractual Obligations for repeated irregularities, including engineering a massive funds transfer to a noted criminal. Great with a laser rifle.

b) **Christy "The Ice Tornado" Streets**—A gigantic-bosomed stripper famous for spinning at high speed while engaging in extraordinarily lewd acts. She's also the ex-wife of the guy who founded Blackstarr's favorite band, Blistering Skidd, and a polymath with a penchant for Samurai culture.

c) **Winnie Culpepper**—A precocious, freckle-faced thirteen-year-old girl with a tremendous wit, encyclopedic knowledge of history, and a passion for solving mysteries. Winnie is a devout environmentalist, plays cello, and is a two-time geography bee champion.

d) **XT-Zenis**—A lifelike omni-gendered android who was created to serve as a sex slave for a corrupt ruler on a rogue starship that Deke won in a high-stakes poker game. XT-Zenis is breathtakingly inappropriate; it makes even the most hardened badass blush.

e) **Uranus Joe Musclecock**—A court-martialed former general, who at one time was rumored to be the wealthiest man in the galaxy, due to his control of Diamond-White—a super-psychadelic that sold for $10,000,000 Koopch per ounce in its heyday.

CONTINUING ED

The 2017 podcast *S-Town*, produced by *This American Life*, focuses on a man with a powerful connection to his hometown Woodstock, Alabama. He goes by John B. An article on *Vox* accurately describes him as "a queer liberal conspiracist who socializes with neighborhood racists; a manic depressive consumed by predictions of cataclysmic global catastrophe; an off-the-grid hoarder of gold who takes in stray dogs; a genius with a photographic memory who's spent his whole life caring for his mother while designing a massive and elaborate hedge maze in his backyard; and one of the most skilled antique clock restorers in the world. All that, and he may be sitting on a fortune in buried treasure."

The podcast begins with the show's producer, Brian Reed, responding to an email from John B. claiming that a murder took place in Woodstock. He alleged the murder was being covered up by the local powers-that-be. But as the show progresses, it becomes more of a deep dive into John's true nature and his relationship to his hometown. Why does John B. refer to Woodstock as "Shit Town"? How do the values, interests, and sophistication of the culture at large clash with John's intellect and passion? How fully is the culture of Woodstock realized by the storytellers—the natural world, businesses, local politics, religion, food, and entertainment? If John B. hates his hometown as much as he claims, why does he stay there? How do John's views on race and sexuality reveal his inextricable link to his setting? Is it possible to imagine John B. being born and raised in a big city like Birmingham, Alabama, or in the wealthy landscapes of Greenwich, Connecticut?

MINI FINAL ANSWER

The correct answer is **c) Winnie Culpepper—A precocious, freckle-faced thirteen-year-old girl with a tremendous wit, an encyclopedic knowledge of history and a passion for solving mysteries. Winnie is a devout environmentalist, plays cello, and is a two-time geography bee champion.** Like a discordant note in a symphony, placing this character in this setting would make no sense and damage the experience. Anyone who tunes into a show like this is looking for a specific kind of dark comedy. To introduce a precocious, happy child onto a ship called "The Galactic Penetrator" would be uncomfortable and offensive in a bad way.

21

Exceed expectations.

"I want to top expectations. I want to blow you away."
—QUENTIN TARANTINO, Filmmaker

QUICK TAKE

When you tell a story, you make a promise to deliver a certain kind of experience. If you ask someone to read your thriller, it's a whole different ball game than asking them to watch your rom-com. This principle is about mastering your medium and genre so that you not only meet your reader/audience's expectations, you exceed them.

Medium is the form your story takes—novel, screenplay, etc. Genre is the style—Western, romance, etc. When people come to a story, they bring a set of expectations based on medium and genre. You, as the storyteller, need to know the inherent strengths of your medium and the conventions of your genre so that when you make a promise—to terrify, crack up, incite, inspire—you deliver what people expect, but in your own unique way.

Think of this like being a pilot. If, right now, you sat down in a cockpit and had to fly a plane, would you rather have a hazy idea of how to get airborne, or total command of what every single button, dial, lever, and joystick in the cockpit can do? Of course you want to be in total command. If you hit a high-altitude storm or just feel like doing a tuck-and-roll, you need to know how to execute the necessary maneuvers. You want to dominate the machine—and take your passengers for a ride.

HOW IT WORKS

In Stephen King's book *On Writing*, he talks with great passion about how much he loves to read. He reads all the time—hundreds of books per year. It's not something he does to study the craft, though that's a by-product. It's just because he *loves* to read. He grew up reading old comic books and watching science fiction and horror movies that blew him away. And when you look at King's awe-inspiring output—he's written over *ninety* novels, almost all of which are science fiction or horror—you can feel the depth of this man's love for his medium and genre.

Never underestimate the power of love. It's everything. When you write in the medium and genre that you love, it gives you the strength, courage, and endurance necessary to become truly great. If you roll your eyes at this, you're making a grievous error. You can only master what you love.

In terms of medium, you can write fiction, screenplays, TV scripts, stage plays, podcasts, graphic novels, comic books, video games, and, as technology races ahead, new formats—virtual reality and mixed media—will surely become more prominent. Each of these has (or will have) its own inherent strengths.

In film—and television, which is quickly becoming indistinguishable from film—it's easy to change locations and time periods. You can warp time, show the same image from different angles, and cover vast distances at high speed. You can zero in on the subtlest facial expressions, race through wormholes, or enter into the human body. And you can mix music and images to create intense emotions.

In fiction, you can string sentences together to do anything one can imagine, but fiction's greatest strength, where it's superior to all other mediums, is in the way it lets you go deep into characters' minds to experience exactly what they're thinking and feeling.

In theater, there's an immediacy and intensity that's not present in any other medium. The stage sits before you like an arena, and it's ideally suited to explore conflict between tight-knit groups of people—family, friends, coworkers, barflies, guests in a hotel—who do battle at close range. It begs for you to populate it with enormous personalities—to give great actors the fuel they need to shake the rafters.

In graphic novels and comic books, there's magic in the way artists make it appear that someone has moved from one panel to the next, or as if time passed. It's a medium that invites attention to detail and depth of thought, as you can study moments that are frozen in time.

In podcasts and radio, the emphasis is on sound. There's something profound that happens when you can hear but not see people and places. There's a purity to the communication, as we experience characters free from the inevitable biases and judgments that come from merely seeing. We can envision a whole scene by just hearing silverware hit plates or wind howling through an open door.

What is it about your unique skill set and the story you need to tell that makes it ideally suited to a given medium? For example, August Wilson started his career writing poetry, and had an intense personality. His characters have a towering presence. Troy Maxson, the protagonist in *Fences*, is an ex-convict who was savagely abused as a child, played baseball in the Negro leagues, and once wrestled death. It was necessary for Wilson to put Troy before a live audience so the enormity of his spirit could be directly felt. August Wilson was a playwright.

Medium is the form your story takes. Now let's talk about genre, the type of stories you tell. The best way to think about genre is in terms of expectation. Depending on whether we watch a family drama, romance, Western, horror, or fantasy, we expect to see certain kinds of characters and settings, to experience certain types of emotions, and to explore certain kinds of ideas in varying degrees of depth and intensity. You watch romantic comedies to have a light laugh and see adorable people driving each other nuts. You read a five-hundred-page science-fiction novel to stir your sense of wonder about the nature of reality and the infinite possibilities of the universe.

Each genre comes with its own set of conventions—a murder mystery has a murderer, victim, and detective. These are the fundamental elements of the genre. They are not clichés. A convention is a necessary element, just as spaghetti and clams are to an entree called "spaghetti and clams." It's a convention when it's written at top of your intelligence and integral to your story. It's a cliché when it's carelessly executed, done without soul, heart, or brains.

We always want to return to the Bruce Lee quote, "Obey the principles without being bound by them." Here this means know the conventions of your genre. If you write Westerns, know every type of character, setting, situation, and theme that's been explored by the vast catalogue of Westerns. You understand what your reader/viewer expects when they settle in to enjoy a Western. To avoid being "bound" by conventions, you need to come up with your own unique take. In the Coen brothers' Western *The Ballad of Buster Scruggs*, there's a duel between a cowboy in a white hat and one in a black hat. It's set on an old, dusty road between two combatants who passionately believe their honor is at stake—a staple of Westerns. But how it shakes out it is completely original, dark, and hilarious. Buster (in the white hat) shoots off each one of the other guy's fingers, then puts him down by firing over his shoulder, looking into a rather dainty handheld mirror he just happens to have with him, while pleasantly narrating his thoughts. It's vintage Coen brothers.

There are no hard limitations on your choice of genre because you can combine them in any way. The classic film *It's a Wonderful Life* is a holiday noir. To my knowledge, it's the only one of its kind. For a Christmastime movie aimed at families, that story gets dark. But it works because, to make its point—that we all add value to the world—it needed to take its hero, George Bailey, who has lost faith, into a nightmare. The film's genre morphs from a holiday film into a film noir and returns to a holiday film. It uses genre to express its idea.

Back to our pilot metaphor. This is about you walking into the cockpit of your plane, staring down the panel and instruments with total command of how every last one works, putting on your badass aviator sunglasses, and letting your passengers know they're about to have an *experience*. You make a promise, then tear ass down the runway, take flight, and deliver.

HOW A MASTER DID IT

30 Rock, "Jack-tor" (2008)
Tina Fey, Robert Carlock

The sitcom *30 Rock* ran on network television (NBC) during prime time for seven seasons from 2006 to 2013. The show was created by comedy writer and actress Tina Fey, and was inspired by her real-life experience as the first woman ever to become head writer for *Saturday Night Live*. It's a comedy about Liz Lemon (played by Fey), a beautiful but lonely woman who is married to her high-stress job. She is the head writer for an *SNL*-like sketch comedy show called *The Girlie Show with Tracy Jordan* (*TGS*), and she struggles to manage her staff and navigate the complexities of doing creative work within the confines of a multinational corporation. At the time the show was produced, NBC was a subsidiary of General Electric (GE).

It's a single-camera half-hour show, which essentially means it looks more like a film than a "multicamera" sitcom shot on a sound stage. (*Curb Your Enthusiasm* is single camera; *Seinfeld* is multicamera.) Because *30 Rock* is single camera, it makes it easier to do multiple storylines, as you can quickly travel to more places and do the rapid-fire cutaways that are more commonly associated with animation.

The genre is comedy. More specifically, it's a workplace comedy on prime-time network television. Though there are satirical elements, it's more send-up than biting satire. It touches on issues of politics, race, and gender, as well as the struggles between creativity and commerce.

The reason I picked a TV show to articulate this principle is because TV shows come with a set of expectations that *must* be met, week in and week out. Admittedly, this principle is not meant to explore the deepest profundities of literature and the human experience. (We'll hit those hard in the last four principles on theme.) This is about the underrated importance of getting the basics right.

The episode we'll break down, "Jack-Tor," is the fifth episode of the first season and is widely considered the series' first great episode. It was written by a veteran TV comedy writer, Robert Carlock. Let's put ourselves in Carlock's shoes and look at the task at hand. Here's what his to-do list might have looked like:

- Lemon (Tina Fey) has conflict with her conservative boss, Jack Donaghy
- Lemon has conflict with her quirky African American *TGS* star, Tracy Jordan
- Lemon has conflict with her narcissistic blond bombshell friend, *TGS* costar Jenna Maroney
- Lemon has conflict with her personal life (or lack of it)
- Multiple storylines
- Cutaways
- Jokes dealing with politics, race, gender, art vs. commerce

- Include at least one bit for all additional characters—the Jimmy Fallon–esque actor-writer Josh; the sloppy man-child writer Frank; the Harvard-educated writer Toofer (as in he's black and went to Harvard); Jack's insanely dedicated assistant Jonathan; Lemon's drop-dead gorgeous assistant Cerie

- Lemon learns something from Jack or Jack learns something from Lemon

- All storylines end on a positive (or positive-enough) note

If this feels like a lot to consider, it is. And in case you're interested in writing for television, keep in mind, this has to be done on tight deadlines while dealing with all sorts of pressures—from producers, actors, agents, and sponsors. Below, we'll go through the episode and I'll note each time the writer checks a box.

(If you're a fan of the show, this is before Kenneth, the page, became such a prominent character and the episode doesn't include Lutz, so neither appears.)

• • •

Before the credits roll, there's a brief three-minute introduction to set up the storylines.

Lemon catches Tracy trying to sneak out of rehearsal. Tracy is not used to the grind of doing a live TV show. He hates rehearsal and doesn't want to have to do a show every Friday night—he's got an orgy coming up on a Friday! Lemon insists that he do his job and asks him to please read the cue cards, but he refuses, comparing himself to the great jazz improvisers. **(Main storyline—conflict with Tracy.)**

Jenna pleads with producer Pete Hornberger to let her perform her song "Muffin Top," which is a hit in Israel. He says she can, as there are a few minutes left at the end of the episode, but she continues pleading long after he says yes, then finally realizes, to her shock, that he agreed.

Jack Donaghy forces the *TGS* writing staff to watch a video he's made of himself encouraging writers to include positive mentions, or "Pos-Mens," of GE products in their shows. For example, it would be easy for a character to say something positive about GE's new offshore drilling equipment. He then lauds the company (himself really) for "setting a new standard of upward revenue stream dynamics." **(Sendup of corporate excess.)**

The staff is mortified. Lemon refuses to have the show's integrity compromised by selling products. **(Conflict between art and commerce.)** But she's interrupted by Pete, who marvels at how delicious Diet Snapple tastes, and several other writers join in to express their passion for Snapple. **(Self-referential joke sends up writers' own questionable dedication to art.)** Lemon continues to refuse to do it, provoking Jack to mock the idea that they're artists like James Joyce. They're just hacks who make cheap jokes about presidents to kill time between car ads. She protests that Josh gets tons of fan mail for his Gaybraham Lincoln. Josh adds effeminately, "Four score and seven beers ago." **(Bit for Josh.)** Lemon then marvels at how cool it is that Snapple puts fun facts on their bottle caps, like that Holland is the only country with a national dog.

And the opening credits roll.

At the start of Act One, Jenna complains to Lemon that Tracy's still not reading the cue cards and suggests that he can't read. Lemon barks, "That's offensive!" and asks Tracy to try a line off a cue card. He's obviously upset by it, refuses, and runs out—through a door clearly marked "Emergency Exit Only." Maybe . . . he can't read. **(Jokes about race, exceeds expectation in that it's pretty damn edgy to suggest a black man can't read.)**

To needle Jenna, Frank and Toofer tell her they heard Jack is going to fire an actor to save money, upsetting her greatly. **(Additional storyline, brings in Frank and Toofer.)**

Pete complains to Lemon about their writing ads into the sketches as a man gets out of the elevator wearing a giant Snapple bottle costume. He asks where Human Resources is, and they casually point the way. In the elevator, Lemon asks Pete if it's possible that Tracy can't read and he insists Tracy is just being typical crazy Tracy. But after they think about his acting in movies—flash to a clip—it does seem like he just makes up his lines. **(Cutaway.)**

They march into Jack's office to find him studying DVDs of the show *Friends*. Though it was on for a decade, and was one of the most popular shows in history, he's clearly never seen it. But he's determined to learn how comedy works, since NBC's comedies are so important to the company. They tell him they're writing a sketch to make fun of the new product integration initiatives and want him to star in it. He's hesitant but he thinks out loud about the whole "self-referential" nature of the bit where he, the corporate titan, is mocked, and agrees to do it. **(Additional storyline and setting up conflict with Jack.)**

Jenna demands to know why Jack Donaghy is appearing in a sketch—clearly the rumors are true that he plans to fire an actor to cut costs. Lemon denies it, but Jenna tells her that she is going to make sure she's not fired by unleashing her secret weapon. Lemon begs her not to say "my sexuality," and Jenna says proudly, "my sexuality." But Jack only likes women half her age who are Asian. **(Additional storyline, conflict with Jenna.)**

Lemon goes off to find Tracy—carrying a giant stack of script revisions she found, unread, in his mailbox. She is now certain he can't read. Here, Lemon is operating at the top of her intelligence—there is overwhelming evidence to support her conclusion and she is consumed with liberal guilt because Tracy's illiteracy is undoubtedly society's fault. She finds him and, with great syrupy condescension, asks if he can read. He is stunned and hurt, but confirms that if he can't read, he will need to be tutored, and the show will have to operate around his schedule. Lemon agrees—she'll do anything to right this wrong. He screams out that a great burden has been lifted now that his shameful secret is out. He is illiterate! He doesn't even know if he voted for Obama! Lemon, a wreck, follows him to the elevator but the doors close before she can reach him. Another person hits the button and the doors pop open. Tracy is reading the *New*

York Post and shaking his head, noting that a conservative pundit just keeps getting more conservative. Lemon is stunned. He just played her like a fool. **(Sendup of liberals.)**

Later that day, Lemon and Pete are interrupted by Jack's devoted assistant, Jonathan, who must show them something—strictly to protect Jack. He insists that Jack can't do a live comedy show because he is the worst actor in the world. He shows them the outtakes from the video Jack did on product integration. It was a disaster that took more than one hundred fifty takes. We see about thirty of his bungles in rapid succession—forgetting his two simple opening words, "product integration," calling it "product integortion," taking a giant fall, yelling at others to shut off their phones when it's his phone ringing. He's the worst actor in history. **(This brings in Jonathan, and the thirty-plus shots of Jack messing up leverage the single-camera medium. This bit exceeds expectations in the fact that Alec Baldwin is widely considered one of the great comic actors of our age. It's fascinating to see him be so convincingly terrible.)**

This takes us to the first-act break.

After the break, Jack tells Lemon he's nervous about the rehearsal and she encourages him to drop out. But he refuses—he doesn't quit. He's both summitted Mt. Kilimanjaro and showered with then–Fox News host Greta Van Susteren. **(Political humor.)**

He goes off to a meeting as Jenna pops out in a slinky dress, ready to pounce. Lemon warns her not to bother Jack, who has a meeting with his boss. Jenna then follows him around the corner and eyes Jack talking to his boss, an old, bald, homely man. Jenna shifts her sights to *him*—he's even higher up. After Jack walks off, she puts the moves on the executive big time, obscenely eating his yogurt and placing the plastic spoon in his stunned mouth. **(Sendup of women who flaunt their sexuality. Since Tina Fey often writes about the struggles of being a woman in a position of power, we don't expect to see her rip into a woman.)**

At rehearsal, Jack is not only a disaster, but he blames his weak performance on the "clunky" writing. Lemon is insulted and sarcastically tells him to do the show, because he will be hilarious. He says that will be a "refreshing change" and practices his terribly unnatural on-screen walk as he goes off. **(Conflict with Jack.)**

Pete and Lemon talk to Tracy, who is still wreaking havoc on the show by missing rehearsals and pretending he can't read. Lemon says she just wants to show him the new poster advertising the show. It features Tracy's smiling face with the copy, "The smallest penis in show business." He recoils, then laughably still insists he can't read it. Pete and Lemon stomp off.

At 3:10 a.m., Lemon gets a call from Jack summoning her to the set. **(This subtly hints at her conflict with her work/life balance—she sleeps alone.)** She finds Jack on stage. He's a nervous wreck, desperately struggling to memorize his lines. She implores him to quit, but this dilemma is destroying him. He can't bear the thought of going on stage—he once played an ear of corn as a kid in a school show, flubbed his line, and barked, "Sonofabitch." **(Cutaway.)** He insists that he's not afraid, he just truly does not understand acting. He flops on the floor, begging Lemon to help. She gloats, this time *he* needs *her* help. He tells her not to gloat as it makes her look "mannish." Then she rips into him, telling him to "nut up" and that any idiot, including Josh and Jenna, can act. He tells her that he'd be turned on by any other woman who said this, and she goes off, disgusted. **(This gets to the heart of the two main characters' relationship. They learn from each other. She learns about the challenges of management and he learns about being an artist. But this exceeds expectations in the sense that we don't expect Lemon to tell the hyper-masculine Jack to "nut up.")**

This brings us to the second-act break.

We come back and Jenna brags to Lemon that she used her sexuality to nail Jack's boss, virtually guaranteeing that she won't be fired. Lemon tells her that he's not Jack's boss, he is just an extra on the show. We flash back to see that what Jenna thought she saw—Jack talking to his boss—was actually Jack and an extra named Ron on separate phone calls. But it looked like they were talking to each other. Ron strolls by and eyes Jenna, who mutters simply, "Ew." **(Cutaway to the memory, additional satire of Jenna's narcissistic sexuality.)**

On the day of the show, Lemon and Pete trick Tracy into walking into a room by posting a sign that reads, "Hot lesbian auditions." He confesses that he can read. Pete and Tracy bond over the fact that they agree Lemon is racist. She winces. Tracy explains that the show is too hard. Pete sympathizes. Then Lemon insists Tracy read the cue cards because she demands professionalism from herself and her staff. As she starts monologuing, Josh, dressed as Gaybraham Lincoln, pops in and asks if he can cross his eyes when he gets kicked in the groin and Lemon tells him it's fantastic. **(Lemon-Tracy conflict ends on positive note.)**

Jenna tries to get back at Toofer for lying about Jack planning to fire a cast member. She attempts to trick him into having sex with her on the roof, but he, at the top of his intelligence, realizes that she plans to trap him naked up there. Not done yet, she goes off to find Frank.

Days later, Jack watches his performance on his DVD player, enamored with himself. Lemon comes in to tell him he did a good job and realizes he's cherishing his performance. He throws her out and is then horrified to see naked Frank appear on the ledge outside his window. Jenna got him. **(Lemon-Jack conflict ends on positive note. Frank gets his comeuppance for being a bad boy, but it's funny and not too mean-spirited.)**

The episode ends with Jenna doing a raunchy performance of her song "Muffin Top," which Pete and Lemon groove to before a live audience, then wonder if Jenna knows they went off the air two minutes ago. **(Jenna gets to do her song, even if not for a large audience.)**

When you factor in everything that the writer, Robert Carlock, had to do to make this episode work—write multiple storylines with fast-paced scenes, capture the voice of each character, explore issues of race and gender, as well as the office power structure, and pack the story with laughs—you see that he delivers exactly what viewers tune in for when they sit down to watch a half-hour comedy (genre) on network television (medium). And he exceeds expectations by pushing the boundaries—that Tracy can't read, that Jenna's abusing her sexuality, and that this time, it's Lemon who must coach Jack—as far as he can without breaking them.

HOW YOU DO IT

The following bullet points will help you think through and execute the principle.

▶ Take stock of your temperament and style. How does your personality align with the strengths of the various media? If, for example, you are obsessed with images, think visually, and love nothing more than watching and studying movies, you're a screenwriter.

▶ Finish this sentence: If I could only experience stories for the rest of my life in one medium it would be . . .

▶ Factor in lifestyle. The life of a television writer, for example, is very different from a novelist's. Do you like to spend time collaborating with other people, or do you prefer to work alone?

▶ List your five all-time favorite stories in any medium. Take your time. You want to list only the ones that you *love* with a near-religious fervor.

▶ If you think about the experiences that had the greatest impact on your life, that most define you, how do they feel? If you were a character in a story, what would that story's genre be? Is your life a comedy, dramedy, a tragedy, or something else?

▶ This is not simply "write what you know." If you've had a hard life, no one has any right to tell you that you must tell miserable stories. You might feel that the whole point of stories is to escape from life's pain. That's fine. Just be aware of how your personal experience fuels what you write.

▶ Make a conscious decision about who you are as a writer. Decide which medium you want to work in and what types of stories you want to tell. The key thing is that it feels right for you. Make the decision consciously, intelligently, and authentically. It will make you stronger, more confident, and help you weather the inevitable storms.

▶ Before you start a new story, list the conventions of the genre, or combination of genres, of your story. What absolutely must happen and how will you avoid clichés? Knowing this will help you start off on the right foot.

MINI FINAL EXAM

Read the following, then answer the question below.

When Stanley Kubrick read Anthony Burgess's novel *A Clockwork Orange*, he was so blown away that he committed instantly to adapting it into a film. Burgess was inspired by the idea that what makes us human is our ability to choose between good and evil. If we lived in a perfect world, free from all temptation, we could not choose to be evil, because evil would not exist. But the trade-off is we would lack vitality and have no need for heroism, invention, ingenuity, or to create art. He believed it's better to live in a world with both art and evil than one that is free from evil but lacks vitality.

So, he created Alex DeLarge, a teen gangbanger in a dystopian future world who is brilliant and poetic and who consciously chooses to be evil. The story tracks society's attempt to "cure"

Alex by training him to associate feeling deathly ill with his violent impulses. This causes him to become a harmless, pitiful creature, incapable of even defending himself.

In the trailer, disturbing images of sex and violence race past, interspersed with the words "Frightening," "Thrilling," and "Bizarre," among others. Kubrick clearly set expectations. This will be a dangerous and darkly comedic film.

Though audiences in 1971 were told to expect a frightening, thrilling, and bizarre film, which of the following exceeded the expectations Kubrick set?

a) The makeup and costumes: Alex wears long false eyelashes on one eye and the gang wear white jumpsuits with huge jockstraps outside their clothes.
b) The language: The gang, called "droogs," speak a language that combines Russian, English, Romany, and rhyming slang with Shakespearean flare.
c) The ultra-violence: Alex and the droogs thrash a homeless man and sexually assault a woman while he croons "Singing in the Rain." Alex also crushes an old woman's head with a sculpture of a penis.
d) The graphic sex: The film includes full-frontal nudity of both sexes, a hilarious threesome edited at high-speed and set to the "William Tell Overture," and several appalling and darkly comedic costumed gang rapes.
e) All of the above.

CONTINUING ED

In 1936, Charlie Chaplin made the film *Modern Times,* a romantic comedy featuring his character the Little Tramp—an impoverished, quirky mess of contradictions with his tiny hat, giant shoes, tight jacket, huge pants, and square mustache. Chaplin, who grew up in extreme poverty, was a champion of the working poor. He was concerned by the brutality of the industrial age and set out to satirize corporate greed and the dehumanizing impact of machines.

Try to put yourself in the mindset of someone going to see *Modern Times* in 1936. Watch the film and consider how the following would meet the audience's expectation to confront and laugh at the excesses of the industrial age, and at the same time exceed those same expectations:

- The harshness of the working conditions
- The invasiveness of technology
- The special effects of the film
- The suffering of the poor
- The degree of chaos the Little Tramp causes

MINI FINAL ANSWER

The correct answer is **e) All of the above**. In his 1971 review of *A Clockwork Orange*, *New York Times* film critic Vincent Canby wrote, "It is brilliant, a tour de force of extraordinary images, music, words and feelings, a much more original achievement for commercial films than the Burgess novel is for literature." The score, locations, clothing, language, and powerful combinations of light comedy, music, and extreme violence all go beyond what the audience anticipates. But what exceed expectations more profoundly are the extreme feelings and complex thoughts stirred by the expression of Burgess's core idea that however awful it is to live in a world plagued by evil, it would be even worse to live in one where evil could not exist, in which humankind had been neutered.

22

Craft actionable dialogue.

"Speech is power: speech is to persuade, to convert, to compel."
—RALPH WALDO EMERSON, Essayist, Poet

QUICK TAKE

When FBI agents use the term "actionable intelligence," it means they can act on it. A witness says he saw a woman at the crime scene and he knows where she works; now the agents can go to her office.

Great dialogue is fueled by strategic battles to achieve specific objectives—by characters trying to get other characters to do things. This heightens emotion, drives the narrative forward, and, above all, reveals who they are. Imagine two little kids who each realize they've broken their mother's will by badgering her for candy. The first one backs off. He says, "I'm sorry, Mom." The second one adds, "I'm taking a soda too." Because their dialogue is clear, specific, and actionable, it comes to life.

If you just get this right, you're well on your way. But let's lay a deeper foundation. To write dialogue that jumps off the page, that's dynamic and revelatory, scintillating, original, and alive, you need to do some work to understand the characters and the situation they're in. We'll break that down next.

HOW IT WORKS

In Chapter 15, "Write characters to the top of their intelligence," we talked about how important it is to have your characters bring their A game to the story. Again, they can make mistakes, even stupid ones. They can get tripped up by their own hidden desires and choke under pressure. But they can't be just plain stupid, or they become uninteresting, repetitive, and dismissible. Characters who operate at the top of their intelligence push each other to reveal more of their true natures. And they're just plain more fun to watch, read, and hear speak.

To write effective dialogue for each character you need to know:

- Their basic biography, worldview, and temperament
- Their emotional state
- How they view their relationship with the other character(s)
- What they need from the other character(s)
- How they expect the other character(s) to respond

Basic biography, worldview, and temperament

The amount of backstory and history you figure out for your characters is a personal decision that varies from writer to writer. Some need to know every single thing they can about their characters before they write. Others trust they'll figure it out as they go and add only the details that they need to tell the story. For now, we just want to get in touch with who this person is on the most basic level: What do they look and feel like? How old are they? How do they see the world? Are they naïve and trusting or hard and cynical? Generally speaking, every character you create should have their own unique temperament. In *The Lord of the Rings*, Gandalf is wise and mysterious; Frodo is sweet and trusting; Aragorn is the strong and silent type; Gimli is loud and combative, etc.

Emotional state

The mood we're in can radically alter our behavior. When my wife has a lousy night's sleep and hasn't had her coffee, it's a bad idea to go near her. You want to consider what your characters were doing before the scene or chapter started. Were they stuck in a horrific Los Angeles traffic jam for hours? Or did they just go for a long jog on the beach? I recently played poker with some old actor buddies. The guy on my right was on a tear—he had just gotten a second killer job offer and was on cloud nine. He was dressed nicely, shaved and showered, and brought an expensive bottle of Scotch to the game. He cracked jokes and was full of compliments about everything. The guy on my left hadn't worked in almost a year. His clothes were rumpled, shoes untied, and he could barely mumble hello. How we feel has a huge effect on how we act and what we say.

How they view their relationship with the other character(s)

Think about reasons they may be open or closed, feel good or bad, comfortable or uncomfortable with the other character(s). A woman is wary about a former colleague joining her new firm because she knows he is a wicked ass-kisser. A man is happy to see his newly sober brother talking optimistically about the future, but also nervous because he's relapsed before and seems vulnerable and twitchy. He might erupt at any second.

What they need from the other character(s)

Whenever human beings spend time in each other's company, we need things from each other. It could be to talk about something important, entertain each other, or borrow ten grand. If we're having a crappy time, our need could be to vent or to simply part ways. Whatever it is, we need something. This is especially true for characters in a story. If dialogue must be actionable, then of course it's essential to know what each character needs in order for the characters to make intelligent decisions about what to say and how to say it.

How they expect the other character(s) to respond

There's an old joke about a guy who wants to borrow his neighbor's lawn mower. As he walks to the neighbor's house, he worries that the guy won't lend it to him, and he'll be embarrassed. He thinks about all the times he lent the other guy stuff, and how rude it will be if he says no. But his gut screams that the guy will refuse and the closer he gets to his house, the angrier he gets. Finally, he rings the bell. The neighbor answers and the man shouts, "Keep your damn lawn mower!" and storms off. What you expect from the people you talk to affects what you say.

• • •

When you know each character's basic biography, worldview, and temperament, their emotional state, where things stand with the other characters, what they need from each other, and what they expect to happen, you have built a strong foundation on which to write dialogue that works. This is essentially the work that professional actors do. They invest a great deal of time into figuring out exactly what their character is trying to do to the character they're talking to. This is worth bearing in mind even if you're writing fiction—you want to write your dialogue so well an actor could perform it. And if you are working with actors, you can now speak a key part of their language and work together to better understand your characters.

The key point is that your characters are not just talking. They're playing actions. If a kid wants his mom to let him eat candy before dinner and asks, "Can I mom? Can I please please please?" his action is badgering her. If she says no and he cries, "Oh man, you never let me have any fun ever!" he's making her feel guilty. If she says, "Not tonight, please, I'm so tired," she's begging him to stop. If she snarls, "Ask me one more time," she's threatening him. There are, of course, other factors—rhythm, consistency, believability, psychology, and poetic flair. I just don't think these things can be taught; they come with practice. Instead, focus on making the dialogue feel clear, sharp, purposeful, necessary, and active.

Though there are no rules on how many people can speak in a scene, the overwhelming majority of them feature just two characters doing most, if not all, of the talking. This is because dialogue is actually far more complex than it seems. Stories often deal with high-stakes situations where intricate, intense emotions are expressed and difficult ideas exchanged. There's a scene in *The Godfather* where Don Corleone meets with Virgil "The Turk" Sollozzo, to discuss a major drug deal. Sonny, Tom Hagen, Clemenza, and Tessio join the Don to hear out the deal. Except for a few lines by Sonny—that turn out to have enormous consequences—*all* of the dialogue is spoken by Don Corleone and Sollozzo. Even in plays featuring large groups of people, like most of August Wilson's work, the dialogue tends to be broken up into sections focused on the interactions of just two characters.

I strongly encourage rookie writers to keep their cast design small and stories simple. To get these complex dynamics between people right takes hard work and deep thought. Think how different the social dynamics are when you're out with two friends as opposed to just one. Three people is a whole different ball game.

Have fun with this. And stay open to what you learn. When you do this work, your characters push each other harder, dig deeper, and force you, as the writer, to go further into their personalities, to reveal more of who they are and what they're truly after. Understanding your characters' intentions is the most important factor in writing killer dialogue. It puts you into a more focused state, which makes it easier to lose yourself and fully inhabit your characters.

HOW A MASTER DID IT

Death of a Salesman (1949)
Arthur Miller

At the start of Arthur Miller's Pulitzer Prize– and Tony Award–winning play, Willy Loman, an aging salesman, returns home from a sales trip late at night, exhausted. He's shaken because he couldn't keep his mind focused, and kept veering off the road. His identity is tied to his job. If he can't sell, he can't earn a living; if he can't earn a living, he feels worthless. Lately, he's been drifting into the past and talking to himself. He longs for the old days when his sons, Biff and Happy, were promising teenagers. The house was full of life. The air was fresher. He earned a good living. He provided for his family. He was the man of the house and his boys looked up to him.

Now his house is dark and too big for just him and his wife. His life makes no sense. He spent his entire life paying down his mortgage but now that his house is almost free and clear, there's no one to fill it. He has no grandkids. His once-promising boys are unmarried, lost souls floundering through their thirties. The younger one, Happy, is a salesman. He's pleasant enough, but immature and fake. He's stuck at a dead-end job with little chance of promotion, and he compulsively sleeps with other men's wives. He has no core values or higher purpose. His father, whom he idolized, always favored his older brother.

The older son, Biff, is a drifter; he's unable to hold down a job and bitterly resents his father. The defining experience of

Biff's life was the day he paid the old man a surprise visit in a hotel on the road—and caught Willy with the other woman. Right there his faith in his father, in his family, in how the world works, was shattered. And he lost his way.

Biff has returned for a visit and Happy came to be with him. They're staying in the house for a few days. Willy is traumatized by Biff's failure to launch and knows, deep down, that he's to blame. But he still holds out hope. Regardless, the boys being home causes him a great deal of stress as they stir his passion for the old days and worries about their future.

The scene we'll break down takes place near the start of Act Two, when Willy meets with his boss, Howard, to ask for a different job at the company, one that would enable him to work at the headquarters so he could stop traveling. Before we unpack Willy's dialogue, let's look at some other key principles in play. Willy is a salesman and always has been. That takes tremendous optimism and the ability to overcome rejection. His plan is to go in and close a deal, just as he's always done. He operates at the top of his intelligence because this is all he knows how to do. His intention is to be affable and connect with Howard, lay out his case, and land a new job. He'll drop his price a little if he has to, but he'll start high, so that will be fine.

The problem with executing this plan is that he is consumed by conflict on every level. His home and car are breaking down. Bills are piling up. His sons are failing and he's riddled with guilt. His mind keeps drifting into the past. He's growing old and there is little to no safety net. He has no pension. And his ego will not allow him to live off charity. His highest ideal is self-reliance.

The scene begins with Willy meekly entering his boss Howard's office. Howard is fussing with a "wire" recorder that he just got and is obsessed with—he makes Willy listen to obnoxious audio of his kids reciting capital cities and other nonsense. Without even looking at Howard's lines, you can tell exactly what happens. Here are fifteen things Willy says, and what the underlying action is:

1. Dialogue: "Like to have a little talk with you, Howard."
   Action: Asking to talk about something important.
2. Dialogue: (re: recorder) "I'm definitely going to get one."
   Action: Propping himself up as an equal, even though he can't afford a newfangled gadget like the recorder.
3. Dialogue: "Well, tell you the truth, Howard. I've come to the decision that I'd rather not travel anymore."
   Action: Easing into the issue at hand.
4. Dialogue: "Remember, Christmas time, when you had the party here? You said you'd try to think of some spot for me here in town."
   Action: Making Howard feel like he's breaking a promise if he says no.
5. Dialogue: "I tell ya, Howard. The kids are all grown up, y'know. I don't need much anymore. If I could take home—well, sixty-five dollars a week, I could swing it."
   Action: Selling a good deal on his labor. He'll lower his offer several times.
6. Dialogue: "God knows, Howard, I never asked a favor of any man. But I was with the firm when your father used to carry you in here in his arms."
   Action: Reminding Howard of his long service, and appealing to him personally.
7. Dialogue: "Look, it isn't a question of whether I can sell, is it?"
   Action: Assuring him he can do the job he seeks.
8. Dialogue: (*desperately*) "Just let me tell you a story, Howard." Willy then tells Howard a story about an inspiring and beloved salesman he once met, Dave Singleton, who died an honorable death. His funeral was attended by hundreds. He adds, "In those days there was personality in it, Howard. There was comradeship, and gratitude in it."
   Action: Pleading for kindness and respect.

9. **Dialogue:** "I'm talking about your father! There were promises made across this desk!"
   Action: Insisting he is *owed* this job. The founder of the company, Howard's father Frank, implied he'd take care of Willy.

10. **Dialogue:** "I put thirty-four years into this firm, Howard, and now I can't pay my insurance! You can't eat the orange and throw the peel away—a man is not a piece of fruit!"
    Action: Demanding recognition and respect for his work.

11. **Dialogue:** "In 1928 I had a big year. I averaged a hundred and seventy dollars a week in commissions."
    Action: Asserting his own former glory.

12. **Dialogue:** "Frank, Frank, don't you remember what you told me that time? How you put your hand on my shoulder, and Frank . . ."
    Action: Escaping into the past—the only place left to go to feel self-respect.

13. **Dialogue:** "Howard, you're firing me?"
    Action: Confirming what he's heard and making Howard say it straight out.

14. **Dialogue:** "All right, I'll go to Boston tomorrow."
    Action: Offering to drop the whole thing, and keep his traveling sales job.

15. **Dialogue:** "I can't throw myself on my sons!"
    Action: Clinging to his last shred of dignity.

Nothing in story works in isolation, and this is particularly true of dialogue. This scene is located in the dead center of the play. As we discussed in Chapter 7, "Max out the middle," this is the place to put the most intensely emotional moments—and Miller does exactly that. The reason the dialogue works so well here is that Miller has a total command of structure, character, and theme. Because he knows exactly what the purpose of the scene is (to break your heart), who the characters are, and what it's about—how a hypercapitalist system grinds out the humanity of the individual—he is able to make his dialogue actionable, and therefore riveting. What ultimately makes this one of the most tragic scenes ever written is that although Willy is pretty much dead from the start, he takes action after action after action to try to save himself. However obnoxious, irritable, and shallow he can be, his passion to live is noble. He gives it everything he's got.

HOW YOU DO IT

The following bullet points will help you think through and execute the principle.

- Writing killer dialogue takes hard work. Make peace with this fact now and commit to doing the work.

- Get clear on the worldview, outlook, and basic biography of every character who speaks.

- Know what they were doing before the scene and how it shaped their mood. What kind of day or night were they having? Did a bus just blow through a puddle and spray dirty water on their new suit? Did they just have some sweet afternoon delight with a loved one?

- Determine how they feel about the person they're talking to. If they love and trust this person, they're likely to behave differently than they would with someone they think is a duplicitous thief.

- What *specifically* do they need? Why do they think they can get it from the person they're speaking to?

- Know what they expect to happen—do they expect the other person to meet their need or reject them? And know how this affects their attitude coming in. This works particularly well with the fifteenth principle, "Write characters to the top of their intelligence."

▸ Show their attitude and expectation in their behavior and their word choices. Make sure their underlying attitude informs the dialogue and, as always, make everything hard for the hero. They've got to work for it. In *The Godfather*, when the undertaker Bonasera pleads with the Godfather, Vito Corleone, to avenge the assault on his daughter, Vito makes him earn it by showing proper love, respect, and gratitude. This forces Bonasera to dig deep, think on his feet, and up his game. As a result, in a brief conversation, we learn a tremendous amount about both characters.

▸ Even if you're writing fiction, write as if your dialogue will be acted. Imagine an actor reading the line. If they can figure out *why* the character is saying the lines, it works. If not, it doesn't. Dialogue exists to help the character obtain what they need. Talking is an action in the same way any physical movement is.

▸ You'll know you have it when your dialogue feels alive, as if an electric charge runs through it, when everything the characters say makes sense given who they are and the situation they're in, and it feels necessary for them to speak—every word feels essential.

▸ Again, we always like to invert, to figure out how to do things by exploring how not to do them. To write vapid, cliché-ridden, boring dialogue, just let characters say whatever you want the audience to know. If you want to say how long a couple's been together, just have one say, "Gosh, we have been together thirty years! Where does the time go?" And make sure you have no clue who this character is, where he's been, what he wants, or who he's talking to. This is an important point—if your dialogue sucks, it's almost always because it's not properly motivated, it's just information sharing. To fix it, make it actionable. For example, she says, "For thirty years I've been taking your shit"—this can work, because she's playing an action: telling him to back off.

MINI FINAL EXAM

Read the following, then answer the question below.

A Navy SEAL commander gathers his squad for a high-risk raid. The target is a terrorist bomb maker, who is guarded by heavily armed militia. He's in a warehouse in the middle of enemy-controlled territory. The SEALs expect to take massive fire—and they're excited about it. The commander gathers all six soldiers around and locks eyes on each one as he speaks.

"All right, we're good to go. Get your shit together—and bring at least six liters of water. I remind you that you cannot power through heat stroke. And I don't want to have to carry you fuckers. Basics, basics. Ammo, grenades, smoke, and make sure your fuckin' headset works. We're going to meet the marines at the *second* checkpoint—and we are going on foot.

"We'll move in groups of two. Get to the corner, sprint your fuckin' ass off to the next corner. For each team, know who's covering which direction. You will be getting some. And it will be heavy. They know we're here. Do not return fire unless you absolutely have to. If we alert the enemy prior to our final attack position, it will be a problem. All right, if there's anything you need to say to anyone back home. . . . And again, know that I could not be more proud to serve with this group of warriors. Your courage and dedication to each other, to your country, and to the world is unmatched and you have my respect. We move out at twenty."

How many different actions does this dialogue include?

a) Seventeen, because there are seventeen sentences and each one is an action.
b) Eight: confirming, instructing, reminding, informing, further instructing, reminding, honoring/revving up, and further informing
c) One, because it's all one big action—to prepare.
d) None, because his words are not relevant to the task at hand.
e) None—his words are inactive because only he talks.

CONTINUING ED

Jennifer Egan's Pulitzer Prize–winning novel, *A Visit from the Goon Squad*, features multiple storylines, all focused on the complexities and cruelties of passing time. The stories track people battling to find their place in the world, overcoming addictions, and building careers, and all touch upon rock 'n roll and its culture of youth. The novel has an inventive structure that jumps from story to story and time period to time period to help develop its theme of passing time. Though it explores many issues, what's really at its heart is the simple attempt to find meaning—and happiness—in spite of all we must endure and the never-ending change time subjects us to.

In the chapter "X's and O's," two middle-aged men, Bennie and Scotty, get together at Bennie's office. They were once bandmates in a punk group called The Flaming Dildos. Their lives have not worked out as expected. Scotty was the leader of the band and he was young and hungry and filled with potential. Bennie sucked. Now, with many years behind them, Bennie has become a successful music producer. And Scotty's become a lost soul. In this chapter, what does Scotty need from Bennie? What does he expect to happen? Carefully go through his dialogue and study what actions he's taking through his words. What does he feel? And what is he trying to do to Bennie?

MINI FINAL ANSWER

The correct answer is **b) Eight: confirming, instructing, reminding, informing, further instructing, reminding, honoring/revving up, and further informing**. You might choose to break this up a little differently—it's not essential to distinguish between informing and instructing. What's important is that you know why your character is delivering each line and that it's written to the top of the character's intelligence.

"All right, we're good to go."
Action: confirming

"Get your shit together—and bring at least six liters of water. I remind you that you cannot power through heat stroke. And I don't want to have to carry you fuckers."
Action: instructing and adding some levity

"Basics, basics. Ammo, grenades, smoke, and make sure your fuckin' headset works."
Action: reminding to check gear

"We're going to meet the marines at the *second* checkpoint—and we are going on foot."
Action: informing

"We'll move in groups of two. Get to the corner, sprint your fuckin' ass off to the next corner. For each team, know who's covering which direction. You will be getting some. And it will be heavy. They know we're here. Do not return fire unless you absolutely have to. We don't need to wake up the neighborhood."
Action: further instructing and informing

"All right, if there's anything you need to say to anyone back home. . . ."
Action: reminding (of the gravity of the situation)

"And again, know that I could not be more proud to serve with this group of warriors. Your courage and dedication to each other, to your country, and to the world is unmatched and you have my respect."
Action: honoring/revving up

"We move out at twenty."
Action: further informing

23

Hide meaning.

"Let the audience add up two plus two and they'll love you forever."
—ERNST LUBITSCH, Filmmaker

QUICK TAKE

In the last chapter, "Craft actionable dialogue," we explored the importance of writing dialogue that is fueled by specific intention so it drives your narrative forward, sparks conflict, and forces characters to respond in a way that reveals who they are. In story, characters don't just talk for no reason. They speak to achieve a specific objective—to entertain, hurt, provoke, share information, etc.

This principle, "Hide meaning," is its sister. When characters are actively trying to influence each other, but the meaning of what they're saying is hidden, things get interesting. Hiding meaning opens up all kinds of dramatic possibilities to move your narrative and characters in compelling directions. The gap between what a character says and actually means is intriguing. If a character says, "I like your haircut, it suits your face," but there's something off about their tone, this raises questions. Are they actually insulting the haircut? Are they angry? Did they definitely say it with a tone? What's going on here? An action has been played, but we don't know what it means. By trusting that your readers/viewers will find the hidden meaning, or even interpret it in their own way, you show them respect. And make their experience more rewarding.

HOW IT WORKS

Let's say two old friends meet for drinks. They hug, thrilled to see each other. And say exactly what they mean:

Ned: My God, you look fantastic, Pat!

Pat: I want to say the same about you, Ned, but you've aged.

Ned: That kind of hurts my feelings.

Pat: I don't want to hurt your feelings. You know I would never do that on purpose.

Ned: I know. Of course you'd age too if you struggled for these last ten years to make ends meet.

Pat: Struggled? But you look so happy on Facebook.

Ned: Who doesn't? It's all hype. I'm in debt up to my eyeballs. They're about to foreclose on my house. How are you doing?

Pat: I'm good. I still like my job. Kate and I are still happily married. Pat Junior's in college—doing okay, some mental health things. He's probably fine but we're keeping an eye on him. He drinks . . . a lot. And to be honest, so do I.

In isolation, this bit of dialogue is quirky and actually more interesting than I thought it would be—it's so unusual for people to come right out and admit to their vulnerabilities that it's engaging. But over the course of a full-length story, this type of on-the-nose conversation is likely to become exhausting and predictable. The onion just peels itself right before our eyes. It's all right there. It makes everything easy for the characters. If everyone says what they really mean, everyone knows exactly where they stand and can act accordingly. When you make life easy for your characters, they don't have to do the work that's necessary to grow. They can just talk through every problem, reach the most obvious conclusions, and move on. For example, if a boss tells a worker, "I'm concerned about your performance," and the worker says, "I'll try harder," and the boss responds, "I don't think you can work your way out of this, but I'll wait until after the holidays to fire you," the worker might be hurt and upset, but at least he knows exactly where he stands and can start looking for another job. The problem with this is it's dishonest. People do not always know what they feel and what they mean, and we all have to work hard to navigate our relationships.

Most spouses can relate to the situation where you're about to walk out the door to a big event and your significant other asks, "How do I look?" You want to respond honestly but what if you're not sure whether the outfit is unique and great or not really working? Or you think it looks terrible, but don't want to hurt your spouse's feelings? We also don't want to initiate conflict. The boss in the example above would almost certainly say, "OK. We'll talk after the holidays," and imply there's a possibility of working this out, even if he knows there is none. We also hide our feelings when we don't want to worry or burden others. Your doctor finds a mysterious spot on an X-ray that needs further testing. And someone asks how you're doing. You say, "Fine," but they sense you're far from fine and wonder what you're hiding. Maybe they worry. Maybe they tell others. Or even wonder if you are hiding something from them. Why? Did they do something wrong? Do you not trust them with a secret?

When characters hide what they mean, it's more entertaining and psychologically interesting. What we hide says as much as, if not more than, what we reveal. And if you think about it, there's only one way to say what you mean. You just say what you mean. But there's an infinite number of ways to hide what you mean. If a character wants to make another character feel insecure, they can bring up a whole array of subjects, say the most seemingly innocuous thing with a certain tone and look.

This principle doesn't always have to be about conflict. When people say things indirectly, they're not always trying to get away with something or to spare someone's feelings. A man texts his fiancé, "Made you something special. It's in the fridge. See you tomorrow." It means simply, "I love you."

HOW A MASTER DID IT

The Remains of the Day (1993)
Screenplay by Ruth Prawer Jhabvala
Based on the novel by Kazuo Ishiguro

Mr. Stevens is the head butler of Darlington Hall, a vast English estate. Dedicated to serving Lord Darlington, he has no life outside his job. He demands perfection from his staff and makes sure every glass sparkles, every fork is placed with precision. His father, whom he greatly admires, was also a head butler. So he was literally born to do this work. He does not allow himself to express emotion, to hold opinions on anything beyond his job, or to conduct himself in any manner that would be detrimental to his labor. His dedication to serving the Darlington estate is so all-encompassing, he even continues working, without distraction, as his father lies on his deathbed. His father would not have it any other way.

A challenge to his carefully constructed world comes in the form of Ms. Kenton, an attractive, articulate young woman who is hired to lead the housekeeping staff. She too is excellent at what she does and devoted to her work. The two are kindred spirits who share an intense attraction, mutual respect, and what seems like true love. The problem is that Mr. Stevens has no room to be in love. He cannot allow himself to be emotional, out of control, vulnerable. It would conflict too heavily with his work.

The story takes place in two time periods: the 1930s, as Hitler is threatening Europe, and the 1950s. In the years following the war, Lord Darlington is exposed as a Nazi sympathizer. It's not clear if he was a true anti-Semite or simply failed to see the threat posed by Hitler. Either way, he supported the appeasement of Germany and an alliance with the Nazis. His reputation is destroyed. The tragedy of this for Mr. Stevens is that he devoted his life to a man who was at best a pathetic fool, calling the entirety of his own existence into question.

In the 1950s he finds himself lonely, growing old, and filled with regret for allowing his one true love, Ms. Kenton, to marry another man. After he exchanges letters with her and learns that she's separated, he attempts to bring her back to the estate, which has been purchased by a wealthy, warm-hearted American. Mr. Stevens dreams of reuniting with Ms. Kenton, and running the estate together, but this time openly in love. Sadly, he'll learn that while she does still love him, she has just found out that her daughter is pregnant. She wants to stay near her to help with the baby. For the good of her family, she will reconcile with her husband, whom she describes as lost without her. Though she would love to return to the estate and be with Mr. Stevens, her commitment to her family must come first. When they part on a rainy night, she gets onto a bus and watches him through the back window, tears streaming. He can only watch helplessly as the one true love of his life disappears into the night.

In the scene below, which takes place in the 1930s, he sits alone in his darkened study, reading. It's daytime but the curtains are drawn. She enters, carrying flowers to place into a vase. He puts down his book and watches her.

Ms. Kenton: What are you reading?

Mr. Stevens: A book.

Ms. Kenton: Yes. But what sort of book?

Mr. Stevens: It's a book, Ms. Kenton. A book.

She reaches for it. He holds it beyond her reach. He gets up and retreats into a corner.

Ms. Kenton: Are you shy about your book?

Mr. Stevens: No.

Ms. Kenton: What is it? Is it racy?

Mr. Stevens: Racy?

Ms. Kenton: Are you reading a racy book?

Mr. Stevens: Do you think racy books are to be found on His Lordship's shelves?

Ms. Kenton: How would I know? What is it? Let me see it. Let me see your book.

She reaches for the book, he holds it close to his chest.

Mr. Stevens: Please leave me alone, Ms. Kenton.

Ms. Kenton: Why won't you show me your book?

Mr. Stevens: This is my private time. You're invading it.

Ms. Kenton: Is that so?

Mr. Stevens: Yes.

Ms. Kenton: I'm invading your private time, am I?

Mr. Stevens: Yes.

Ms. Kenton: What's in that book? Come on, let me see.

Pause. She inches closer, carefully.

Ms. Kenton: Or are you protecting me? Is that what you're doing? Would I be shocked? Would it ruin my character?

Pause. He silently grants her permission to move even closer.

Ms. Kenton: Let me see it.

He flinches as she reaches for the book, clutched tightly in his hand. As she slowly pries his fingers from the book, he watches her closely. Their eyes meet as she takes it from his hand. She inspects the book, breathless. Then . . .

Ms. Kenton: It's not scandalous at all. It's just a sentimental old love story.

Mr. Stevens: Yes. I read these books, any books, to develop my command and knowledge of the English language. I read to further my education, Ms. Kenton. I really must ask you, please, not to disturb the few moments I have to myself.

Ms. Kenton collects herself, turns, and exits the room.

On the surface, this is a scene about a book. Ms. Kenton mistakenly assumes it is a racy book. Mr. Stevens says it is not. She checks for herself and discovers he's telling the truth. He says he reads for education and asks her not to disturb him. That's all that is said. And yet, this is widely considered to be one of the most heartbreaking scenes in film, the ultimate metaphor for missed opportunity, for choosing the wrong path in life.

Mr. Stevens desperately wants to express his true feelings, but can't. They are buried too deep to access. He longs to tell her how he feels, but to do so would destroy his identity. This is not a scene about a book. She doesn't want to see the book. She wants him to express his true feelings, to finally turn loose his passion and sexuality. She wants to make love with him, and he wants to too, but he can't. He is a strong-willed man. If he were not interested in her, he would never have crept into the corner and allowed her to get so close. When she asked about his book, he would have just showed it to her. When she asks if it is a racy book, he doesn't say, "No it's not." He asks, "Do you think racy books are to be found on His Lordship's shelves?" He is prolonging the intimacy of the encounter. This is a man who runs a very large staff with an iron hand. Yet here, he can barely bring himself to speak, and feebly asks her not to invade his space. When he tells her that he reads books to further his command of the English language, what he means is that he does not share her penchant for romance and won't allow himself to be seduced.

When he firmly asks her not to disturb him, he definitively rejects her advances. Though she says nothing, she is humiliated, hurt, and feels like a fool. She too values professionalism and control. And this is her boss. This encounter is devastating to her on every level.

Now let's look at how the scene would work if they said what they meant.

Ms. Kenton enters to find Mr. Stevens reading.

Ms. Kenton: Put your book down please, I've something to say.

He looks up at her.

Ms. Kenton: I can no longer hide my feelings. I'm in love with you. And I want us to be together . . . in the most intimate fashion.

Mr. Stevens: I can't. It makes me too uncomfortable. I have no room in my life for love. Service to His Lordship is my life.

Ms. Kenton: You could serve me. And I you. We can serve each other.

Mr. Stevens: I wish I could—my God, I love you so. I truly do—but I can't. You're so lovely. I am fiercely attracted to you, but I would be vulnerable. I could be hurt. Then I could slip up at my job and that would wreck my sense of self.

Ms. Kenton: I'm burning for you.

Mr. Stevens: You're making me angry because on the one hand I want you terribly, but on the other I cannot do it. I just cannot do it!

Ms. Kenton: Ravish me this minute.

Mr. Stevens: I said no. Are you deaf, fool?

Ms. Kenton: You're really, truly, saying no?

Mr. Stevens: Get the hell out!

Ms. Kenton: I feel humiliated, rejected, and heartbroken.

Mr. Stevens: So be it.

Ms. Kenton runs off.

Though this is kind of hilarious, it fails on many levels. First of all, if these two lived in a world in which they always expressed exactly how they felt, things could never reach a boiling point. In the original their repressed sexuality fuels their desire, but here nothing is repressed. They also fail miserably when it comes to operating at the top of their intelligence. If they are both clear in their desire to be together, and he explains that he fears being vulnerable, she would surely make the case that she would not hurt him and that her love would make him an even more effective butler. Since *Remains of the Day*'s genre is a hybrid of drama and romance, the utterly direct dialogue doesn't work. It doesn't match the tone or mood of the story. All that said, writing out what the characters actually mean is a terrific way to sketch a first draft to make sure you've got a firm grasp of what's hidden below the surface.

HOW YOU DO IT

The following bullet points will help you think through and execute the principle.

- When we write dialogue, we venture into psychologically complex territory. You, as the writer, may not know what your characters mean. When you get into that primal place where hours pass in seconds, things erupt from the depths of your psyche. Therefore, consciously deciding to hide the meaning of what characters say requires patience and reflection. How much information about the characters and plot you reveal adds even more complexity to these choices. So you need to always be in conversation with yourself about what it is you're exploring.

▶ Write out the first draft of dialogue stating exactly what the characters mean. Then return to the draft and work backward to hide what they really mean.

▶ Think carefully through each line. Exactly why are the characters hiding what they mean? Is it due to fear? Shame? Or maybe even they don't know what they're trying to say.

▶ This principle, of course, is a sister to "Craft actionable dialogue." All the work you did there—understanding who the characters are, what they're feeling, what their relationship is to each other—applies here as well. And, again, not every character is the type to hide what they mean, at least not to the same degree, and not every line must be packed with hidden meaning.

▶ Break out a pen and paper, and instill hidden meaning in the following line: "Let's get a cup of coffee." What might this line actually mean? Virtually anything, right? I'll start. It means, "I need to talk to you about something big." Do you feel how this builds tension by asking a dramatic question? Write five to ten alternate meanings.

▶ You'll know you have it when you feel that your dialogue is filled with hidden meaning, but not so much hidden meaning that it's impossible to decipher what the hell is going on. Great dialogue makes you think about the nuances of your characters and the layers of your theme, and also drives your narrative forward.

MINI FINAL EXAM

Read the following, then answer the question below.

A middle-aged son, who some might uncharitably but accurately call a "doofus," visits his hypercritical, judgmental, razor-tongued mother. He knows he's going to be mercilessly criticized—for what he says, does, wears—everything about him sets the old lady off. He prepares accordingly. He makes sure to wear a nice belt that matches his polished shoes. He checks and double-checks that his pants cuffs are not too high and touch his shoes at exactly the right location. He combs his hair and carefully fingers in exactly the right amount of gel. Then, he coaches himself in the mirror, vowing not to let her get to him. He acts out awful things she might say and meticulously crafts unruffled responses.

On the bus ride to his mother, he deliberately tries to recall the most pleasant times they've had together—the strolls to the farmers' market, the long hours seated at the library reading the classics beside each other, the time she let him have two cupcakes on his twenty-third birthday. The two have brunch at Mom's favorite diner, where she eats after church every Sunday—and Tuesday, Wednesday, and Friday. Maybe she'll be in a good mood for once and it won't be too awful.

Throughout the meal, Mom says the following lines. Identify all those that could express disappointment in her son:

a) "That shirt is nice. They have it in blue? I love how you look in blue."
b) "Are those the shoes I bought you?"
c) "Remember Martha Davidson? Her son just got married. Oh! Is he tall. So tall and handsome!"
d) "Egg whites have fewer calories."
e) All of the above.

CONTINUING ED

In the Coen brothers' 2007 film *No Country for Old Men*, serial killer and hitman Anton Chigurh stops for gas in a rural Texas town. Chigurh is a wild-eyed madman who has a relationship with a nefarious company that he's helping to recover stolen money. He has a thick face, a piercing gaze, and a long, odd, sweeping side part. The scene begins with Chigurh buying gas. The gas station owner, a sixty-something, pale-skinned, pleasant man, asks if they've been getting any rain "up your way." Chigurh coldly responds, "What way would that be?" The man says, "I seen you was from Dallas." To this Chigurh replies, "What business is it of yours where I'm from, friend-o?" What is at stake during this scene? How does Chigurh feel about the gas station attendant? In what year does the story take place? After Chigurh encourages the man to call heads or tails on his coin flip, the man asks some questions about what he stands to win or lose. How does Chigurh feel about this man and what does the man stand to lose? Note how indirectly it's all expressed.

MINI FINAL ANSWER

The correct answer is **e) All of the above**. Each of those lines of dialogue could express disappointment. There's a way to read them as wishing his shirt was a different color, chastising him for not wearing the shoes she gave him, looking down on him for being unmarried and not tall and handsome enough, and pointing out that he's overweight.

24

Hunt big game.

"Get after it."
—JOCKO WILLINK, Navy SEAL Commander

QUICK TAKE

This principle is about deciding what to write about. It's about taking on the issues, incidents, and people that are essential to you. They're personal.

You can't escape the fact that the stories you tell define who you are. Storytelling is a revealing art. This is what makes it so terrifying—what if the world rips off your mask and finds you lacking? In *The War of Art*, Steven Pressfield popularized the term "resistance"—a force that does whatever it can to keep you from completion. The more important the work, the more powerful the resistance. The degree of resistance you feel toward a subject is a reliable indicator of its importance.

If you envision your essential being as a target, you want to write about those things that hit the bull's-eye—the things that keep you up at night, fuel your obsessions, get your blood flowing. There's an expression in martial arts—the monk runs *at* the barking dog at night. You face your fears. The subjects you need to write about are like those barking dogs. They'll stalk and torment you until you confront them. The sooner you accept this, the sooner you can get after them. And gain all the insight, confidence, and self-respect that comes from showing courage.

HOW IT WORKS

Sometimes you get a blast of inspiration and immediately know with absolute certainty what you must write. A streak of light races into the woods and you have to follow it in. Awesome. Go for it, always. Here though, we're going to consider some key factors that will help you decide what to write when divine inspiration hasn't yet struck. This includes your biography, personality, and defining experiences. The key word here is alignment. You want to see a clear, direct, and compelling connection between who you are, what matters to you, and what you're writing about.

When you read a story you love and then learn about the author—or meet them—it always makes sense that *this* person wrote *that* story. In all the research I did for this book, I never once found myself crying out, "*She* wrote *that*?! Wow! How could that be?" This alignment between author and subject is not always as readily apparent as it is, for example, between Eugene O'Neill and his autobiographical play about his alcoholic father and brother and drug-addicted mother, *Long Day's Journey Into Night*. But when it's not, it usually only takes the slightest peek behind the curtain to find it.

J. K. Rowling thought up the idea for her magical world centered around the Hogwarts School of Witchcraft and Wizardry while working for the human rights organization Amnesty International. There, she learned firsthand how much carnage evil leaders can inflict on innocent people. This inspired her to write about the true nature of good and evil. It wasn't a topic she picked out of thin air. The good wizard, Dumbledore, represents humility, acceptance, transparency, freedom, and inclusivity, and the evil wizard, Lord Voldemort, represents arrogance, secrecy, domination, and exclusivity. She wrote about this because she knew the horror of what happens to good people trapped under the tyranny of evil regimes. This authenticity radiates through the novels and into the films.

Look through all twenty-seven masterworks in this book, and you will see a tight alignment between the storyteller, their history, defining experiences, passions, personality, and the subjects they return to throughout their career. Alison Bechdel spent seven years meticulously studying her father in her graphic novel *Fun Home* (see Chapter 17), because it was necessary for her to get him out of her head. He was demanding and emotionally abusive, pushing her to become something he wanted her to be, based on his own repressed needs. Until she dealt with his impact on her, she could not feel truly free.

Junot Diaz spent eleven years writing *The Brief Wondrous Life of Oscar Wao* (see Chapter 20)—about a Dominican "ghetto nerd" and his tragic quest for love. It was necessary for him to write because of his personal history—as a Dominican American immigrant, as a child of parents who lived under a dictatorship, as a man who has struggled in his relationships with women, and as a man who was sexually abused as a boy. To better understand himself, his family, and his culture as a whole, he needed to tell this story.

Neither Bechdel nor Diaz told their stories to win awards or get famous. But that's what happened. Both have known astronomical success. Diaz won the Pulitzer Prize and a MacArthur "genius" grant. Bechdel's graphic memoir was adapted for the stage—something she never dreamt of—and it won the Tony Award for Best Musical. This doesn't mean you have to spend a decade working on your story, or that you must confront your darkest secrets. Arthur Miller wrote the first act of his two-act play *Death of a Salesman* (see Chapter 22) in one night. The second act took him six weeks. He was fascinated by the tragic nature of American everymen who feel extraneous once their utility runs out in our capitalist culture.

HOW A MASTER DID IT

Beloved (1987)
Toni Morrison

Toni Morrison's *Beloved* won her the Pulitzer Prize and, as her masterpiece, was a key reason she was also awarded the Nobel

Prize in Literature. In 2006, more than two hundred critics polled by the *New York Times Book Review* named it the best American novel of the past twenty-five years.

The novel is set in a town on the outskirts of Cincinnati, Ohio, in 1874, right after the Civil War. Sethe is a former slave who lives with her emotionally stunted, but dynamic and quietly intelligent, eighteen-year-old daughter, Denver. She has two sons, Howard and Buglar, but they ran off, in part because Sethe's home is haunted by the enraged ghost of a child.

One day, a man named Paul D. shows up to visit Sethe. He knew her and her husband, Halle, who fathered her children, when they were slaves on a plantation in Kentucky known as Sweet Home. It was run by Mr. and Mrs. Garner, who were relatively kind for slave owners, but after Garner died, the plantation was run by a sadistic and virulently racist white man known as Schoolteacher and his equally repugnant nephews. Paul D. is a strong and profoundly decent man who, like Sethe, has known extraordinary suffering. Her back is covered with thick scars that look like a tree from repeated lashings. He carries so much pain with him that he describes his heart as a tobacco tin where he keeps his worst memories hidden.

Sethe and Paul D. understand each other in a way that only those with a shared history of suffering can. Though Sethe loves Paul D., she is determined to protect Denver from the horrors of her past. So she's fully aware of the danger of having someone from Sweet Home around. They can't help but talk about the past—what they saw and what was done to them. For example, Paul D. confides in her that he knows why her husband, Halle—a kind, intelligent man—went mad. He witnessed Sethe getting raped by Schoolteacher's nephews. He was hiding in the rafters of a barn and the sight of them stealing the milk meant for their children broke him.

After Paul D. and Sethe begin a relationship, he moves in and quickly chases off the ghost haunting the house. Though Denver is at first skeptical of him, he begins to win her over. The three spend a joyful day at a local carnival and return home to find a young woman waiting for them. She calls herself Beloved. And this sets up the conflict at the heart of the novel.

Beloved is a strange character. She has no history, and knows very little about herself, but a great deal—including things she could not possibly know—about Sethe, with whom she is obsessed. Sethe takes her in, and Beloved and Denver become friends. But there's really no room in this home for Beloved and Paul D. Her odd presence and her intense attraction to Sethe make him profoundly uncomfortable, and they drive a wedge between Paul D. and Sethe. He becomes emotionally distant and begins sleeping apart from her.

Another former slave, who goes by the name Stamp Paid, feels obligated to share a secret about Sethe with his friend Paul D. Years ago, when she had just made it to freedom with her four young children—Howard, Buglar, a daughter, and then-infant Denver, four slave catchers showed up to reclaim Sethe's family under the Fugitive Slave Act, which allowed slave owners to track their "property" into free states. Rather than allow her children to be condemned to a life of degradation and abuse as slaves, Sethe violently turned on them, beating the boys and sawing off the head of the girl. She'd have killed them all if she hadn't been stopped. The slave catchers, figuring she'd lost her mind and was now worthless, left without them. And the community allowed Sethe to care for her three remaining children, Howard, Buglar, and Denver. It's possible that Beloved is a runaway slave who truly doesn't know her own history, but Beloved is most likely Sethe's murdered child, somehow returned to her as a young woman.

Paul D. moves out of the house into a cold church basement and, over time, Sethe becomes consumed by her relationship with Beloved. The home begins to feel as if it's sickened, and eventually Denver ventures out to seek help. When a group of women from the community learn what's going on with Beloved and Sethe, they gather before the house and burst into song. It's not just a song, but an exorcism that drives Beloved off. Paul D. returns and vows to care for Sethe, who has lost her grip on reality.

Beloved explores the psychological terrain of slavery, capturing how it felt to be a slave, to be African American in the mid-nineteenth century. A moment that stands out in terms of raw emotional power is Paul D.'s description of being made to wear "the bit"—a piece of iron fitted into the mouths of slaves to degrade them, to silence them, but still keep them working. He talks about walking past a rooster while he's wearing it and feeling as if the rooster is freer than he is. He's made to feel less than an animal.

One time Paul D. talks with his friend Stamp Paid and almost goes over the edge. Morrison writes,

> "Tell me something, Stamp." Paul D.'s eyes were rheumy. "Tell me this one thing. How much is a nigger supposed to take? Tell me. How much?"
>
> "All he can" said Stamp Paid. "All he can."
>
> "Why? Why? Why? Why? Why?"

In three fiercely poetic chapters late in the book, Morrison takes us deep into the minds—even souls—of Sethe, Denver, Beloved, and the millions of human beings who suffered indescribable pain and degradation as slaves. I don't believe in "best of" lists when it comes to art—it's subjective, not a competition, and the criteria never make any sense. But the reason *Beloved* feels to so many as if it is the "best" is because Morrison set the bar so high. As a writer, you can't hunt bigger game than to capture how slavery felt and to heal what seems like it can never be healed. An interviewer once asked her if a mother can ever recover from the trauma of killing her own child. And Morrison answered, with a warm smile and unaffected conviction, "Yes." The interviewer asked, "How?" And Morrison said, "Grace." Though few reach the intensity of the pain Sethe felt, we sense that if she can be healed or redeemed, so can we, so can anyone, so can the world—no matter how bad things get.

• • •

So, that's a basic summary of one of the most critically acclaimed and revered stories ever told. Now, let's look at how she came to write it. Greatness is never an accident.

In 1974, Morrison was editing *The Black Book*, which collected various items from black history, and she came across an article from 1856 entitled "A Visit to the Slave Mother Who Killed Her Child." It was about a woman named Margaret Garner who escaped from slavery with her husband and four children to Ohio. But when she made it to her uncle's farm, she still wasn't safe because slave catchers descended on her uncle's farm. In response, Garner violently turned on her own children and slit her little girl's throat with a butcher knife, killing her. She was apprehended before she could finish off the others.

Morrison could not forget Garner, who was interviewed by the reporters and was entirely rational, even serene. She was certain of her decision. In a 1987 interview with PBS's Charlayne Hunter-Gault, Morrison said, "The article stayed with me a long, long time. And seemed to have in it an extraordinary idea that was worthy of a novel . . . Anything that Margaret Garner would have chosen to do was a disaster. It was a perfect disaster. I didn't know how to judge her. I thought the only one who could judge her would be the daughter she killed."

The idea of exploring the character of the child appealed to Morrison. She could imagine the daughter returning to "claim what she'd been robbed of, which is a mother's love and life and also to accuse her mother. She is the only one who could say, 'How would you know death is better?' Maybe it isn't."

When you watch and read interviews with Morrison about *Beloved*, it feels almost as if a perfect storm formed around, or inside, her that provoked her to write the novel. When she read the article on Garner in the mid-1970s, a lot of her friends were swept up in what was called the women's liberation movement, and had come to believe that motherhood was a kind of prison to be avoided. But Morrison, a devoted single mother of two young boys, felt exactly the opposite. She felt that to love and raise and nurture her own children was the very essence of freedom—a freedom that was denied to Margaret Garner. She couldn't imagine ever killing her boys, but she couldn't imagine allowing slave catchers to take them, either. She found Garner's act abhorrent, but also a powerful statement of ownership, of saying to the world, "these children belong to me."

The idea of bringing Garner's murdered child to life in a novel spoke to her in two other important ways. Educated at Howard University and Cornell, Morrison had become disconnected from her spiritual life. Like many in the African American community, her mother believed in spirits, viewing them as elders who could help guide one through life. Her mother swore she'd seen a ghost in the woods as a child. And Morrison came to see the idea of spiritual guides as a source of great comfort and narrative possibility. She was also fascinated by the way the past intrudes on the present and said,

> The ghost in *Beloved* is not only because the people believed in ghosts. It's not only because Sethe needs the ghost. It's also structurally a way to say memory can come in and sit down next to you at the table. And even though you don't want to remember. And you're trying very hard not to remember, it's always been there. It's always with you. And sometimes the situation arises in which you cannot put it off any longer.

Interestingly, this quote captures Morrison's feelings about confronting slavery. She didn't want to deal with the inevitable pain it would take to tackle this subject. But she felt the past intruding upon her, and a responsibility to the upward of sixty million people who suffered so much horror. She knew that if she was going to confront this subject, she had to find a way into it that was uniquely her own. She said,

> Slavery is so intricate, so immense, so long and so unprecedented that you can let slavery be the story, the plot and you know what that story is and it is predictable. And then you can do the worst thing which is when the center of it becomes the institution and not the people. So, if you focus on the characters and their interior life it's like putting the authority back into the hands of the slaves rather than the slave owner.

At this point in her career, in the mid-1980s, Morrison had appeared on the cover of *Newsweek* (in 1981). So you have an African American woman, a major literary force, a towering intellect, who is transfixed by Margaret Garner, who is fascinated by how the past intrudes on the present, who doesn't feel the story of slavery has been properly told, who now has the talent and experience required to handle such a monumental subject, and one day she finds herself sitting in her backyard, which overlooks a river. She has a vision of a young black woman walking out of the river wearing a straw hat. And she knows *this* is Margaret Garner's dead child and the character she must write about. This is Beloved.

She told the story that the historical moment seemed to require. She set out to explore a woman, Margaret Garner, who struck the deepest chord within her, and took on what remains one of the most haunting legacies of not just the black community, but of America and the world as a whole. She set out to hunt big game—and brought down a fuckin' T-Rex.

HOW YOU DO IT

The following bullet points will help you think through and execute the principle.

▶ This is about intensity, about refusing to settle for a subject to write about that's just good. Good enough is not good enough. You want to write about subjects that are essential to you.

▶ Imagine you're alone at a boring cocktail party. You're just waiting until you've stayed long enough to avoid hurting the host's feelings with your departure. Then you hear two people talking about something that gets your blood flowing. What could they be talking about that would change your entire attitude and excite you to get in on the conversation?

▶ Do you have a favorite subject, or one you're fascinated by, that comes up often in the stories you like? For example, I've always been interested in prison. To me it seems like the worst thing in the world. What fascinates you? It could be a person, historical period, a place, or institution. Have you ever thought about why this particular thing is so interesting to you?

▶ We talked above about the tight alignment between writers and their masterwork—briefly sketch out your biography. Include your age, race, gender, and some basic information about your upbringing—who were the key people and what was the vibe? There's no judgment here; as always, you can write about anything that inspires you. You just want to be curious about how well things align when you find a subject worth writing about. You just want to ask, to openly consider, why would someone with my biography write about this subject?

▶ Once you find a subject, generate story ideas by riffing on "What if?" questions. For example, if you're interested in the subject of old age you might come up with "What if we had suicide parties for people when they turned eighty?" or "What if a twenty-year-old kid woke up as a ninety-year-old?"

▶ Don't settle for mediocrity. None of us knows how long we've got to live. Think of your time as an investment—and value it high. The billionaire investor Warren Buffett encourages investors to make thoughtful decisions by imagining they get a punch card and can only punch it twenty times. That means you'd only get to invest in twenty companies over the course of your entire life. Imagine you can only write five stories for the rest of your life. Set the bar high—never write about anything you're not fully inspired by.

MINI FINAL EXAM

Read the following, then answer the question below.

This famous author was only three years old when he and his siblings were called to gather round the bed of his beautiful, twenty-four-year-old mother, Eliza, an accomplished actress who was stricken with tuberculosis. After bouts of spitting blood and struggling to breathe, she died. The boy was separated from his siblings and put in the care of foster parents, John and Frances. He was not close to his adoptive father but cared deeply about his adoptive mother, Frances, who by all accounts was loving and kind. At age twenty-eight, while he was in the army, he learned that she was ill, probably also with tuberculosis. A newspaper clipping described her illness as "lingering and painful." But by the time he made it home, she had already passed. He then fell in love with and married his young cousin, Virginia. The two had a happy marriage, but one day, while playing piano, Virginia began coughing up blood and became bedridden and suffered greatly before finally succumbing, at age twenty-four, to the same illness that took his mother and adoptive mother.

These three tragic deaths were among the defining experiences of which of the following authors:

a) Nikolai Gogol, who wrote the short story "Diary of a Madman," about an underachieving civil servant's descent into madness.
b) Franz Kafka, who wrote the short story "The Burrow," about a molelike creature who digs a labyrinth of underground tunnels and attempts to protect his stuff from invaders.

c) Mark Twain, who wrote the short story "The Celebrated Jumping Frog of Calaveras County," about two men who place a bet on frogs and the dirty deed one does to the other's frog.
d) Herman Melville, who wrote the short story "Bartleby the Scrivener," about a productive office worker who one day responds to his boss's request with "I would prefer not to" and ultimately gives up entirely on life and dies alone in prison.
e) Edgar Allan Poe, who wrote the short story "The Masque of the Red Death," about a prince who attempts to hide out from a deadly plague, "the Red Death," and hosts a masquerade ball that is visited by a mysterious guest in a blood-spattered robe . . . who brings death to all.

CONTINUING ED

In the 2003 South Korean film *Memories of Murder*, two detectives, Park and Cho, are confronted by the nation's first known serial killer. Inspired by a true story, the film is set in a small industrial town in 1986. It begins when a woman's bound dead body is found in a large drainage pipe. The two detectives are utterly unprepared to deal with the murder. The police station has no forensic testing equipment—nor, for that matter, virtually any modern technology. Park believes that he can tell if a suspect is guilty merely by looking in their eyes. And Cho, a former military officer, believes he can simply beat confessions out of suspects. As the body count rises, Park and Cho are joined by Seo, a detective from Seoul who believes in modern technology and making decisions based on evidence. At first, Park and Seo clash, but as they track and desperately try to stop a sadistic killer, they develop a mutual respect.

How does the subject matter of this film qualify as "big game" for director Bong Joon-ho, who was then thirty-four years old? If you look closely at each detective—Park, Cho, and Seo—how might their characters be viewed as a comment on modern South Korean society, which transitioned from a military dictatorship in the 1980s to a democracy? Put yourself in the young director's shoes. Realistically, how could he have possibly hunted bigger game?

MINI FINAL ANSWER

The correct answer is **e) Edgar Allan Poe, who wrote the short story "The Masque of the Red Death" about a prince who attempts to hide out from a deadly plague, "the Red Death," and hosts a masquerade ball which is visited by a mysterious guest in a blood-spattered robe . . . who brings death to all.** Poe wrote the story when his beloved wife, Virginia, had recently become ill. She was bedridden and suffering, which upset the author greatly, shattering his nerves and driving him to return to drinking, a problem that would torment him for the rest of his life.

Look at how tight the alignment is between the author and the subject of one of his most powerful stories. Here, you have an author whose beloved wife was being destroyed—bloodied—by a disease he was powerless to stop. And he tells the story of a prince who attempts to have a ball as the world is being ravaged by plague. To a happily married person, your spouse often feels like your world. When they're suffering greatly, you can't imagine ever feeling happy again.

25

Amplify your theme.

"Sing loud, sing proud."
—DROPKICK MURPHYS, Celtic Punk Band

QUICK TAKE

When you tell a story with a clearly asked Central Dramatic Question, the way the story resolves—i.e., how the question is answered—is meaningful. As the story unfolds, you may want to telegraph that meaning to varying degrees. Some writers feel intense passion about their ideas and need to state them boldly and often. Others are more subtle and may simply wish to insert them in bits of dialogue or use visual cues—an image in the background, a billboard on the highway, a slogan on a T-shirt.

We usually think of the word "amplify" as meaning to make louder, but it also means to expand. You can also insert references to your theme that add nuance and texture, that express it with different feelings. Or, as you finish writing, you may just sense that there are multiple ways to interpret your story and you prefer one over another, so you choose to tip the scales toward your ideal interpretation by amplifying it with references and cues.

HOW IT WORKS

To amplify your theme, you focus on the overriding idea that is expressed through the events of your story and reinforce it with images, dialogue, allusions, and sounds.

You may have other ideas that will be expressed through secondary storylines, compelling characters, single scenes, little moments, or a killer line of dialogue. But the story itself expresses one main idea. Because Elliot, the boy hero of the 1982 film *E.T. the Extra Terrestrial*, so tightly connects with his alien buddy, he risks his own life to save him—and becomes more fully human in the process. Over the course of the film, he transforms from someone who lacks empathy—he hurts his newly divorced mother when he callously tells her his father/her ex-husband has a new girlfriend—into a very empathetic little guy. Thus, the theme is we become more fully human when we develop empathy.

You've probably heard the expression "use every part of the animal"—which comes from the American Indian practice of showing respect for animals they've hunted by literally using every single part—meat for food, fur for clothing, bones for tools, etc. In story, your characters pass signs in shop windows, walk through rooms, listen to each other talk, and hear music playing and sounds in the street. Make all of this count. Toward the end of *The Godfather, Part II*, mob family boss Michael Corleone is at the height of his spiritual crisis. He senses that he's losing his wife—and his soul. He walks alone across the family's Lake Tahoe compound. The ground is covered with ice and snow. Crows caw madly overhead. The crows calling and ice crunching beneath his feet seem like harbingers of death.

So often, what you see in great writing is a density of thought—elite storytellers waste nothing. Every location, costume, sound, color—everything—is specifically chosen to add nuance and texture to the central theme. In Chapter 13, "Layer conflict," we looked at the moment Kamala Khan, a teenage kid from Jersey City, sneaks out late at night to go to a party. She is lost—both literally and figuratively. A green mist envelopes her.

As she passes out on a deserted street, her hand rests on a telephone pole that has a little flyer for a missing child nailed to it. These details are noticeable—without overtly calling attention to themselves. It's entirely believable that a missing child poster would be affixed to a pole in the city, and this amplifies the message that Kamala, at this point, is profoundly lost.

In an episode of *The Sopranos* entitled "College," mob boss Tony Soprano takes his daughter to visit colleges in New England, and by pure chance spots a "rat" in hiding, a guy who testified against the family and then went into witness protection. After Tony sneaks off and strangles the man to death, he visits the campus with his daughter. While waiting for her, he looks up at a wall to see a quote from Nathaniel Hawthorne that reads, "No man can wear one face to himself and another to the multitudes without finally becoming bewildered as to which may be true."

Keep in mind, this is an exercise for one style of writing, in which expressing an idea is important to the writer. Some writers, like the famous playwright Neil Simon, just wrote and *never* focused on theme. Simon said he found out what his plays were about by reading reviews. In Chapter 27, "Transcend thought," we'll explore writing purely to express a feeling. But for now, this principle is about clearly and unapologetically expressing an idea you believe in.

HOW A MASTER DID IT

Double Indemnity (1944)
Screenplay by Billy Wilder, Raymond Chandler
Based on the novel by James M. Cain

When insurance salesman Walter Neff, in his mid-thirties, pays a sales call to a prospect named Dietrichson, he finds that Mr. Dietrichson is out. Instead, he encounters Mrs. Dietrichson, also mid-thirties, returning from the pool in just a towel. After an intense flirtation packed with sexual innuendo, the two begin a torrid affair. Intoxicated by lust, and convinced that Phyllis is abused by her husband, Walter decides to help her kill him. But he's determined not only to kill the man, but to do it in such a rare way the insurance company will have to pay double on her claim. The two will then make off with the money and live happily ever after.

This won't be easy. They'll have to trick Mr. Dietrichson into signing off on a new life insurance policy, then pull off a complex murder. Mr. Dietrichson plans to take a train from the LA area, where the story is set, to his alma mater, Stanford, in northern California. He's a big guy who played football in college. And so is Walter. The plan is for Walter to hide in the back seat of the Dietrichsons' car when Phyllis drives her husband to the train. He'll strangle Mr. Dietrichson from behind on the way and dump the body on the train tracks. With the collar on his overcoat pulled up and hat pulled down, he'll assume Mr. Dietrichson's identity and board the train. He'll make his way to the back and, when it's moving slowly enough, jump off, meet up with Phyllis, and drive off.

For a moment it looks like their plans are thwarted when Mr. Dietrichson breaks his leg. But the gruff man insists on traveling anyway. This is perfect. Walter will tape up his leg to look like it's in a cast and bring a pair of crutches. If anything, this will make the story of him "accidentally" falling off the train all the more believable.

But, as if murdering someone, assuming their identity, and hopping off a moving train without getting caught isn't hard enough, there's a whole other level of complexity. Since Phyllis will be filing a double indemnity claim—in other words, a very expensive one—the insurance company will put their best claims investigator on the job. This is Barton Keyes, a legend who is married to the job—he eats, sleeps, and breathes his work. He hates insurance fraud; it literally makes him sick. When he gets a fake claim, it feels to him as if a little man is gnawing his guts from within. He will examine every detail of this incident and not hesitate to grill Phyllis hard to make sure she had nothing to do with it. Also, further complicating things for Walter is the fact that Keyes is a father figure to him, a mentor, a true friend who genuinely loves him. If ever there are characters who must operate at the top of their intelligence, they are Walter and Phyllis.

The Central Dramatic Question is "Will Walter and Phyllis get away with murder/fraud?" The theme is evil deeds unite evildoers until death. When you commit murder with someone, you're tied to them forever, your fate is in their hands. Throughout the film, the phrase "right down the line" is said once, "straight down the line" five times, and "end of the line" three times. We'll look at each one and explore how the writers used it to amplify the theme. (The film also contains images that accentuate the theme—for example, the train tracks embody it.)

• • •

The term, "right down the line" is said in Walter and Phyllis's initial encounter, after she asks him if he sells just auto insurance or all kinds.

Walter: All kinds. Fire, earthquake, theft, public liability, group insurance, industrial stuff and so on **right down the line**.

This seems harmless enough. But Phyllis has been thinking about knocking off her husband for a long time. When Walter enters the picture, she immediately begins to speculate about the possibility of not only killing her husband but making some real money off it. If Walter's company did not offer life insurance, their relationship would likely end here. But it does offer life insurance. Her intentions are as wrong as can be—and he quickly catches her drift. He's very intelligent, but he's also burning with desire, and it's clouding his judgment.

• • •

The first and second uses of "straight down the line" occur at the end of Act One, when Walter agrees to help Phyllis commit the murder.

Walter: . . . watch your step. Every single minute. It's got to be perfect, understand. **Straight down the line**.

Phyllis: **Straight down the line**.

Here, "straight down the line" conveys a commitment to detail. But in repeating the line to each other, it also serves as a commitment, binding them to each other like a wedding vow. The word "down" has a double meaning. The murder's about to go down and they're spiritually descending. When you think of the term "straight down," you think of a rapid descent, like a plane doing a nose dive. The word "straight"—especially in film noir—implies being honest and direct, as opposed to hiding your true meaning and being "crooked." When you "go straight," you commit to living within the law. This relationship is backward. It's evil. Despite all the meaning packed into these four tiny words, the dialogue is perfectly natural. No one hears this line and shouts, "Theme!"

• • •

The third use occurs when Phyllis calls Walter just before the murder to let him know what her husband is wearing, so that Walter can assume the man's identity.

Phyllis: This is it, Walter. I'm shaking like a leaf. But it's **straight down the line** now for both of us. I love you, Walter. Goodbye.

Here, she uses the phrase to further tie the two of them together. It's a declaration between two lovers hoping to break free. And it implies there's no other choice now, that they are heading one way—toward murder.

• • •

The fourth use occurs after the murder. The two have been separated because they know Keyes is watching Phyllis like a hawk, as she stands to make a fortune off her husband's death.

Phyllis: What's the matter, Walter. Aren't you going to kiss me?

Walter: Sure, I'm going to kiss you.

Phyllis: It's **straight down the line**, isn't it?

Phyllis kisses him. In the kiss, he is passive.

Walter is shaken by what he's done. To commit the murder, he hid in the back seat while Phyllis drove Mr. Dietrichson to the train. As she honked the horn to let Walter know they arrived at the track, Walter sprang from behind and choked the poor bastard to death, breaking his neck. It was a nasty, intimate, cowardly murder.

Sensing Walter's distance, Phyllis turns the phrase into a loaded question. She needs him to renew their vow. They are lovers but now also coconspirators, criminals who are equally guilty. She's afraid of losing him, because she knows full well how dangerous it is if he goes soft. He could rat her out. He's the first one who used the phrase "straight down the line," and made a big deal about going all in. She's questioning his manhood by reminding him of what a big shot he was when they cooked up the plan.

• • •

At first, the plan goes smoothly. Keyes believes that Mr. Dietrichson fell from the train. He has analyzed the incident and everything checks out. He informs his superiors at the company, to their horror, they'll have to pay out. They have no choice. But as time passes, Keyes turns the case over and over in his mind. The "little man" in his belly senses fraud. Keyes—always operating at the top of his intelligence—figures out the train was moving too slowly for Dietrichson to have been killed by such a short fall. He knows he was murdered elsewhere and dumped on the tracks. After Keyes tells Walter he knows it was murder, Walter realizes they are in serious trouble. If Phyllis tries to collect on the claim, she'll be arrested for murder, and if she goes down, she'll take him take with her.

They meet at a grocery store and pretend to shop. He wears his hat pulled down low, she wears dark sunglasses. Walter explains that they must abort the plan. His logic is flawless. But she refuses. They separate, and she wanders down another aisle. The very tall Walter looks over the shelves at her. She coldly says,

Phyllis: I loved you, Walter. And I hated him. But I wasn't going to do anything about it, not until I met you. It was you who had the plan. I only wanted him dead.

Walter: Yeah, and I was the one that fixed him so he was dead. Is that what you're telling me?

Phyllis takes off her dark glasses and looks at him with cold, hard eyes.

Phyllis: Yes. And nobody's pulling out. We went into it together, and we're coming out at the end together. It's **straight down the line** for both of us, remember?

When Phyllis slowly removes her glasses and stares at him, it is one of the great femme fatale moments in noir. She now uses the phrase as an ice-cold threat. When she says, "We're coming out at the end together," she still thinks there's a chance they'll get away with it—or die trying. Once she realizes that Walter is definitely not going along for the ride, and he realizes she most definitely is, they each decide the only way out is to kill the other.

• • •

Toward the end of Act Two, the phrase transitions to "end of the line." Keyes knows that Phyllis is guilty, and he knows she had an accomplice. But he could never imagine it's Walter. He tells his protégé:

Keyes: They think it's twice as safe because there are two of them. But it's not twice as safe. It's ten times twice as dangerous. They've committed a murder and that's not like taking a trolley ride together where each one can get off at a different stop. They're stuck with each other. They've got to ride all the way to the **end of the line**. And it's a one-way trip, and the last stop is the cemetery.

At one point during the film, Walter walks at night and imagines he can't hear his own footsteps. He's a dead man walking. Though he might fool himself into thinking he still has a shot, deep down, he knows Keyes is right. You can feel the writers twisting the knife. The phrase began as a comment about insurance, morphed into a wedding vow, and now suggests his funeral.

• • •

The line's repeated twice during Walter's final showdown with Phyllis.

Walter: I have a friend who's got a funny theory. He says when two people commit a murder, they're kind of on a trolley car, and one can't get off without the other. They're stuck with each other. They have to go on riding clear to the **end of the line**. And the last stop is the cemetery.

Phyllis: Maybe he's got something there.

Walter: You bet he has. Two people are going to ride to the **end of the line**, all right. Only I'm not going to be one of them.

Walter guns Phyllis down after she wounds him with a bullet that will later kill him. He had planned to frame another guy, and might have gotten away with it. But in a final act of redemption, he warns the man to get away from Phyllis and saves his life.

The theme of the film is when you commit a crime with someone else, you put your life in their hands. The writers come back to the idea nine times. Each time it is expressed, it's clearly and powerfully motivated. And because the context changes, the idea is expertly developed. The writers pull off the rare feat of both showing and telling. It makes a cowboy wanna tip their hat. World-class storytelling.

HOW YOU DO IT

The following bullet points will help you think through and execute the principle.

▶ To amplify your theme, you need to, of course, define it. If you know it, write it out in a simple sentence using as few words as possible. For example: All men are traitors. Killing animals is murder. Love makes life worth living. Monogamy always fails. Whatever it is, it must boldly express your take on a subject. This is not a theme: marriage. That's a subject. You have a subject and your theme is your take on the subject.

▶ If you've written a draft and are not sure what your theme is, carefully analyze the basic action. If an ant moves a rubber tree plant because he has high hopes, it means high hopes fuel great triumphs. Express your theme in as few words as possible. The theme of Shakespeare's *Macbeth* can be expressed in three words: Blind ambition kills.

▶ In every scene or chapter, look for opportunities to highlight your theme through phrases, key words, music playing in the background, sounds, or visuals—in needlepoint on a pillow, inscribed in a tattoo. Make it prominent enough to be noticed, but not so prominent that it hits the audience over the head.

▶ Consider your story's genre, or general feel. Some types of stories—comedy or melodrama—make it easy to blatantly express what you need to express. The TV series *South Park* often has one of its main characters declare, "You know, I learned something today," then state the theme. More serious fare, like family dramas, requires greater subtlety.

▶ The amplification must be believable within the context where the theme's expressed. If your hero takes the bus to work every day, they will likely see the giant advertisements plastered on the sides. You might consider using these to add color and nuance to your theme.

▶ After you complete a draft, list every reference that you've included—audio, spoken words, visuals—and make sure they work together, in concert, to amplify your theme, not just making it more pronounced, but so the full expression of it includes different tones and textures.

MINI FINAL EXAM

Read the following, then answer the question below.

A full-length feature film about marriage includes the following bits of dialogue: When the couple first discuss getting married, the man nervously asks, "Do you know how long the long haul really is?" She laughs and says she does. Months into their marrige, they hit a rough patch when their initial burst of wild lovemaking loses its zest. The man says, "It's all right, there are bound to be some bumpy roads when you're making the long haul."

Years go by and the couple feels like they're drifting apart. One night they're out to dinner and have nothing to say to each other. After a long stretch of silence, the wife sighs and jokes, "You'd need a big rig to haul that silence." They grow old. He develops a serious condition. She cares for him, and he apologizes for becoming a burden. She gently kisses his forehead—as a large truck rattles the windows when it drives by. The two share a laugh. He thanks her for being a wonderful wife. And she thanks him for always being there when she needed him, despite the hard times.

The theme of this story is best described as:

a) Marriage is a difficult commitment, but ultimately rewarding.
b) Marriage is a bitter pill to swallow, and always ends in sorrow.
c) The story has no clear theme.
d) Marriage is a sacred institution.
e) Marriage no longer makes sense in the modern world.

CONTINUING ED

In Shakespeare's 1606 tragedy *Macbeth*, the title character returns from battle with his comrade in arms, Banquo. They're greeted by three witches who appear on the heath and address them by titles above the ones they hold. When they tell Macbeth he'll become king, something snaps within him. He's tormented by their prediction and Banquo immediately notices that something's not right. After all, this news should be a good thing. This prediction starts Macbeth and his wife, Lady Macbeth, down a very dark road, and provokes him to savagely murder King Duncan, whom Macbeth has actually always held in high regard.

This is a tragedy bordering on outright horror that explores the dark side of ambition. How does Shakespeare amplify his theme? How many references are there to strange and unnatural occurrences? What time do most scenes take place? How's the weather? How are the animals in this world doing? How often do blood and weaponry come up? To fully appreciate how far Shakespeare pushes the envelope, try to list every single dark reference, then look them over to analyze their consistency and extremity.

MINI FINAL ANSWER

The correct answer is **a) Marriage is a difficult commitment, but ultimately rewarding**. The idea of marriage being a long journey is expressed four times, each in a subtly different way. These combine to amplify the story's incontrovertible theme.

26

Attack your theme.

"Thinking is when you adopt the opposite position from your suppositions and make that argument as strong as you can possibly make it. And then you pit your perspective against that and you battle it out."
—JORDAN PETERSON, Psychologist

QUICK TAKE

When you know what you want to say—when you've discovered an essential truth about the nature of life—you strengthen your argument by showing that you are in command of the case *against* that truth as well for it. Just as you want to create fierce antagonists who come at your hero with everything they've got, you want to present the counter ideas to your main idea, or theme, as intelligently as possible. This will push you to fully explore your theme, sharpen your take on it, and ultimately make your point stronger.

It's the same with people—when someone has strong opinions, they are much more convincing when they show that they take opposing views into consideration. Plus, they're far more enjoyable to spend time with. Consider how differently you feel about someone who is intelligent, is a good listener, and weighs others' viewpoints, as opposed to an opinionated loudmouth. When you express the counter idea to your theme, without dumbing it down, you make your story more engaging and your theme more persuasive, because you've shown that you have honestly considered the case against it.

HOW IT WORKS

As your hero battles mightily to acquire their object of desire, they move closer to and further from their goals. How things end determines what the story means. It's like the old routine where the lovestruck fellow plucks petals from a daisy, saying, "She loves me. She loves me not." If he says "she loves me" on the last petal, she loves him. If he says "she loves me not," she does not. This is a little story with the meaning shifting back and forth with each petal, until the dramatic conclusion arrives when the final petal's plucked.

In the Johnny Clegg song "Warsaw 1943," two boys are fighting in the Resistance against the Nazis. One night, soldiers swarm one of their homes and take the boy away. Though he's described as having "iron" in his heart, he's subjected to physical torture and psychological manipulation as the Nazis press him to give up names. He hangs tough, but just when he's sure he's about to be killed, he whispers his best friend's name. His friend is hauled in and they're both stuck in a prison cell to await execution. We don't get their names, so to make things clear we'll call them the "Kid" (who gives up the name) and the "Best Friend" who is betrayed. The CDQ is "Will the Best Friend forgive the Kid?" In the hook, the Kid swears he didn't betray his Best Friend. He was just too scared to die alone. It's a brilliantly complex idea. It is a fact that the Kid betrayed his friend. But did he, really? He's a boy being tortured by sadists. Terrified and exhausted, is he really responsible for breaking at the very last second, under unimaginable pressure? Of course not. And his friend knows this. Just before the firing squad guns them both down, he forgives his guilt-ridden friend.

The theme is that forgiveness is a sacred and beautiful thing. It resonates because Clegg gave the betrayed kid the most powerful reason imaginable *not* to forgive. The ultimate sin in their world is to rat out your best friend. Therefore, when the CDQ is answered and the Best Friend uses his dying breath to forgive and comfort the Kid, it's devastating. Here are boys who have more courage, compassion, and honor than their killers can fathom. And though they are defeated, you sense that they have won a more important battle to stay fully human.

"Attacking" your theme doesn't necessarily mean putting a character up on a soapbox to give voice to the entire counter-argument. Obviously, a lyricist writing a rock song needs to be more economical than a novelist or screenwriter. But Clegg's skill at executing this principle is extraordinary. He captures the boy's "attack" through his silence. It's a silence that screams, "I will never forgive your sin. It is unforgivable." When the "traitor" mournfully denies his betrayal, the focus, through the sheer magic of storytelling, is on the Best Friend listening. And when he finally speaks and gives his forgiveness, it sets the story's theme off like a bomb.

What makes Clegg's story work so well is that he understood how hard it is to forgive. "Attack your theme" is a close sister principle to both "Provoke dilemma" (Chapter 12) and "Motivate fierce antagonists" (Chapter 18). If your theme is too simplistic, if the answer is too obvious, it's impossible to have the dynamic, intellectual battles that are essential to executing this principle. For example, if your theme is "protect our noble grannies," you can't make a legit counterargument. Only a maniac would argue for harming noble grannies. Therefore, the story has nowhere to travel to because we already agree at the outset. So, it's essential for you to ask yourself questions that truly confound you. Toni Morrison's masterpiece *Beloved* was inspired by an escaped slave who slit her own daughter's throat to protect her from being enslaved. The question at the heart of that novel is, "Can a mother be forgiven for killing her own child?"

These fundamental choices you make early in the creative process often determine whether or not your story works. Let this thought sink in for a second. If your story is founded on a theme that is so obvious it's not possible to attack it with a counterargument, the story's doomed from the start. Set yourself up for success from the outset by exploring complex ideas that are worth deep exploration and fierce debate in a story. You're writing a story, not a bumper sticker. Make it count.

HOW A MASTER DID IT

The Brothers Karamazov (1879)
Fyodor Dostoevsky

In 1878, the great Russian novelist Fyodor Dostoesvky began his final novel, *The Brothers Karamazov*. This was just seventeen years after Emperor Alexander II had issued the Emancipation Edict that freed twenty-three million serfs—Russian peasants who were essentially slaves, with few rights. The concern was that if they were not freed from "above" by the emperor, they would be freed from "below"—by revolution. Try to imagine the psychological impact on a society of sixty-two million people of freeing more than a third of the population. The serfs had been oppressed for a very long time, had little education, had been denied their dignity. They didn't just waltz out happily, healed, and ready to enjoy life; nor did the wealthier classes all welcome them with open arms. This was bound to be a rough ride. Just twenty-six years after *The Brothers Karamazov* was completed, the Bolshevik, or workers', revolution overthrew the Russian monarchy and started a civil war that ultimately led to the formation of the Soviet Union.

It's in the period between these momentous historical events, when the air was charged with the fever of dawning revolution, that Dostoevsky serialized his novel in a magazine called *The Russian Messenger*. He was deeply concerned with the dissolution of the Russian family, which he viewed as a symptom of people turning away from the church. He saw what he considered a "fashionable atheism" sweeping across Russia, and was well aware of the political fervor rising, particularly in young men. But he was equally concerned with the flaws and outright corruption of the church. He disliked fanaticism and believed in humility, ethics, and refraining from judgment. For Dostoevsky, it was essential to believe in Jesus Christ as a supernatural force, not an abstract idea or ideal. To be fully human, to find contentment in this life, to build a more just, loving society, we must have unshakable faith in God.

He wrote this novel to prove a point—that faith in Christ is essential to human happiness and the evolution of humankind. This, he believed, was our only hope of building a just, kind, compassionate society. To make his point, he set up a central conflict between Christian faith and reason in the novel. What we'll explore here is the attack he put on his underlying belief. Its power and brutality are astonishing. In fact, when the chapter we're going to explore was published, his friends who shared his Christian faith were stunned, and feared it would undermine the point of the book. But it didn't. It did exactly the opposite. It's his attack on faith that makes his ultimate embrace of faith so profound—and convincing.

• • •

The story focuses on five characters—Fyodor Karamazov, mid-fifties, and his four sons. Three of these are recognized: Dmitri Karamazov, mid- to late twenties; Ivan Karamazov, early- to mid-twenties, and Alyosha Karamazov, who turns twenty during the novel. Dmitri, Ivan, and Alyosha are Fyodor's legitimate sons, but only Ivan and Alyosha share a mother. It is highly likely that Fyodor has a fourth son named Smerdyakov. Fyodor is almost certainly the man who raped a mentally ill homeless woman the town called "Stinking Lizaveta," who gave birth to Smerdyakov.

We'll quickly introduce the characters, do a stripped-down summary of the plot, and then get to the red meat—Dostoevsky's attack on his own theme.

Fyodor is a "sensualist"—a selfish, hateful, cynical, greedy man who cares about no one but himself and satisfying every one of his urges, no matter how immoral, scandalous, or despicable. He was a terrible father to his sons, an awful husband to their mothers, and although he is intelligent and apparently well-read, he is a vile human being.

Dmitri, his eldest son, is a soldier, a brawler who is in perpetual battle with his urges, passions, and extreme personality. He weeps openly at the drop of a hat, and will pummel other men for the slightest reason, even in front of their terrified children. His lust and appetites know few bounds. Although he shares his father's passionate nature, he is much kinder, more honest and open, and after he commits some unseemly or violent act, he is tormented by guilt and the desire to confess his sins.

Ivan, the middle son, is a true intellectual. He is a brilliant young man who has made a name for himself as a writer and political thinker. His most notable accomplishment is that he has written articles about ecclesiastical, or Christian, courts and their role in society. An argument was raging then about whether the society should be ruled by the church or state. Ivan writes articles that make such powerful and convincing cases, each side feels that he supports their cause. Though Ivan is an atheist, he realizes there are many positive sides to church teachings and is able to articulate them with the full force of his intellect.

Alyosha is the youngest son. Throughout his life, he has possessed a deep-seated love for people. He could never judge others harshly or speak ill of anyone—not even his repulsive father, who would have been happy to let him and his older brothers starve. Alyosha has always believed in God. It's as is if he were born faithful—the truth of God's presence is as real to him as air or water. He lives in a monastery under the tutelage of Father

Zosima, a kindhearted and popular religious figure who some believe has healing powers. Alyosha plans to become a monk, but Zosima feels he must experience life in the real world before making that decision.

Smerdyakov, Fyodor's bastard son, was raised by Fyodor's servant, Grigory, and his wife, Marta. They brought him up as a servant, or "lackey," in his real father's home. He is understandably resentful of the bad hand he was dealt, but there is something dark and ugly in him that feels as if it springs not just from his awful upbringing, but from his soul. As a child, he took delight in hiding pins in a ball of bread, tricking dogs into eating them and watching the dogs writhe in pain and howl with fear.

The story revolves around the murder of Fyodor, and the trial of his oldest son, Dmitry, who is accused of killing him. Dmitry hates his father and believes that Fyodor stole money he was entitled to inherit. The two are in love with the same beautiful young woman, Grushenka, who takes pleasure in driving both father and son wild with lust. On the night of the murder, Grushenka plans to meet up with Fyodor. Smerdyakov tells Dmitry about his father's planned rendezvous, knowing this will enrage him. Dmitry shows up in Fyodor's garden that night and beats his father with a pestle (a tool used to crush foods), leaving him in a pool of blood.

The next day, Fyodor's body is discovered, and Dmitry is arrested for murder. The novel then becomes a courtroom drama focused on Dmitry's trial, where he faces being shipped off to Siberia to do hard labor for rest of his days. Dmitry insists that he just gave the old man a good beating, but didn't kill him. Alyosha stays by his side and believes him without hesitation or doubt. Dmitry is passionate and can be violent, but he is not a liar. The evidence against him, however, is so overwhelming that he is found guilty. Grushenka is wracked with guilt at having contributed to his downfall, repents for her sins, and promises to follow Dmitry to Siberia, where the two of them will find redemption through their suffering. Though Dmitry seeks redemption, it is for his sinful ways, but not for the murder. He did not do it.

Smerdyakov found Fyodor wounded later that night and finished him off. Prior to the murder, he had become friends with Ivan, whom he greatly admired. The two talked about atheism, and Smerdyakov came to believe that Ivan was right, there is no God, and thus that anything human beings do is permissible. So, he killed Fyodor to impress Ivan, who is horrified and punches Smerdyakov in the face. Before Ivan can help bring the real killer to justice, Smerdyakov kills himself. Ivan is traumatized by his guilt and suffers a nervous breakdown, or "brain fever," which may prove fatal.

At the end of the book, Fyodor has been beaten to death, Dmitry will go to prison for life for a crime he did not commit, Ivan suffers a breakdown that may kill him, and Smerdyakov is dead from suicide. It's only Alyosha, the man of faith, who survives both literally and spiritually. When we last see him, he is comforting a group of boys who have just stood by a dying friend. Alyosha makes a beautiful speech about faith and goodness. The boys are so moved, they cheer his name. And all go off to a dinner celebrating the life of the fallen child.

• • •

The theme of the book not only deals with the moral righteousness of faith, but the *intelligence* of it. Alyosha is not just the only one who survives, he's the only person who gets it right. Despite the mountain of evidence against Dmitry, Alyosha simply needs to look in his brother's eyes to know that he is not guilty. There is wisdom in his faith and refusal to judge others. He can see the truth that can't be found by logic and reason.

And this brings us back to the principle at hand, Attack your theme. What makes this ending so powerful, and Dostoevsky's commitment to faith so extraordinary, is that in a chapter called "Rebellion," Ivan meets with his beloved younger brother Alyosha in a restaurant and explains to him why he rejects faith. It is a blistering attack. And it's delivered by a very charismatic and likable character. Ivan is handsome, loving, and widely admired. If Dostoevsky were a weak writer, or less confident in his position, he could have put the attack on faith in Fyodor's nasty mouth to bias the reader against it. But like Alyosha, who listens with an open heart and mind, Dostoevsky's conviction was strong enough to take the very best shot the other side could give. Think of this like pushing a ball as deep into water as you can. The further you push it down, the higher it shoots back up.

Ivan respects and loves Alyosha dearly, and he recognizes that Alyosha looks up to him as an older brother. Ivan also knows Alyosha is studying to become a monk, and says, "It's not that I want to corrupt you and push you off your foundation; perhaps I want to be healed by you." Alyosha senses the depth of his brother's torment, and wants to hear his ideas because he would like to help him bear his burden.

With the skill of a prosecutor, Ivan lays out his case for why he "does not accept the world." Essentially he says the following:

Saints suffer because they are required to by some kind of duty or punishment or force. He talks of "John the Merciful" lying down with a sick man and breathing into his diseased mouth. Regular men can't do things like this, as men can't bear each other. We don't like other guys' faces or how they smell, and we bear hostility toward others for stepping on our feet. We can't stand each other, let alone love each other.

Ivan then turns to children. He loves them and feels kids aged seven and younger are so innocent and free, they're almost different beings. He can't bear to see them suffer. He tells Alyosha that he collects stories that he's pulled from newspapers and needs to share. (A word of warning, these are *extremely unpleasant* and true. Dostoevsky actually did collect such stories. I'm going to go into excruciating detail here to accurately express how well the principle is executed.) Ivan recounts atrocities committed in a war in Bulgaria, between Turks and Circassians, in which they cut infants from living mothers' wombs, tossed the babies in the air, and caught them on bayonets. They also put guns up to the babies' heads, got them to giggle and play with the barrel, then shot them in the face. He says that to compare men to animals is an insult to animals. When a tiger mauls someone, it could never be so "artistically cruel."

As Ivan tells these stories, his emotional state alternates between bouts of sorrow and wild-eyed mania. He talks about an illegitimate child in Switzerland who was given to a shepherd to raise in the mountains. He was treated like an animal—barely clothed, left without food for days. He was often so hungry, he'd pray for a chance to steal some slop from pigs. He grew up to become an unstable thief, and one day killed a man. He was tried and sentenced to death. In prison, he was surrounded by church groups who taught him to read and write and study the gospels. They "exhorted him, persuaded him, pushed him, pestered him, urged him, and finally he himself solemnly confessed to the crime." All of holy, pious Geneva rushed to his side to celebrate the fact that he was saved. And though he was raised like an animal, and had no knowledge of God, and really wasn't the one at fault for his sins, he was hauled up to the scaffold and, with the crowd cheering his journey to God, had "his head whacked off in brotherly fashion."

Ivan then details a wealthy, well-educated couple who savagely flogged their small child. They beat her with a stick covered with little twigs so it would "smart" more. They liked inflicting pain. "I know for certain there are floggers who get more excited with every stroke, to the point of sensuality, literal sensuality, more and more, progressively, with each new stroke." By some fluke, the couple ended up in court, but they hired an eloquent attorney who railed against the courts' interfering in family matters, and got them off without punishment. The crowd cheered the acquittal. Ivan adds bitterly, "Ah, if I'd been there I'd have yelled out that they should establish a scholarship in honor of the torturer."

He then tells two more awful stories. One is about parents who thrashed a five-year-old girl for wetting her bed. They beat her so badly her body was covered in bruises, they smeared her face with feces, and locked her in the cold, wet, dark outhouse. Ivan rages angrily about the poor little child who had no clue what was happening to her or why, praying to God to help her—and her prayers going unanswered. If that's not gruesome enough, he tells the tale of a wealthy landowner, a general, who owned hundreds of dogs. An eight-year-old serf was playing and accidently struck a dog with a stone. When the general heard what happened, he had the boy locked up. The next morning, the general showed up with a crew of men on horseback, all ready to go out for a big hunt. He had the mother trot out the boy, who was stripped naked and told to run. The general then let loose a wild pack of wolfhounds, who raced to the boy and tore him to pieces in front of his traumatized mother.

Ivan gazes at Alyosha. "What to do with him? Shoot him for our moral satisfaction?" Alyosha says, "Shoot him!" And Ivan cries out "Bravo!" Alyosha tries to walk this back, claiming what he said is absurd. Ivan says, "The world stands on absurdities." When Alyosha is unable to bear any more, he asks why Ivan is doing this to him. Ivan says, "You are dear to me. I don't want to let you slip, and I won't give you up to your Zosima." (Zosima is the revered monk Alyosha's studying under.) Ivan insists that he understands one day all will be forgiven, that one day the murdered will embrace the murderer and all will cry out to God, "how just thou art!" but he cannot accept this, that nothing, not even eternal peace among all humankind, can justify savagely beating a little girl, smearing her with feces, and locking her in an outhouse. He says that no one, not even God, has the right to forgive such torture. And that no future harmony that comes about as a result of such suffering could justify it.

> "I don't want harmony. I'd rather remain with my unrequited suffering and my unquenched indignation, *even if I am wrong*. They have put too high a price on harmony, we can't afford to pay so much for admission. And therefore I hasten to return my ticket. And it is my duty, if only as an honest man, to return it as far ahead of time as possible. Which is what I am doing. It's not that I don't accept God, Alyosha, I just most respectfully return him the ticket."

Then he challenges Alyosha to admit that even if he could alleviate all human suffering by torturing a single child, it would not be worth it. Alyosha agrees this is true. This ends Ivan's assault on faith.

Try to put yourself in Dostoevsky's shoes. You're a famous novelist and a man of faith. You feel society as a whole teetering on the brink of disaster—the twentieth century would bring unimaginable bloodshed to Russia—and you want to espouse the merits of faith. You're serializing your masterwork. Imagine the courage it takes to roll this chapter out, to put this kind of beating on what you so fervently believe. Just think of the confidence he had to have as a man of faith and as a storyteller to believe he could still win his argument. It's awe-inspiring.

HOW YOU DO IT

The following bullet points will help you think through and execute the principle.

- As you did in the last chapter, start by defining your theme in a clear, simple sentence using the fewest words you can. For example, the road to hell is paved with good intentions.

- If you don't know your theme, analyze the main actions of your last draft. If the drug addict dies alone in the gutter, it means drugs kill. If the drugs cause him to expand his perception of reality, it means responsible drug use can expand your mind.

- If you're not sure what your story's about, write out a simple idea you're interested in or believe in. It's never a bad idea to put some muscle into it. For example, it's okay to kill people to protect the environment.

- For the sake of this exercise, commit fully to defending your idea. Write out why you believe, with true conviction, that this idea is gospel truth. For example, consider the idea that wrathfulness destroys the wrathful. It's true that wrathfulness destroys the wrathful because one can't think clearly when enraged and looking for someone—anyone—to blame. Rage has negative physical effects—on sleep, diet, drug and alcohol use, relationships—and it darkens or destroys everything it touches.

▸ Now, imagine you're attacking the idea that wrathfulness is sinful. The key is to have the same genuine conviction from the opposite side. Come hard. Two sons are savagely beaten throughout their childhood by a sadistic father. As they reach adulthood and struggle with the effects of the trauma, one brother attempts to convince the other to murder their father. He rails at him about how the strongest nations dominate the weak ones, how dictators crush dissent, and multinational corporations obliterate the environment and wipe out whole species. The world is fueled by wrath. To the wrathful go the spoils. And even if wrath is a sin, there's only one way to get it out of their systems once and for all—to unleash it on the man who put it there. Your goal here is to genuinely—not playfully, *really*—shake your own convictions.

▸ You'll know you have it when the argument strikes a nerve. To tell a story, you pay a price. That price is the discomfort of having your most cherished ideas, the ones that ground you, fully tested.

MINI FINAL EXAM

Read the following, then answer the question below.

A writer wishes to write a novel about the nature of reality. Her theme is that reality is absurd, a bad joke, an illusion. And the only hope for happiness is to escape into what few objective truths you can find in mathematics.

She creates a character, a math professor, Maggie McRuin, who finds beauty only in complex formulas and calculations that lead to objective truth. Though Maggie is attractive, she is repulsed by the idea of "brute pig" men eyeballing her—especially if they're students. So she makes herself as unappealing as she can. She owns seven sets of the same drab outfit, one for each day, and adds a puffy lime green jacket with a yellow ski hat when it gets cold. She has tenure at a community college and lives alone, so no one cares what she looks like as long as she teaches her students enough basic math to move them through the system.

The story is an antiromance, a harsh tale of unrequited love. After Maggie is diagnosed with a chronic illness, she treats herself to a week at a spa in New Mexico. There she meets Eduardo, a war veteran who now works the night shift at the front desk. They strike up a conversation when he sees her wandering the lobby alone at 2:45 a.m. He falls instantly in love with her, as he can sense that she is hiding a deep, wounded soul beneath her contrived "ugly" appearance. He longs to help her learn to love life. They share one romantic night. Though she is tempted by his kindness, she ultimately decides romance will bring nothing but absurdity, and shatters his heart by slipping a note under his windshield wiper that reads only "Thx but no thx."

To attack the author's theme, which of the following works best:

a) Late one night, in a trance-like state, Maggie sees a series of numbers that lead her to discover a glitch in the Law of Quadratic Reciprocity.
b) Eduardo tells her about the kids he met while doing his second tour of duty—kids who have seen things she can't imagine. And warns her that it's a sin to say their suffering is not real or is absurd.
c) Eduardo tells her about the horrors he witnessed in war, and toasts her conviction that nothing has any meaning.
d) Eduardo recites a poem to her that he wrote in seventh grade when his father died. That was the day he realized we are all doomed and there's nothing we can do about it.
e) After Eduardo asks her out, Maggie treats herself to the most expensive spa package and shows up to their date looking drop-dead gorgeous.

CONTINUING ED

Anton Chekhov's 1891 novel, *The Duel*, is set in a small town in the Crimea along the Black Sea. A young couple, Laevsky and Natasha, are in a scandalous, bohemian relationship. He is a neurotic, immature, spoiled aspiring writer who fell in love with her and stole her away from her husband. Natasha is young, beautiful, and filled with sexual desire. She is either not fully aware of the lust and rage she provokes in men, or is aware and enjoys it. Either way, she stirs up trouble when her romantic dalliances with a police captain and another young man provoke them into aggressively pursuing her. Laevsky is depressed, lost, anxiety-stricken, and longs to get rid of her as soon as possible. The two, in short, are a mess. Their free-spirited ways infuriate a German zoologist, Von Koren, who is also staying in town. He so deeply despises Laevsky that he wants to kill him.

The theme of the story is, ultimately, that we cannot know the truth—therefore we must be humble, compassionate, and never too certain. This is a discovery Von Koren makes after the duel is fought. However, prior to that, he is certain that he knows the truth—that the world would be a better place if he could just murder Laevsky and wipe his ilk off the face of the earth. How boldly does he state his case against Laevsky and how convincing does it seem? What is the appeal of Von Koren's initial attitude and how does this reveal the way Chekhov executes the principle by attacking his theme?

MINI FINAL ANSWER

The correct answer is **b) Eduardo tells her about the kids he met while doing his second tour of duty—kids who have seen things she can't imagine. And warns her that to say their suffering is not real or is absurd is a sin**. This is the only one of the choices that offers a strong challenge to the story's theme that reality is absurd, a bad joke, an illusion. The kids' suffering is all too real.

27

Transcend thought.

"The truth of a thing is in
the feel of it not the think of it."
—STANLEY KUBRICK, Filmmaker

QUICK TAKE

Lord Byron called poetry "the lava of the imagination whose eruption prevents an earthquake." Isaac Newton called it "ingenious nonsense." And Edith Stillwell said it's "the deification of reality." There is a place in reality where things make sense and feel true, but we can't fully articulate why. One can't explain "the deification of reality" any more than one can explain Mozart or Miles Davis to someone who can't hear. But it's a powerful definition of poetry.

The point is that you must not rely exclusively on rational thought to tell your story. We are not putting together puzzle pieces to create identical pictures. The structures, patterns, visions, incidents, and moments that you write can't all be analyzed by an algorithm, proven or disproven by a theory. Some things work just because they work, because you feel them intensely, and they provoke a sense of awe that leaves you speechless.

If you're 100 percent certain of how everything works, what motivates people, and what it all means, you leave no room for mystery and wonder. Just because a story makes sense doesn't mean it has a life force, a spirit, or, if you will, a soul. This principle is about unbinding yourself from the chains of rational thought, unleashing your imagination, and venturing into the places you don't understand.

HOW IT WORKS

We talked earlier about the "math" of story, how A + B = C. If Mary studies hard and aces her science test, it means hard work pays off. This is logical. But it's important not to focus exclusively on logic. Story is about the fusion of intelligence and *emotion*. A + B = C says nothing about how science makes people feel a sense of awe about the trillions of galaxies that exist, the way cells regenerate, or what makes up dark matter. Again, we started this book with the Bruce Lee quote "Obey the principles without being bound by them." What can make you feel bound in story is trying too hard to control every last detail, so it all makes perfect sense and leads to an indisputable conclusion. When you overemphasize logic, you risk making the work simplistic, predictable, didactic, and worst of all, boring.

Because the first twenty-six principles essentially ask you to think through every choice, they come with an inherent danger of strangling the life out of your story. This principle doesn't contradict those, it provides a vital and necessary complement. Here, we're championing the inexplicable, the poetic, what can't be neatly defined. There's an important reason for doing this. Storytellers can be too certain that they know the truth. This feels wrong because it fails to respect the fact that human beings cannot know what is objectively true.

Over 2,500 years ago, the Buddha theorized that the world is created as a representation of our minds. Philosophers, including Immanuel Kant and David Hume, have reached similar conclusions. Neuroscientist Eric Kandel has written about how we use our brains to disassemble and reassemble art using an array of different brain areas and systems. This means that everyone perceives art and stories in different ways. Quantum physics and Einstein's Theory of Relativity suggest there is not one fixed reality. Therefore, to be too certain of anything is questionable at best. This principle is about respecting the indescribably complex nature of reality in order to tell more authentic stories.

Some stories demand that you create events that do *not* flow with a logical progression of cause and effect, characters who *don't* think and behave the way rational people normally do in real life, and worlds that *don't* adhere to the laws of physics as we currently understand them. When you transcend thought, you create with total freedom. Anyone can do anything for any reason or no reason. But whatever you create must be fueled by authentic feeling. David Lynch's surreal 1977 masterpiece, *Eraserhead*, takes place in a terrifying, industrial urban wasteland and deals with the emotional trauma of starting a family, having sex, and breeding new human beings. There's enough thematic consistency and forward motion in the narrative to derive meaning from the film, no matter how utterly bizarre it gets. And it gets *bizarre*.

This principle is about absence of information—deliberately excluding reason in order to provoke emotion. In *Pulp Fiction* the hit men, Jules and Vincent, recover a briefcase for their boss. When Vincent opens the briefcase, light emanates from it and Jules asks, "We happy?" Vincent is awestruck by whatever's in the briefcase and doesn't respond. Jules calls out, "Vincent," and Vincent, inspired, replies, "Yeah, we happy." By not telling us what's in the briefcase, Tarantino provokes our sense of wonder. In the absence of a clean explanation, the contents of the briefcase are infused with *feeling*. If we saw it were money or precious gems, this might raise all sorts of logical questions and thoughts—what would we do with them? What will they do with them? But when we don't know what's in there, we have room to simply *feel* the importance. And it's entertaining to speculate on what's in there. Many fans of the film are convinced there's a supernatural element to the briefcase, in part because Vince unlocks it using the combination 6-6-6.

When you attempt to transcend thought, you do so because logical thought can't express what you need to express. If anything, it's a hindrance, a veil you've got to pierce. You just need to accept that whether or not these moments actually "transcend" is, like beauty, in the eye of the beholder. What matters most is that you feel it intensely—it strikes a nerve. it feels at least intuitively connected to your narrative and theme, it inspires a sense of awe and wonder *in you*—if that happens, that's good enough.

HOW A MASTER DID IT

Fever Dream (2017)
Originally published in Spanish as
Distancia de rescate (Rescue Distance) in 2014
Samanta Schweblin

Samanta Schweblin is an Argentinian short story writer who was inspired to write her first novel, *Fever Dream*, after watching a French documentary on the devastating effects of pesticides. This was of particular concern to her, as Latin America has a poor track record of agrochemical regulation. But although the work began with a clear, specific objective—to warn people of the dangers of toxic chemicals—Schweblin felt that fiction works best when it goes beyond the rational mind. In a 2017 interview with the literary magazine *Full Stop*, she discussed her conscious decision to avoid writing an overtly political tract, stating, "People always forget about numbers, names, all kinds of information, but they never forget a strong feeling."

With a clear objective in mind—to instill a feeling of great unease, of *terror*, about the perilous state of our relationship with the natural world—Schweblin wrote 183 blistering pages that blur reality, dreams, memory, and identity. There are no breaks of any kind—no chapters, not so much as the slightest pause. Nothing anyone says can be fully relied on, yet everything, even what seems to be supernatural, rings true.

The entire short novel is an extended dialogue between a young mother, Amanda, and a strange boy, David, who is the nine-year-old son of a woman named Carla whom Amanda met while on vacation in a small farming town outside Buenos Aires. The story begins with Amanda lying on a cot in an emergency clinic. She can't see, can't move—not even enough to adjust the sheets bunched up under her back. David kneels beside her and pushes her to figure out exactly when she felt the sensations of worms entering her body. This is the moment she was contaminated. He tells her that "it's very important for us all" to figure out the exact moment she *felt* sick. He's pushing her hard to be specific, as the smallest detail could lead them to figure out what has sickened her. They don't have time to waste because she is hours, if not minutes, from death. She understands the mess she's in and is surprised by her ability to handle it. His character seems devoid of emotion as he aggressively questions her and passes judgment on what he deems important or not important, regardless of her feelings or needs.

Over the course of their dialogue we learn that Amanda had rented a house earlier in the week and brought her daughter, Nina, who is about three or four, slightly precocious and good-natured. Her husband, whose name we never learn, will drive up for the weekend. While there, Amanda befriended another mother, Carla, and they spent a few days together sunbathing and talking. Carla is about ten years older than Amanda and, though she is kind and attractive, there's something about her Amanda finds repellant. Carla wanted to learn to drive and Amanda was happy to teach her. One day, pulled over by a pool, Carla dropped her head on the steering wheel and asked if she could tell Amanda a story. She was worried that this story would make Amanda want to stop seeing her and no longer allow Nina to play with David. Amanda assured her it wouldn't.

Carla told a long story, but we experience it through Amanda's dialogue, in which Amanda essentially becomes Carla. It happened six years ago. Her husband, Omar, was breeding race-horses, which can bring in a lot of money. Amanda mentioned that she saw Omar drive past her in his truck, but he didn't return her wave. Carla said, "That's Omar." He no longer smiles.

One day, while Omar was out and Carla was alone with their then-three-year-old, David, she noticed the stallion was missing. She grabbed David and raced around until she found the stallion in some nearby woods drinking from a stream. She put David down and tenderly patted the stallion until she could grab the reins. Greatly relieved, she started the horse back toward their farm when she saw David crouched in the stream, sucking water off his fingers. Feeling somehow responsible for the horse's escape, and disgusted with herself for placing David near a dead bird, she didn't tell Omar what happened. The next morning, Omar found the horse on its side, with its eyes swollen shut, dying. Carla immediately realized that David drank the same water as the horse, and raced to his crib. She lifted him out and rushed him into her bed where she prayed over him like a crazy woman. He was covered in sweat and burning up.

Without telling Omar, who was tied up with the fallen horse, she scurried the boy out of the house and ran him to "the woman in the green house." In this town, it can take hours for doctors to arrive at the emergency clinic and they're rarely well-trained. People go to the woman for all sorts of ailments, especially for the many miscarriages that take place here. She's some kind of alternative healer who can read people's energy and sense where illness lies in the body.

Throughout Carla's story, Amanda kept a close eye on Nina, who was playing just outside near the car, by the pool. Amanda talked about "the rescue distance," which is a calculation she does to determine exactly how long it will take to reach her child should something bad happen. She imagines a rope between her and Nina. The more dangerous a situation seems, the tighter she feels the rope pull and the closer she keeps her child. She does this because her mother and grandmother always taught her that eventually something terrible will happen.

At the green house, the woman told Carla that the horse was dead. Carla was taken aback, as she said nothing about the horse. The woman said the poison was attacking David's heart, and the only hope to save his life was to do a "transmigration." She needed to move his soul into someone else's body, and when the soul left, it would take enough of the toxin with it to render it harmless in both David's body and the new body he would inhabit. In doing this, another soul, or part of another soul, would move into David's body and though he would be irrevocably changed, Carla would still have to care for him. Carla was desperate to know where David's soul would go, but the woman insisted it was better not to know and, with David's eyes swelling, his body burning, and her panic rising, Carla agreed to do it rather than let him die.

For two eternal hours Carla stayed completely frozen, waiting. Finally, the door opened, and the woman came out. It went well, she said, better than expected. The woman couldn't stop yawning. And then, the little boy, dazed, with his wrists scratched from the rope, staggered out. He had spots on his skin. And though he looked basically the same, he walked differently and had an odd look in his eyes. He didn't hug his mother like before; in fact, he'll never hug her again. The boy yawned too, as the woman said, "let it all out." Carla was horrified and only wanted to run away from this "monster."

Amanda doesn't believe in transmigration and is mortified that a mother would turn away from her own small child who is sick and in shock. In the present, she and David have the following exchange—his dialogue is in italics as it is throughout the book.

> It must be very sad to be whatever it is you are now, and on top of that your mother calls you a monster.
>
> *You're confused, and that's not good for this story. I'm a normal boy.*
>
> This isn't normal, David. There's only darkness, and you're talking into my ear. I don't even know if this is really happening.
>
> *It's happening, Amanda.*

This bizarre exchange is emblematic of the entire book. Though Amanda doesn't believe in transmigration, she refers to him as "whatever you are now." He claims to be a "normal boy," though he speaks with the precision of an adult and the command of a leader. This could be due to the wisdom one acquires by having teetered on the edge of death, or an actual transmigration of his soul. For all we know, he actually has the soul of an adult. Amanda claims not to know if any of this is happening, but we have every reason to believe it is. Nothing in this world is safe—not even pure running streams. She suddenly recalls that she doesn't know where Nina is now. David coldly insists that this doesn't matter. She cries out that it's all that matters, and he threatens to leave her alone if she doesn't get back to the story of exactly how she got sick. Terrified of being left hopelessly alone to die, she continues with her story.

Schweblin feeds the reader just enough narrative to hope for a solution, an explanation, a way out of this tortured reality. The Central Dramatic Question "Will David figure out what made Amanda sick?" lingers in the air, but their dialogue, the story Amanda tells, moves so fast, and is infused with so much emotion, it's impossible to think straight. Consider all that's going on here. Both Carla and Amanda are separated from their kids. Amanda is blind, frozen, in a clinic that can do very little to comfort or heal her. This is a mother so obsessed with protecting her child that she calculates a "rescue distance" every time her daughter moves. And now, as she lies here, inches from death, she doesn't even know where Nina is or if she's okay. On top of this, she just told the most terrifying story about a traumatized, terrified, and guilt-ridden mother, Carla, who blames herself for losing her little boy. And that little boy, that "monster," kneels beside her and bullies her for information.

On one level, the narrative feels like an old-time thriller in which a noble doctor attempts to overcome impossible odds to stop a fast-moving plague. If only he can find the exact moment when the plague started, he can vaccinate the populace! On another level, this situation is so perverse, it makes no more sense than a nightmare. David, this "transmigrated" or somehow enlightened *child*, is going to do exactly what if he finds out how and when Amanda was poisoned? Why isn't there a team of toxicologists, medical experts, and military personnel racing to cordon off the area? Is David employed by the hospital? Does no one care that a bizarre child is harassing a dying mother? Rational responses to the situation don't exist. The people just accept the carnage of living in a toxic world the way others accept that rain falls from clouds.

Let's go back to Schweblin's quote: "People always forget about numbers, names, all kinds of information, but they never forget a strong feeling." What she suggests here is that by cutting out the forgettable stuff—the facts and figures—she increases the intensity of how the story feels. When she says "all kinds of information," it's important to include adjectives and excessive explanation here. The filmmaker Stanley Kubrick once said, "I cut everything to the bone." Schweblin's writing does the same thing. Here's how Carla describes the moment the woman brought David back to her after the transmigration:

> Then I heard his footsteps, very soft on the wood. Short and uncertain, so different from how David walked. They stopped after every four or five steps; hers would stop as well while she waited for him. They were almost to the kitchen. His little hand, dirty now with dry mud or dust, fumbled over the wall as he leaned against it. Our eyes met, but I looked away immediately. She pushed him toward me and he took a few more steps, almost stumbling, and now he was leaning on the table. I think I'd stopped breathing for that entire time.

Because there's no description of his response, we can *feel* how utterly foreign he's become. In Carla's inability to breathe, it's easy to access her storm of emotions—terror, guilt, sadness, pity, and rage. We never learn why David's hands are dirty, but our minds, programmed to fill in blanks, to add story where none exists, attempt to supply reasons. Perhaps the woman rubbed dirt on them, or somehow the migration of souls kicked up dust. Or we picture his little hands pressing into the table as he writhes in pain with his wrists bound. Had Schweblin larded this procedure with information by having the woman in the greenhouse say, "I'm going to rub nutrient-dense mud from the South Atlantic on his palms to facilitate the soul dispersion . . . ," our minds would turn against her story. "That's bullshit! Mud nutrients play no role whatsoever in transmigrating souls. No way. I'm out." And with our critical minds activated, we feel nothing, because we're thinking about whether or not we believe the information coming at us.

• • •

The novel ends with David "pushing" Amanda to envision a final scene. He tells her that before she dies, "There will be only a few seconds of clarity." In this final scene, her husband returns to this town from the city to visit with Omar and David. Carla has left them. And Amanda is dead. It's noon, but the sky is dark. Amanda's nameless husband hopes that Omar can help him figure out what happened to Nina. Omar can tell him nothing. He's got his own problems. There's a nightmarish quality to their disconnected conversation. Neither can offer any insight or friendship.

Amanda's husband angrily returns to his car, feeling he wasted his time. David gets in the back seat. Amanda describes the moment:

> He [the husband] wants to leave right now. Upright against the seat, you [David] look him in the eyes, as though begging him. I see through my husband, I see those other eyes in yours. The seat belt on, legs crossed on the seat. A hand reaching slightly toward Nina's stuffed mole, covertly, the dirty fingers resting on the stuffed legs as if trying to restrain them.

David, here, sits exactly the way Nina sat. Amanda's husband is disgusted and tells the boy to get out. Omar all but yanks the kid out of the car as David's "eyes desperately seek out my husband's gaze." Omar returns to the house with David, and Amanda's husband drives back to the city. These are the story's final apocalyptic lines:

> He doesn't notice that the return trip has grown slower and slower. That there are too many cars, cars and more cars covering every asphalt nerve. Or that the transit is stalled, paralyzed for hours, smoking and effervescent. He doesn't see the important thing: the rope finally slack, like a lit fuse, somewhere; the motionless scourge about to erupt.

This harrowing conclusion suggests that Nina's soul has been moved into David's body. But trying to logically track all these time changes and shifting voices is ultimately beside the point. We can't possibly determine what's happened here through logic and rational thought. Yet the logic of the story is clear in the sense that it is a warning—an alarm bell to wake up the world. The level of disconnection has become too great to bear.

This principle is called "Transcend thought," which doesn't mean ignore it. Schweblin's intellect, attention to detail, and craftsmanship are astonishing. It's as if logical thought is a stepping-stone to a higher realm: the pure expression of a feeling. Ultimately, *Fever Dream* works so well because the feeling expressed is profound and resonant. Anyone who has ever felt helpless and unable to protect a loved one, especially a child, can relate on the most personal level. But beyond the parent-child relationship, the story touches on every kind of disconnection—between people and the environment, government and people, companies and people, spouses, and friends. In this novel's terrifying world, we can't rely on anything—not even our own identity. And one is left with this intense and sickening feeling that our existence, every last bit of it, hangs by a thread.

HOW YOU DO IT

The following bullet points will help you think through and execute the principle.

▶ When your focus is on expressing an idea with clarity and precision, as Dostoevsky does in *The Brothers Karamazov*, you structure events to lead to an indisputable conclusion. Because Alyosha practices Christian humility and has true faith, he can endure life's traumas with dignity. This is not what we're after here. The goal is to authentically and intensely express a *feeling*. Which feelings do you feel most intensely but don't fully understand? These are worth writing about.

▶ Since you're working on a narrative, telling a story, not writing a poem, you still need to build a track for the story to ride on. You build this track by asking a Central Dramatic Question (CDQ). You know the drill. Identify your protagonist and their object of desire, then phrase it as a question: Will (character) acquire (object of desire)?

▶ Tie your CDQ to the feeling you need to express and explore. For example, if you're feeling enraged, a CDQ might be "Will a man escape justice after he kills another man in a bar fight?"

▶ Continuously challenge yourself to up the intensity of the feeling you wish to express. See how tightly you can "pack the cannon." For example, why does this main character not just dislike, not just hate, but despise the man he kills in the bar fight? If you were this man, in this situation, what could push you over the edge? Keep going until you, as the writer, truly feel what you need to feel to make the situation and character authentic.

▶ Free yourself from reality and the logic of cause and effect. The bar killer's dead mother, Satan, aliens, his alter ego, historical figures—anyone imaginable can enter his world. And he may need to step through Hell itself on his way from the bathroom to the bar. Let characters and the world respond in unpredictable ways.

▶ Seek the negative spaces that come from removing information and explanation. As your story develops, constantly explore what you can take out—about the world, the characters' biographies and motivations, the situation, etc. Remember that your readers/viewers will fill in blanks. Explore how removing information increases feeling. But don't go so far that you remove any semblance of narrative structure. It's still a story.

▶ Inspiration is contagious. You're looking to put yourself in a heightened state. Consciously seek out those people, places, things, and activities that make you feel open, engaged, and more fully alive. Build a list and do things—inspiration doesn't come in a gift-wrapped box. You stalk it. You meditate, pray, go to mountaintops, read poetry, hang out with inspired people. Above all, trust yourself. Be courageous. And know that if you feel these feelings, you're not the only one.

MINI FINAL EXAM

Read the following, then answer the question below.

A kitten with a wild assortment of colors and patterns—a striped leg, browns and blacks with bright white streaks—trotted into the room and stared into his eyes, seeming to grow larger as the minutes passed. He checked the vial in his pocket—the liquid was gone. He tried to pour some onto his tongue, but nothing. In the corner, a woman wearing a black suit and thick-framed spectacles gazed forward and said that she could see better without her glasses.

Outside the window, he could hear someone moaning, but whether it was in pain or . . . something else, he could not tell. He put his fingers under the little handles at the bottom of the window and lifted, but it was stuck. The moaning grew louder and more mournful. He yanked up hard and the window shattered into a million pieces, but each fell softly, like snow, and refracted rainbows of light throughout the room. The moaning bled into wind. Outside, the meadow was covered with ice. A little girl in white skated across, spun gracefully, and disappeared below the ice. He was thirsty. He wanted to lick the ice. The man in the corner said, "I knew your mother." His heart raced. This line always made him nervous. So, he took a seat, bowed his head, and slowly closed his eyes.

To further disconnect this scene from the laws of cause and effect and rational thought, which of the following should you cut:

a) A kitten with a wild assortment of colors and patterns—a striped leg, browns and blacks with bright white streaks—trotted into the room stared into his eyes, seeming to grow larger as the minutes passed.
b) He put his fingers under the little handles at the bottom of the window and lifted, but it was stuck.
c) He checked the vial in his pocket—the liquid was gone. He tried to pour some onto his tongue, but nothing.
d) The woman in the corner said, "I knew your mother." His heart raced.
e) So, he took a seat, bowed his head, and slowly closed his eyes.

CONTINUING ED

In Kono Taeko's 1963 short story "Night Journey," Fukuko and Murao are a married couple at home on a summer Saturday night waiting for their friends, Utako and Saeki. Murao, the husband, is upset that the couple didn't come after dinner as promised. They could not have forgotten the plans that they made. Utako is Fukoko's childhood best friend and Murao is openly attracted to her, which is fine with Fukoko. In fact, Fukoko wishes that Murao would have an affair with Utako so that she could live happily with her best friend and husband. Before Saeki came into the picture, Utako used to get drunk and dance for her married friends. Murao and Fukako decide to take a short train ride to visit Utako and Saeki.

Ultimately, all that happens is a couple looks for their friends and winds up walking at night through a graveyard. The story ends with this sentence: "Fukoko realized that she'd been in a particular mood for some time now, a mood that would keep her walking beside Murao into the night, walking on and on until they became the perpetrators—or the victims—of some unpredictable crime."

The author never explains why Utako and Saeki failed to show up or where they went, nor does she define the "particular" mood Fukoko's been in or the type of crime they might commit. How does this missing information make it more difficult to determine what this story is about—and place the emphasis more on feeling than thought? How does the vibe on the train, in the streets, near the graveyard heighten the couple's sense of isolation? The story deals with the relationship between sexuality and aggression. Which for you is more prominent—an intellectual idea or a feeling? There's no right or wrong here, but just consider whether this ambiguity appeals to you as a storyteller.

MINI FINAL ANSWER

The correct answer is that the best line to cut to *avoid* grounding the scene with logic is **c) He checked the vial in his pocket—the liquid was gone. He tried to pour some out onto his tongue, but nothing**. This grounds the narrative by strongly suggesting this hallucinogenic experience is the result of a drug. Our focus in this chapter is on emotional intensity, infusing your stories with powerful metaphors, and using sounds and images to create dreamlike states. It's about giving your audience a unique experience that is beyond the boundaries of logic, cause and effect, and reason. If you strip out the bits of information that ground a story with reason, you create space for mystery and wonder. Remember, people will form their own narratives and put things together in ways that might unveil truths even you didn't know lurked below the surface. Once your story leaves your hands, it's no longer yours. It's surrendered to the world.

CONCLUSION

The Necessity of Story

I hope you learned much more than you thought you would when you picked up this book. And I hope you feel inspired to write what's essential to you. But more important, I hope you'll explore the subject of story further. I feel profoundly changed by the experience of writing this book. I had always known that story was important, but I never realized just how important.

In a 2002 article entitled "The Power of Story," the biologist E. O. Wilson wrote, "With new tools and models, neuroscientists have joined cognitive psychologists in drawing closer to an understanding of the conscious mind as a narrative generator. Working on the same questions from different perspectives, neuroscientists, cognitive psychologists, and even evolutionary biologists are converging on a common theory of the brain. It develops stories to filter and make sense of the flood of information that we are exposed to every day." In other words, we couldn't make sense of the world, or stay sane, without our ability to tell stories.

In his bestseller *Sapiens, A Brief History of Humankind*, Yuval Hariri argues that stories are necessary to build civilizations. "The truly unique trait of 'Sapiens' is our ability to create and believe fiction. All other animals use their communication to describe reality. We use our communication system to create new realities." What he means by "new realities" are religions, nations, laws, corporations . . . entrenched as they feel, these are all just stories we agree to share. That my wife and I are "married" is a story we tell. If I come home and she says she no longer buys the story, this thing we call a marriage ceases to exist.

I was also taken aback by how profoundly the stories in this book affected my own beliefs. I have never been a particularly religious person, but I find the case that Fyodor Dostoevsky builds through the narrative of *The Brothers Karamazov* to be a convincing argument in support of faith. And I was moved by story's power to heal. Yunior, the narrator of *The Brief Wondrous Life of Oscar Wao*, says that he's telling Oscar's story as a "zafa," or counter-spell, against the curse he fears has been inflicted on the Dominican people. When I first read the book several years ago, the idea that a story can protect someone made no sense to me. But since then, Diaz has written eloquently about his experience of being raped as a child and how it damaged his sense of self. Rereading the novel with this incident in mind is a different experience. The two men at the heart of the novel, Oscar and Yunior, represent aspects of Diaz's personality—one who is desperate to be loved but finds only rejection, and the other who must repeatedly assert his masculinity. Yunior's idea to tell his story as a counter-spell is *real*. Evil relies on suppressing stories. As Diaz brings his story to the light, you can sense its power to heal, not only himself but other victims of abuse as well.

Everywhere I look now I see the power of story play out. As someone who enjoys investing in individual stocks, I carefully watch CEOs in interviews and read through corporate marketing material. Telling a compelling story is essential to inspiring a workforce, explaining the value proposition to customers, and closing deals—and it's grossly underrated, since it can't be cleanly quantified. I have seen, firsthand, how a well-told story can add—or, in absence, subtract—billions of dollars to—or from—a company's market cap. From day one, Reed Hastings, the CEO of Netflix, told a story of how he would stream movies and TV shows onto every device around the world, and he has never once wavered from that story, building Netflix up from nothing to one of the most valuable and powerful media companies in history.

I've also been struck by just how deeply stories affect our personal lives. If a relationship goes through a rough patch, and one partner constructs a narrative that blames the other, this is a serious problem. And think about the setbacks you've endured. If the story you tell is about what a loser you are, it's a whole other ball game than one that celebrates your power to reset and move forward.

Merriam-Webster defines story as "an account of incidents or events." This doesn't do it justice. I'd like to offer a more complete and hopefully inspiring definition:

A carefully constructed series of events, featuring a willful and compelling character, in a specifically designed world, who undergoes a profound change. This change is brought about through a journey, which is emotionally charged and resolves in a way that is surprising but credible and meaningful. The result is a discovery by the storyteller, audience—and often the character—of a deep-seated truth. This transcendent, shared experience is called story.

Aim high. You got this.

Acknowledgments

To my agent, Lisa DiMona, the most loyal, fun-spirited, intelligent, and empathic partner a writer could ask for. I'm grateful for your hard work, and faith.

To my editor, Margot Herrera, for your dedication, limitless insight, and kindness. And to the good people of Workman Publishing—I'm proud to be a member of this tribe.

To my father, Richard, for always making art, culture, and literature essential to our home.

To my mother, Judith, for taking no bullshit, about anything, ever. This made me a writer.

To my brother, David, for the endless insights and conversations that helped me crystallize ideas.

To Ma, Pa, and my Frederick family, for the faith, laughs, and love.

To Anna and Ian Barford, for always helping me focus on process, acceptance, and grace.

To Perry Iverson, for teaching me about focus, patience, and playing the long game.

To Linda Halperin, for your wisdom and compassion.

To Shihan Marcello and the Senseis of the AKMA, for your lessons on courage, discipline, and commitment to fundamentals.

To Alexa Junge, for your mentorship and generosity.

To Connie and Kenny, for your love and support.

To all my students who trust me with your stories—I learn more from you than anyone. Special thanks to Ashton, Brandon, Erin, Ann, Teddy, Marjie, Chris, Cindy, and Scotty B.

To Bassim El-Wakil for your eloquence and friendship.

To Josh Kaufman for your worldly wisdom and friendship.

To Todd and Lori, for your love and dedication.

To Kim Mikkelsen for your old-school Brooklyn loyalty and friendship, staying up all night to help with my first workshop—which became this book.

Index